Joseph G. Schloss

Making Beats The Art of

Sample-Based Hip-Hop

With a New Afterword

Foreword by Jeff Chang

Wesleyan University Press
Middletown, Connecticut

Wesleyan University Press, Middletown, CT 06459
www.wesleyan.edu/wespress

Originally published in 2004
Text design by Julie Allred, BW&A Books, Inc.
Printed in the United States of America
ISBN for this edition: 978-0-8195-7481-7

The Library of Congress cataloged the original printing as:
Schloss, Joseph Glenn.
Making beats : the art of sample-based hip-hop /
Joseph G. Schloss.
      p. cm. — (Music/culture)
Includes bibliographical references (p.),
discography (p.), and index.
ISBN 0-8195-6695-0 (cloth : alk. paper) —
ISBN 0-8195-6696-9 (pbk. : alk. paper)
1. Rap (Music)—History and criticism. 2. Hip-hop.
3. Turntablism. 4. Sound recording executives
and producers—United States. 5. Turntablists.
I. Title. II. Series.
ML3531.S35 2004
781.64'9149—dc22   2004043013

5 4 3 2

To my parents,
John and Suzanne Schloss,
and to our ancestors

Contents

New Foreword

Jeff Chang

When, at the turn of the millennium, Joe Schloss completed the dissertation that would become this groundbreaking book, the biggest question facing the field of hip-hop studies was, "So what?"

Rap music was at the very peak of its commercial impact, and hip-hop's global cultural influence was inescapable. Those facts only gave that question its weight. The academy, having grudgingly granted that hip-hop was not a fad, resisted the idea that the kinds of knowledges it preserved and produced were worthy of study. What, they asked, could hip-hop teach *us* in the academy?

But perhaps the strongest skeptics of hip-hop studies came from within the movement. What, they asked, can the academy teach *me* about hip-hop that someone in hip-hop couldn't teach me better? What could intellectuals offer my movement but patronization and mummification?

These skeptics were people like Schloss himself—committed hip-hop heads concerned they might be pimping their own culture, engaged scholars questioning the relevance of their careers to the communities from which they had come. For Schloss, choosing to write critically about hip-hop meant confronting "So what?" every day he woke up. And if he and his peers—and I count myself alongside him as part of what might be called the second generation of hip-hop scholars—could not find satisfactory answers, the field of hip-hop studies certainly would fade out like a fad.

By now, there was a foundational canon of works by people like Nelson George, David Toop, Steven Hager, Sally Banes, Henry Chalfant, Martha Cooper, Jim Prigoff, Bill Adler, Craig Castleman, and Jack Stewart. Members of the second generation had devoured the works of the pioneers of hip-hop studies like Tricia Rose, Mark Anthony Neal, Harry Allen, Robin D. G. Kelley, James Spady, and Brian Cross. We checked for elders who *got it*—people like Houston Baker, Juan Flores, and Henry Louis Gates Jr. And we were handing each other new books by Billy Wimsatt, Michael Eric Dyson, Cheryl Keyes, Raquel Z. Rivera, and S. Craig Watkins.

There were also lots of "scholarly" pieces about hip-hop that were garbage. (In truth, the number might be smaller than I recall—I can't and won't spend much time in the dustbin of that particular history.) What I do remember is having a classically hip-hop chip-on-the-shoulder ambivalence about imminent institutionalization. When the Brooklyn Museum mounted an exhibition in 2000 entitled *Hip-Hop: Roots, Rhymes, and Rage,* I was more outraged at seeing The Notorious B.I.G.'s stage wear and childhood 45 singles collection behind glass than I was by the fact that it had taken so long for a major museum to take hip-hop seriously. I chalk it up now to youth, but I can still remember that silent scream in my head—*Here we are a mile straight shot from Biggie's home, him just three years in the grave, and they've turned this shit into a mausoleum. We all ain't dead yet.*

But behind the (misdirected) attitude was a fear that our native knowledges might never be honored, much less documented or advanced. At that moment, hip-hop scholarship mostly focused on rap, forget music or any other forms of hip-hop art. Framed by the urgency of the ongoing culture wars, the ever-present concern over Black invisibility and erasure, and a cultural-studies-styled bow to timeliness, this scholarship often utilized narrow textual and/or sociological approaches. Inevitably the writings were sorely—sometimes pathetically—dated by the time they reached publication.

It is true that the academic publishing enterprise is not built for real-time relevance. It also discourages "community review" in favor of "peer review." But we would often joke bitterly that you could rate a "scholarly" hip-hop article or book by the average number of factual errors per page, the same kinds of mistakes that might end our careers if we had published them in the then-booming hip-hop media. For us there were stakes to advancing hip-hop knowledge that many scholars could afford to ignore. They didn't even know what they didn't know.

Many of us were also mad that few scholars saw fit to interview actual hip-hop practitioners. If they did, we chuckled, it would become quickly clear who the real scholar was. They were watching videos, buying albums, and going to shows just so that they could speak to each other. Armchair hip-hop writing, we called it. We didn't want to have our movement translated *for* the academy. We wanted our movement to transform the academy.

Paradoxically, that meant taking up a position that pulled us closer to our community. "'Hip-hop writers' are often accused of being 'too close' to the music and to the scene. Hell yes, we're close to it," the journalist Danyel Smith once wrote of hip-hop journalism, whose late-2000s collapse would accelerate the development of hip-hop studies.[1] "Where else to be but close to the truth? Close to art and mystery and metaphor. To the singularity of voice. The magnificence of ingenious sampling."

And so we all struggled with the question, "So what?" *Making Beats* was Joe Schloss's amazingly inspired, deeply personal answer.

He had also asked himself: What research approach might help push the discussion around hip-hop ethics and aesthetics further? How can I write something that adds to hip-hop knowledge, and does not reduce it?

Thinking about these questions led him to make some important choices—to decenter hip-hop scholarship from the Great Men model of history; to get close to his "consultants," his more respectful name for his interviewees; to respect their knowledge, ethics, and aesthetics, sometimes at the expense of that held by those validated by the academy; and to establish a critical position that still allows a loud and proud kind of advocacy.

In short, he took a side. He did so gracefully—with none of the angst or edge of people like, say, me—and absolutely without apology. In doing so, he offered a model for an engaged intellectual inquiry that yielded as much for the hip-hop community as it might for the academy.

He wrote, "The producer embodies hip-hop history through the use of deejaying, in whatever way he sees fit: scratching, looping, digging for rare records, philosophizing. The producer chooses to become part of the collective history every time he makes a beat."

It's not hard to read this now—knowing that, while hip-hop music has continued to evolve and the hip-hop movement continued to grow,

Making Beats has become a classic of second-generation hip-hop scholarship as well as a fixture on the bookshelves of new generations of emerging beatmakers—as the perfect description of his own achievement.

Note

1. A decade-long plunge in ad pages led to a sharp narrowing of mass print outlets in hip-hop journalism, marked by the sudden—if temporary—closure of the largest title, *Vibe* magazine, in 2009. Four years later, when SpinMedia bought a revived *Vibe*, its circulation had plunged to 301,000, less than a third of its peak number.

Acknowledgments

First and foremost, I would like to thank the producers, deejays, MCs, and others who worked with me on this project. The term "consultant" is sometimes used as a semantic gambit to avoid the negative implications of the word "informant," but in this case those who worked with me were consultants in the fullest sense of the word. They not only informed me of things but also sent me magazine articles and useful phone numbers, critiqued (and in one case pretty much copyedited) early drafts of this work, and introduced me to people, situations, and ideas I would never have found on my own.

The Seattle stage of my research was facilitated by consultants DJ B-Mello, Jake One, King Otto, Kylea, Mr. Supreme, Negus I, Samson S., Strath Shepard, Specs, DJ Topspin, Vitamin D, and Wordsayer. In various combinations, many of them also constitute crews that have worked for years to keep Seattle's independent hip-hop scene vital. Particularly helpful to my project were Conception Records, Tribal Productions, the True Believers Crew, and Jasiri Media Group. A debt of gratitude is owed also to all the others who collectively keep hip-hop in Seattle (aka the Wetlands, the H206, Seatown, and the Two-O-Sickness) moving.

A number of people who work for hip-hop in various capacities across the United States served as consultants on this work as well: Harry Allen, the Angel, Beni B., Karen Dere, Domino, DJ Kool Akiem Allah Elisra, DJ Mixx Messiah, Prince Paul, Steve "Steinski" Stein, and Phill "The Soulman" Stroman.

As a relative latecomer to this culture ("golden era" 1987), I must also honor and thank the pioneers of hip-hop itself (far too numerous to mention), particularly those who have labored to create and maintain a positive vision and path for us to follow, who are our living connection to a time when, as Fabel says, "hip-hop was free."

I would also like to thank the first generation of hip-hop writers and scholars, who have been an incalculably deep influence not only on this work but also on the fact that it is even possible to do scholarship on hip-hop in the first place: Tricia Rose, Stephen Hager, David Toop, Craig Castleman, Cheryl Keyes, Rob Walser, Michael Eric Dyson, Nelson George, Greg Tate, William Eric Perkins, Russell Potter, and many others.

I have been lucky enough to amass a peerless group of academic advisors—some official, some not—all of whom have affected my work profoundly: Howard Becker, Sue Darlington, Shannon Dudley, Ter Ellingson, Bernard Z. Friedlander, David Reck, Hiromi Lorraine Sakata, David Sanjek, Cynthia Schmidt, and Chris Waterman.

My contemporaries in the academic world, especially those who have one foot in the hip-hop community, have also guided and abetted me. They are the Dynamic 2 + 3 (Jeffrey O. G. Ogbar, Lizz Mendez-Berry, Jeff "DJ Zen" Chang, and Adrian Gaskins), Jon Caramanica, Kyra Gaunt, Meta DuEwa Jones, Felicia Miyakawa, Dawn Norfleet, Guy Ramsey, Ryan Snyder, and Oliver Wang.

In various capacities, my work has been supported by a number of institutions, including the University of Washington Ethnomusicology Department; the Tufts University Music Department; the University of Virginia Music Department; the Jazz and Contemporary Music Program at New School University; the Performance Studies Department at Tisch School of the Arts, New York University; Bob George and the ARChive of Contemporary Music; and the Carter G. Woodson Institute for African and African American Studies. An early foray into this material was supported by a University of Washington Dissertation Fellowship.

All of my students have influenced me, but I would especially like to thank those from my "Hip-Hop and Performance" graduate seminar at New York University, all of whom are substantial scholars in their own right: Wonderful G. Bere, Jalylah Burrell, Rhiannon Fink, and Amma Ghartey-Tagoe.

My editors at Wesleyan University Press were extraordinarily helpful, and their work is much appreciated. They are Matthew Byrnie, who guided me through the early stages of my book's publication, and Suzanna Tamminen, who guided me through the late stages.

My friends—like (one hopes) everyone's friends—are so essential to my ability to work that the idea of thanking them for it is almost absurd in its failure to convey the magnitude of their contributions. Thanks anyway: Andy Brown, Elle Chan, Chris Coleman, Njeri Cruse, Veronica Eady,

John Elstad, Lee Ford, Daniela Garaiz, S. K. Honda, Mae Jackson, Malaika Lafferty, Mira Levinson, Spyridon "Iron Spyder" Nicon, Sandra Pai, Lorri Plourde, Mike Singer, Aaron Tucker (wherever you are, dude), Jessamyn West, and Gretchen Yanover.

Finally, people often say that you can't choose your family, but even if you could, I would still choose mine, 'cause they're the best: John Schloss, Suzanne Schloss, Sara Schloss Stave, and Channing M-L Stave.

Making Beats

chapter 1

Introduction

> Joe: I wanted to get you to tell that story about when you were talking to your mother-in-law about painting. . . .
>
> Mr. Supreme: Oh yeah, and we were arguing, 'cause she was saying I didn't make music. That it's not art. . . . She really didn't understand at all, and we argued for about two hours about it. Basically, at the end she said . . . if I took the sounds, it's not mine—that I took it from someone.
>
> And then I explained to her: What's the difference if I take a snare drum off of a record, or I take a snare drum and slap it with a drum stick? OK, the difference is gonna be the sound. Because when it was recorded, it was maybe a different snare, or had a reverb effect, or the mic was placed funny. It's a different sound. But what's the difference between taking the sound from the record or a drum? It's the *sound* that you're using, and then you create something. You make a whole new song with it.
>
> And she paints, so I told her, "You don't actually *make* the paint." You know what I'm saying? "You're not painting, 'cause you don't make the paint." . . . But that's what it is; it's like painting a picture.
> (Mr. Supreme 1998a)

Some people make beats. They use digital technology to take sounds from old records and organize them into new patterns, into hip-hop. They do it for fun and money and because their friends think it's cool. They do it because they find it artistically and personally fulfilling. They do it because they can't rap. They do it to show off their record collections. Sometimes they don't know why they do it; they just do. This book is about those people and their many reasons.

Beats—musical collages composed of brief segments of recorded sound—are one of two relatively discrete endeavors that come together to form the musical element of hip-hop culture; the other element is rhymes (rhythmic poetry). This division of labor derives from the earliest hip-hop music, which consisted of live performances in which a deejay played the most rhythmic sections of popular records accompanied by a master of ceremonies—an MC—who exhorted the crowd to dance, shared local information, and noted his or her own skill on the microphone. When hip-hop expanded to recorded contexts, both of these roles became somewhat more complex. MCs began to create increasingly involved narratives using complex rhythms and cadences. And although deejays continued to make music with turntables when performing live, most also developed other strategies for use in the studio, and these eventually came to include the use of digital sampling. As these studio methodologies gained popularity, the deejays who used them became known as producers.[1]

Today, hip-hop is a diverse and vibrant culture that makes use of a variety of techniques and approaches to serve many communities throughout the United States and, in fact, the world. There remains, however, a surprisingly close bond among producers regardless of geographical or social distance. They see themselves as a breed apart, bearers of a frequently overlooked and often maligned tradition. This book is about these hip-hop producers, their community, their values and their imagination.

I have relied heavily on ethnographic methods such as participant observation to study these questions. As a result, the picture that emerges in this study expresses a rather different perspective from that of other studies of hip-hop or popular music in general. It does no disservice to previous work to say that it has tended to focus on certain areas (such as the influence of the cultural logic of late capitalism on urban identities, the representation of race in popular culture, etc.) to the exclusion of others (such as the specific aesthetic goals that artists have articulated). Nor is it a criticism to say that this is largely a result of its methodologies, which have, for the most part, been drawn from literary analysis. We must simply note that there are blank spaces and then set about to filling them in. Ethnography, I believe, is a good place to start.

Due to the approaches I have employed, common issues of poststructuralist anthropology—such as the social construction of "the field," the effect of the power relationships that exist between a researcher and his or her subjects, and the subjectivities of academic writing—have exerted a decisive influence on the way my study is framed. Conveniently, these are also issues that are rarely addressed in studies of popular music simply because most academics who study it do not use ethnography. But I believe that—beyond self-critique—such questions have much to contribute to our understanding of the social world from which popular music emerges. The recent ethnographic work of scholars such as Harris Berger (1999), Kai Fikentscher (2000), Dawn Norfleet (1997), Norman Stolzoff (2000), and especially Ingrid Monson (1996) have been particularly influential on me in this regard.

In preparing this study, I have spent time with a variety of producers (as well as MCs, deejays, businesspeople, and hip-hop fans). Although I have tried to collect a wide range of opinions on the issues I address, most of the producers I interviewed tend to hold certain qualities in common. Though some of the artists I spoke with are well known to hip-hop fans, most are what could be called "journeymen": professionals of long standing who are able to support themselves through their efforts, who have the respect of their peers but have not achieved great wealth or fame. Virtually all are male, a fact which exerts a huge, if underarticulated, influence on the musical form as a whole. Although my consultants include a relatively small number of women, I believe that their representation in these pages is actually disproportionately large when compared to their actual representation in hip-hop (at least in the capacities with which I'm concerned).

Another significant demographic aspect of my sample is its ethnic diversity, which I feel accurately reflects the diversity of the community itself. That said, however, one of the foundational assumptions of this study is that to the extent that one wishes to think in such terms, hip-hop is African American music. Hip-hop developed in New York City in neighborhoods that were dominated by people of African descent from the continental United States, Puerto Rico, and the West Indies. As a result, African-derived aesthetics, social norms, standards, and sensibilities are deeply embedded in the form, even when it is being performed by individuals who are not themselves of African descent.

Scholars such as Robert Farris Thompson (1996), Kyra Gaunt (1997), and Cheryl Keyes (1996) have demonstrated this in very specific terms on both abstract and practical levels. Thompson (1996: 216–218), for example, traces the intervening steps between traditional dance forms in the Congo and b-boying or b-girling (also known as breakdancing), and Gaunt (1997: 100–112) connects rap's rhythms to those of "pattin' juba," a tradition that goes back centuries. As I will demonstrate, traditional African American aesthetic preferences, social assumptions, and cultural norms inform producers' activities on many levels.

Geographic diversity is another significant factor affecting the producers' sense of community. I interviewed individuals from Atlanta, Los Angeles, New Orleans, New York, Oakland, Philadelphia, and Seattle for this study. Virtually all of them knew each other, either directly or indirectly. This is a small community held together by phone, the Internet, and regular travel. Although such abstract communities have always existed to some degree, the increasingly global nature of communication and the international flow of labor and capital has made the nonlocal community an increasingly common affair (see Clifford 1992, Appadurai 1990, Slobin 1992). Benedict Anderson (1983), in fact, convincingly argues that even such an accepted political formation as the nation-state constitutes an "imagined" community. While this may have its practical difficulties for the ethnographer, it means that relationships are driven by the needs and sensibilities of the individuals in question more than by their proximity to centers of traditional power.

The ease with which such relationships can be maintained still surprises me. When I travel, I am regularly asked by hip-hop artists to deliver records and gossip to individuals in other cities. And as I write this, the Rock Steady Crew, a legendary b-boy/b-girl collective, is preparing to mark its twenty-fifth anniversary with a weekend of parties and performances here in New York City; two of my Seattle-based consultants will be deejaying there. And, of course, the Internet is probably the most powerful tool for communication between individuals and dissemination of general information; new Web sites appear every day.

In order to reflect this state of affairs, my research took a path that was unusual but entirely organic to the processes that I was studying. I began by interviewing hip-hop artists in Seattle, Washington, because I had preexisting ties to that community and because I believe that Seattle is exemplary as a node of the national network I am trying to portray. It is both large enough to support a substantial community of musicians and small enough to be constantly aware of its place within the greater social context. My consultants in Seattle introduced me to producers in other cities, allowing me to explore the network in a fashion similar to that of any other community participant, moving from the local to the universal. This is a practical example of the way the process of performing fieldwork can have a very abstract influence on the way a study is structured.[2]

In other words, my fieldwork was very similar to the educational process that a hip-hop producer would undergo, the primary difference being that I was producing a book rather than music. But the experience of meeting producers, convincing them of my sincerity, going digging and trading records with them, communally criticizing other producers' beats, learning about production techniques and ethical violations through discussion and experimentation, and eventually being introduced to nationally known artists parallels the common pedagogical experience of hip-hop producers themselves in many important ways. I would argue that the shape of the knowledge expressed in this book—what I know and don't know—is largely the result of this approach, and thus reflects the epistemological orientation of hip-hop production—or at least my own experience of it. A researcher setting out to interview the "great producers of hip-hop" or to produce a formal history of hip-hop production may well produce a different picture.

Finally, most of my consultants share a somewhat purist attitude toward the use of digital sampling for hip-hop production. While digital sampling has historically been the primary technology used for making beats, it is not the only one; some forms of hip-hop use synthesizers or live instrumentation as their foundations. One of the major premises of this project is that the distinction between sample-based and non-sample-based hip-hop is a distinction of genre, more than of individual technique.[3] Hip-hop producers who use sampling place great importance on that fact, and—as I will show—find it difficult to countenance other approaches without compromising many of their foundational assumptions about the musical form.[4]

In fact, as I complete this book, sample-based production—once the central approach used in hip-hop—is becoming increasingly marginalized. This, in turn, has led some producers to become more open to other approaches, while others, in response, have become even more purist than they were when I began my research. There are two major reasons for these intertwined developments. First, due to the growing expense of sample clearance (i.e., securing permission from the owner of a copy-righted recording) as well as a general aesthetic sea change, many major-label hip-hop artists are increasingly rejecting the use of samples in favor of other sound sources. While many producers have embraced this change, it is seen by others as a threat to their aesthetic ideals and has caused them to redouble their efforts to emphasize sampling in their work. Second, the increased availability of PC- and Macintosh-based sampling programs has allowed large numbers of individuals who have not been socialized into hip-hop's community or aesthetic to become in-volved in its production. This, too, has led those who already used sam-pling to articulate the previously unstated social values of the community, a trend which can be seen, for example, in the founding of *Wax Poetics,* a journal devoted entirely to various aspects of the search for rare records to sample (a pursuit known as "digging in the crates"—see chapter 4). Ultimately, then, this work—like all ethnographies—reflects the way a particular community defined itself and its art at a particular time.

Ethnography is well suited to address these and many other issues in popular music. It can ground general theoretical claims in the specific experience of individuals, lead the scholar to interesting questions that may not have arisen through observation alone, and call attention to aspects of the researcher's relationship to the phenomenon being stud-ied that may not be immediately apparent. This can deeply affect the work that is produced. And, perhaps most importantly, it can help the re-searcher to develop analyses that are relevant to the community being studied. This is especially valuable in the case of hip-hop, as the culture's participants have invested a great deal of intellectual energy in the devel-opment of elaborate theoretical frameworks to guide its interpretation. This is a tremendous—and, in my opinion, grievously underutilized—resource for scholars. Engaging with the conceptual world of hip-hop via participant observation has been one of the most rewarding aspects of this project, and I have tried to reflect that in the pages that follow.

Another benefit of using participant observation to study popular music is that it allows the researcher to exploit the huge body of critical work on scholarly subjectivity that has emerged from the discipline of anthropology over the last thirty years. Critiques of reflexivity, the abstraction of human activity, and the idea of a discrete and bounded "field" are largely absent from writings on popular music because they are simply not relevant to the theoretical approach of most popular music scholars. Ethnography can bring these issues into the discourse.

I am particularly indebted to a recent piece entitled "You Can't Take the Subway to the Field" (Passaro 1997), which discusses the definitional problems that arose when a researcher chose to do fieldwork among New York City's homeless population. As Passaro suggests, the primary difficulty in this endeavor was maintaining a distinction between the subject of one's study and the other aspects of one's life, including the analysis of one's data. The origins of this distinction, its nature, and its use as an instrument of postcolonial power have been discussed at length in the anthropological literature (most notably Said 1978, Fabian 1983, Marcus and Fischer 1986, Gupta and Ferguson 1997) As Johannes Fabian (1983) in particular has convincingly argued, the idea of an objective and distinct "field" removes the culture of the researcher from the study's purview, despite the fact that it is often a deep and abiding influence on the processes being studied.[5] One of the aims of this work is to use the particular nature of my own experience, particularly moments of social discomfort or awkwardness, to implicitly question the value of the distinction between "home/academia" and "the field." In short, I feel that a researcher's self-conscious confusion over the nature of social boundaries can help to highlight the extent to which the researcher imposed those boundaries in the first place. With that in mind, I would like to address briefly some of the factors that came into play in this study.

Perhaps the most obvious feature working against the researcher who wishes to maintain the separation between these two worlds is that they often occupy the same physical space. This alone cannot help but illuminate the extent to which the separation is an ideological one. Another reason for disorienting overlap is that the scholar is often not the only individual who moves back and forth, and the resulting malleability of social barriers tends to blur any strict distinctions. A number of individuals who had a professional interest in the hip-hop world (including S. K. Honda, DJ Topspin, DJ E-Rok, Jake One, and MC H-Bomb) attended the University of Washington while I was studying hip-hop as a graduate student there. Seven of the people I interviewed for this project (Word-sayer, Kylea, Strath Shepard, Mr. Supreme, DJ B-Mello, Harry Allen, and Steinski) have lectured to classes I taught.

Perhaps the best example of this phenomenon in action was a festival of African American music that I attended in Seattle in the spring of 1999. The chair of my doctoral committee, a visiting artist, and several graduate students from my department performed Trinidadian pan music; they were immediately followed on the same stage by a hip-hop show that featured a number of my consultants from an earlier investigation of this subject. In between sets, I found myself in a conversation with two members of my committee and two of the people I was "studying," all of whom saw themselves simply as fellow participants in a musical event.

The inherently problematic nature of my relationship to the field served as an organic critique of the study itself at every stage of the process. Many of my consultants have approached me with new information or critiques that they wanted to share, sometimes years after I had initially interviewed them. At least one of the formal interviews as well as many informal discussions for this project were conducted in my home, a setting that in many ways reverses the power dynamic between interviewer and interviewee. Finally, I often unwound from a long day of writing by discussing my ideas with consultants in the backs of loud, smoky nightclubs in between their deejay sets. In other words, my fieldwork was itself a social process that interacted in manifold ways with the social processes that were the intended focus of this study. While this is of course true for anyone performing fieldwork, the difference in the case of Americans who study American popular music is that there is no formal beginning or end to our research; our participant observation (i.e., experiencing popular music within the context of American society) covers roughly our entire lives, as do the relationships that we rely on to situate ourselves socially.

I began to listen avidly to hip-hop in the mid-1980s and became actively involved in the Seattle hip-hop scene when I moved there to begin graduate school in 1992. Since then I have attended over five hundred hip-hop performances, club nights, or other events (an average of one per week for ten years). I began writing for Seattle's now-defunct hip-hop magazine *The Flavor* in 1995, and I have subsequently written about hip-hop for the *Seattle Weekly* and the magazines *Resonance, URB,* and *Vibe.* After I began this book, I bought a sampler of my own and began to make rudimentary beats, sometimes playing them for my consultants. It is perhaps more significant at my beginner's level of development that I have also found myself with an increasingly obsessive devotion to digging in the crates for rare records. In fact, when I attend academic conferences in different cities, my fellow hip-hop researchers (particularly Oliver Wang) and I often schedule an extra day to go record shopping. So when I'm digging through rare funk 45s on the floor of a tiny, dusty baseball-card store in Detroit with two people who were on my panel earlier in the day and a local hip-hop deejay, am I in the academic world or the field? I hope never to be able to answer that question. The use of participant observation and ethnography also means that the text that one produces is itself part of the social world one is studying. Its literary conceits often embody the relationship between the author and the context. I would therefore like to briefly discuss some of the choices I have made in transforming my research into a written text.

One decision that I have struggled with has been to refer to producers with masculine pronouns in most cases. This is not intended to be in any way prescriptive. *I do not believe that producers "should" be male.* But I do believe that most producers *are* male. Furthermore, it is clear (as I will discuss in chapter 2) that the abstract ideal of a producer is conceived in masculine terms and that this has a substantial effect on how individuals strive to live up to that ideal. I believe that the use of gender-neutral language would create a distorted picture of this process.

Similarly, I believe that specifying the ethnicity of particular producers who I quote in the following pages would also add distortions because the producers themselves did not make any such distinctions to me.[6] I am not suggesting that ethnicity is never a concern for these individuals or that history and culture do not affect the musical choices that artists make. But I am saying that the producers themselves tend to deemphasize its significance to their conduct *as producers.* As I argue throughout this study, there are no consistent stylistic differences between the practices of producers from different ethnic backgrounds. If there were a white or Latino style of hip-hop production, I think distinctions would be more justifiable. But, as I argue throughout this book, all producers—regardless of race—make African American hip-hop. And those who do it well are respected, largely without regard to their ethnicity. Given the charged nature of most multicultural interactions in American society, this facet of hip-hop culture is particularly remarkable. That fact became clear in my conversation with Steinski, a producer who is universally respected despite falling well outside of hip-hop's presumed "black youth" demographic; he is white and, at the time of our interview, fifty-one years old.

> Joe: Maybe I'm just being idealistic, but that's something that
> I really like about . . . hip-hop. Which is like, "People liked it
> because it was good. End of story."
> Steinski: Totally. I mean, that's been one of the best things about
> hip-hop. You know, that there's a lot of room in it for new shit,
> for anomalous shit, for all kinds of stuff. You know, like, "Here
> we have some of the best deejays on Earth, and they are all
> Filipino American!" Well, you don't see GrandWizzard Theo-
> dore sitting around going, "Those cats aren't authentic—they're
> not *black!*" It's like, they're *hip-hop*—that's the only thing that
> matters, man. . . .
>
> Yeah, I think that part of it's wonderful. That it's kind of like,
> "OK, anyone who can drag themselves in over the windowsill—
> they're in." I mean, that's really great—it was great then [in the
> 1980s], and it's great now. That part's really great. 'Cause other-
> wise, I'd be some asshole with a sampler, fifty-one years old,
> and who listens to me?[7] (Steinski 2002)

Questions of what it means to "be hip-hop" and the relationship of that state of existence to African American culture in general are at the heart of this study and at the heart of hip-hop production itself. But it is clear that this is a deep connection that hinges on the aesthetic assumptions and implications of the work that any given artist produces, rather than, for example, on the espousal of Afrocentric beliefs. Cultural background, while influential, is not determinative. Stated in the most simplistic terms, the rules of hip-hop are African American, but one need not be African American to understand or follow them.

This openness is not simply a matter of largesse on the part of hip-hop arbiters. Rather, it is a result of social processes that are intrinsic to the act of making beats, particularly the complex set of ethical and aesthetic expectations that producers must follow in order to be taken seriously by others. To follow the rules, one must first learn them from people who already know. In order to learn them from people who already know, one must convince them that one is a worthy student.[8] Thus the mere ability to follow the rules in the first place demonstrates that the individual in question has already undergone a complex vetting process, and the willingness to undergo that process demonstrates a commitment to the community and its ideals. This is presumably what Steinski is referring to when he mentions producers "drag[ging] themselves in over the windowsill"—there *are* dues to be paid, but once one is in, one is considered a full member of the community.

It is certainly possible that the apparent color-blindness of the producers' community is an artifact of my own racial point of view (as a Jew, I would be considered white by most Americans). But given the nature of my personality and those of my consultants, it is difficult for me to imagine that they would downplay racial issues simply to avoid making me uncomfortable.[9] In fact, I have discussed various racial questions with almost all of them in other contexts. Ultimately, though, this issue—whether I am underrepresenting the influence of race on individuals' approach to hip-hop production—can only be answered satisfactorily by a nonwhite researcher. From a purely logical standpoint, I cannot assess my own blind spots—if I could, they wouldn't be blind spots.

Another factor that particularly stands out in interview-based research is the disjuncture between the oral language of those who were interviewed and the written language of the author and secondary sources. In other words, my consultants' comments were initially presented orally, improvisationally, and in response to questions that they had not seen beforehand, while scholars' comments (both my own and quotations from other writers) were presented in written form, with (presumably) much forethought and revision. Moreover, many of my consultants speak African American English, even if they write Standard (i.e., European) American English. If one is not familiar with it, a written approximation of African American English—nonstandard by definition—may make the speaker appear to lack full linguistic competence. While such judgments are entirely the result of social prejudice, they may be reinforced by the textual juxtaposition of a quotation from a speaker of African American English and the broader text written in Standard American English. Generally speaking, I have followed Monson (1996) with regard to transcribing the speech of my consultants:

> I have chosen to use nonstandard spellings very sparingly. . . . I include such spellings when they seem to be used purposefully to signal ethnicity and when failure to include them would detract from intelligibility. Since African Americans frequently switch from African American idioms to standard English and back in the same conversation . . . orthographic changes can represent linguistic changes that carry much cultural nuance. For the most part I have preserved lexicon, grammar, and emphasis in the transcription of aural speech.[10] (Monson 1996: 23)

Beyond transcriptional choices, I have used three strategies to try to account for the occasionally jarring nature of these oppositions (oral versus written, African American English versus Standard English, improvised versus prepared), the first of which is simply to call attention to them. A second strategy has been, as often as possible, to include my own side of the conversation when I quote from interviews. In this way, I am able to present a record of my own oral expressions as an implicit point of comparison to those of my consultants.

Finally, I have shown drafts of this work to all of my consultants, in order to see that they are comfortable with the way their words are being presented as well as to make sure that my interpretations of their statements are consistent with what they actually meant. I believe that this is important, not only for ethical reasons, but also for simple accuracy. It is precisely the things researchers take for granted—our own assumptions about the way the world works—where we are most vulnerable and where our consultants can exert a decisively positive role.

The reader will also note that—unlike previous academics who have discussed hip-hop production—I tend to shy away from transcribing musical examples. Transcriptions (that is, descriptive graphic representations of sound) objectify the results of musical processes in order to illuminate significant aspects of their nature that could not be presented as clearly through other means. The core of this book is concerned with the aesthetic, moral, and social standards that sample-based hip-hop producers have articulated with regard to the music that they produce. I believe that transcription—or any other close reading of a single completed work of sample-based hip-hop—is more problematic than valuable for my purposes. There are four general areas of difficulty that bear on this question: the necessary level of specificity of a transcription, the ethical implications within the hip-hop community of transcribing a beat, the general values implicit in a close reading of a beat, and the specific deficiencies of transcription as a mode of representation with regard to hip-hop.

With regard to the level of specificity, most of the significant aesthetic elements I discuss are too general, too specific, or too subjective to be usefully analyzed through the close reading of any one beat. An example of an element that is too general is the myriad conceptual changes that a linear melody undergoes when it is "looped" or repeated indefinitely. An example of an element that is too specific is the microrhythmic distinctions that result in a beat either sounding mechanical or having what producers often refer to as "bounce." Finally, there are a number of psychoacoustic criteria that must be fulfilled for a sample to have "the right sound." All of these issues, I believe, are more usefully addressed through the producers' own discourse than through the objective analysis of a given musical example.

Transcribing a beat also has ethical implications. In the community of sample-based hip-hop producers, the discourse of aesthetic quality is primarily based on the relationship between the original context of a given sample and its use in a hip-hop song; that discourse consists of assessments of how creatively a producer has altered the original sample. For various reasons that I will discuss, however, the community's ethics forbid publicly revealing the sources of particular samples. Thus, while various techniques may be discussed, it is ethically problematic to discuss their realization in any specific case. This also means that when any two people present a producer's analysis to each other they are each implicitly confirming their insider status. This valence is one of the most significant aspects of the analysis (it is manifested in record knowledge and technical knowledge as well as aesthetic knowledge). In other words, the prohibition and what it represents are as significant as the information being protected.

Finally, previous transcribers of hip-hop music, who were acting (implicitly or explicitly) as defenders of hip-hop's musical value, have naturally tended to foreground the concerns of the audiences before whom they were arguing, which consisted primarily of academics trained in western musicology (see Walser 1995, Gaunt 1995, Keyes 1996, Krims 2000). This approach requires that one operate, to some degree, within the conceptual framework of European art music: pitches and rhythms should be transcribed, individual instruments are to be separated in score form, and linear development is implicit, even when explicitly rejected. While Adam Krims (2000) has moved the analysis away from specific notes and toward larger gestures, he has retained the rest of these conventions. I am not saying that these transcriptions are inaccurate, or even that the elements that they foreground are insignificant, only that they represent a particular perspective, which is, as I said, that of their intended audience: musicologists. My work, by contrast, is more ethnographic than musicological. As a result, I wish to convey the analytical perspective of those who create sample-based hip-hop music as well as those who make up its primary intended audience: hip-hop producers. Their analysis, I would argue, is not best served through transcription.

Most significantly, to distinguish between individual instruments, as in a musical score, obscures the fact that the sounds one hears have usually been sampled from different recordings *together*. Take, for example, a hip-hop recording that features trap drums, congas, upright bass, electric bass, piano, electric piano, trumpet, and saxophone. These instruments, in all likelihood, were not sampled individually. The overwhelmingly more plausible scenario is that the piece was created from a number of samples, one of which may feature upright bass and piano; another of which might feature drums, electric bass, electric piano, and trumpet; another of which may use only the saxophone; and another of which may feature only congas and trap drums. To present each instrument as playing an individual "part" is to misrepresent the conceptual moves that were made by the song's composer. But it is not possible to understand these conceptual moves through listening alone, even if one is trained in the musical form. One can only know which instruments were sampled together by knowing the original recording they were sampled from, which brings us back to the ethical and social issues raised by revealing sample sources.

Similarly, pitches, as elements at play within a framework of tonal harmony, are rarely conceived of as such and even then are rarely worked with individually; rather, entire phrases are sampled and arranged. Choosing a melody to sample (after considering its rhythm, pitch, timbre, contour, and potential relationship to other samples) is very different from composing a melody to be performed later.

The use of ethnography also raises questions about the subjectivity of the researcher. For white people writing about African American music, of course, this is an age-old question. Unfortunately it is often answered with guilty soul-searching, a confident recitation of one's credentials, or somewhat perfunctory admissions of outsiderness, all of which tend to be so particular to the individual in question as to be of little value to readers. One begins to move beyond the constraints of these strategies when one senses the underlying issues implicit in William "Upski" Wimsatt's rhetorical question (which arose when he reflected on his own experiences in hip-hop culture), "Hadn't I just been a special white boy?" (Wimsatt 1994: 30). In other words, when a white person does manage to forge a relationship with African American culture, there is a temptation to attribute this to some exemplary aspect of our own personality. While there may be some truth to this, it would be foolhardy—as Wimsatt convincingly argues—to ignore the larger forces at play. The difficulty lies in the fact that these forces manifest themselves primarily through our daily activities and interactions; it is often quite difficult to distinguish between one's own impulses and the imperatives of the larger society.

I believe that the most productive approach to this issue is for scholars to create a framework in which their particular paths may be interpreted as case studies of individuals from similar backgrounds pursuing similar goals. In other words, reflexivity is not enough: one must generalize from one's own experience, a pursuit which requires researchers not only to examine their relationships to the phenomena being studied, but also to speculate on the larger social forces to which they themselves are subject, a process that I would term "self-ethnography." I have found the work of Charles Keil (particularly his new afterword to Urban Blues [1991]) and William Upski Wimsatt (1994) to be particularly valuable as models for such endeavors.[11] To that end, I wish to discuss several aspects of my own life that may contribute to a broader understanding not only of my own project, but also of other such works created by researchers from similar backgrounds. In making this choice, I am intentionally avoiding the impulse to give a comprehensive explanation of my approach in favor of focusing of a few specific factors that I believe have been less exhaustively discussed elsewhere. These aspects include my ethnic and cultural background, social approach to scholarship, and age.

I was born in 1968 and raised in a predominantly white, Christian suburb of Hartford, Connecticut. I was introduced to participant observation at the age of five, when, according to my parents, I browbeat them into taking me to see Santa Claus at a large downtown department store. After a long wait, I made it to Santa's lap and was asked what I wanted for Christmas. "Oh, nothing," I replied, "We're Jewish."

This anecdote suggests to me that the experience of fieldwork was known to me at an early age and that it was used to define my own identity as a Jew in America. In other words, I was trying to understand what I was by engaging with what I was not. I knew Santa Claus wasn't for me, yet I wanted to experience and understand him anyway. And I would suggest that for American Jews in general, day-to-day living in an ideologically Christian society (not to mention conscious self-definition) is always, to some degree, a process of participant observation. I believe that this social impulse combined with a general Jewish predisposition toward scholarship as a mode of social interaction (see Boyarin 1997) may help to account for the disproportionate Jewish representation in fields that make use of ethnography, such as anthropology and ethnomusicology.

A more specific social aspect of this particular project and its value to me personally is the scholarly approach that hip-hop producers themselves take toward collecting old records for sampling purposes. This dovetails nicely with my own tendencies as an ethnomusicologist, insofar as I enjoy collecting records, talking about the minutiae of popular music, and making distinctions between things that are so fine as to be meaningless to the vast majority of people who encounter them. To put it another way, I am a nerd. In a surprising number of cases, this was common ground upon which my consultants and I could stand.

Another useful approach may be to see my attraction to hip-hop production as a delayed effect of the cultural environment in which I was raised—particularly that of 1970s television. As David Serlin (1998) has pointed out, children's shows of that era (especially *Sesame Street*, *The Electric Company*, and *Schoolhouse Rock*), presented multicultural utopias held together by what was, in retrospect, extraordinarily funky music.[12] While hip-hop samples from a variety of sources, there is a particular focus on music that was originally recorded in the early 1970s, an era that corresponds to early childhood both for me and for many of the most influential hip-hop producers. I imagine that at least some of the pleasure we derive from hearing a vibrato-laden electric piano or a tight snare drum comes from the (often subconscious) visions they conjure up of childhood and the mass-mediated friendships of Maria, Gordon, Rudy, and Mushmouth, who smiled at us through our TV screens.

In addition to its sociohistorical context, this book also exists with the academic tradition of scholarship on hip-hop. The development of a cohesive body of literature on hip-hop music, though still in its early stages, has already been characterized by a number of discernable trends. These trends have been extensively documented by Murray Forman (2002b). I would like to focus on a specific aspect of the academic literature that has influenced this study: the dispersal of the literature on hip-hop's precursors among a variety of academic disciplines, a situation that has unintentionally created an inappropriately fragmented portrait of hip-hop's origins.

Hip-hop's ancestors, when they have been studied at all, have been studied in ways that are not particularly related to music or to each other. I would distinguish five primary factors that contributed to the birth of hip-hop music: the African-American tradition of oral poetry; various kinesthetic rhythm activities, such as step shows, children's clapping games, hambone, and double Dutch; developments in technology for the recording and reproduction of music, culminating in the use of digital sampling; attitudes in African American cultures regarding the value and use of recorded music; and general societal (i.e., social, political, and economic) conditions that made hip-hop an attractive proposition for inner-city youth. Any useful scholarship on hip-hop that wishes to be grounded in the literature is therefore necessarily interdisciplinary because it must begin by integrating the literature on these diverse subjects. Of the five areas I have delineated, only one—societal conditions— had been extensively investigated prior to the birth of hip-hop. This, I believe, is one of the reasons that its significance relative to the other four factors is frequently overstated in many discussions of hip-hop culture.

Scholarship that ties the remaining four areas to the birth of hip-hop is sparse, a state of affairs I would attribute to two factors: first, for various social reasons (particularly race, class, and gender), precursors to hip-hop, such as toasts, double Dutch rhymes, and so on, have not until recently been seen as warranting academic attention, and second, because this material was inconsistent in many ways with academic ideas of "music," the literature that does exist is scattered among a variety of other disciplines, such as folklore and sociology. The literary tradition relating to hip-hop's precursors, then, seems to encompass the literature of every discipline *but* music, from African American oral poetry (folklore) to the rhythms of double Dutch (developmental psychology and sociology) to the technological developments of South Bronx deejays (history, sociology, and postmodern literary theory). Hip-hop—as music— becomes literally unprecedented. This may create an unbalanced environment for hip-hop scholarship because the scholar must explain how a musical form such as hip-hop could appear instantly from nowhere.

While few address this question directly, it does emerge in the literature in the form of a striking ahistoricality. As Keyes has noted, "Postmodern criticism tends to define rap music in modernity, thereby distancing it as both as a verbal and musical form anchored in a cultural history, detaching it as a cultural process over time, and lessening the importance of rap music and its culture as a dynamic tradition" (1996: 224). When I refer to the ahistoricality of much of the contemporary literature on hip-hop, I am referring to the difficulties of putting hip-hop music into the context of a larger *musical* history and the resulting implication that hip-hop as a musical form is sui generis. There have been several excellent works that strictly concern the development of the broader culture (see Castleman 1982, George 1998, Hager 1984, Toop 1991). Craig Castleman's work—essentially an ethnography of the graffiti-writing community in New York City (including police officers who try to stop graffiti writing)—has been a particular influence on this study. But most works on the musical facets of hip-hop present it as a discrete moment in time, and the few that do take a larger historical view almost universally follow the development of rapping, to the exclusion of other hip-hop arts. This has its benefits as well as its liabilities.

The primary benefit of such ahistoricality is that it implicitly presents history (i.e., a developmental paradigm based in linear time) as only one of a variety of possible settings for analytical work on hip-hop. Many of the works cited above primarily emphasize economic, social, and cultural contexts, all of which are valuable approaches. The liabilities emerge, however, when history is summarily excluded as a paradigm due to the paucity of source material or the requirements of a theory. While some scholars find that historical context is not relevant to their particular arguments, many imply that historical context *cannot* be relevant because hip-hop's use of previous recordings from different eras automatically voids the paradigm of historical development. This, I believe, is a mistake. As Keyes notes above, hip-hop's aesthetic is deeply beholden to the music of other eras, and an understanding of these sensibilities can only enrich our understanding of contemporary practice.

Furthermore, the boundary between hip-hop insiders and outsiders can be rather porous, a state of affairs that may be obscured when hip-hop is removed from its larger context. As I will show, the nature of the producers' art requires them more than other hip-hop artists to explore beyond the genre boundaries of hip-hop. The producer Mr. Supreme, for instance, rejects the notion that a "true hip-hopper" should listen only to hip-hop music: "If you're a real true hip-hopper—and I think a lot of hip-hoppers aren't—like I always say, 'It's all music.' So if you really are truly into hip-hop, how can you not listen to anything else? Because it comes from everything else. So you *are* listening to everything else. So how can you say 'I only listen to hip-hop, and I don't listen to this.' It doesn't make sense to me" (Mr. Supreme 1998a).

In fact, every producer I interviewed cited older musical forms as direct influences. An extreme example of this phenomenon arose in an interview with Steinski, who was a heavily influential figure in the development of sampling, particularly with regard to the use of dialogue from movies, commercials, and spoken-word records:

> Joe: If you weren't the first, you were one of the people that really
>   popularized that idea of taking stuff. . . .
> Steinski: Oh, cut-and-paste shit? Yeah.
> Joe: Were you the first person to really do that?
> Steinski: I don't think so.
> Joe: OK, I guess "Grandmaster Flash on the Wheels of Steel"—
> Steinski: Buchanan and Goodman. 1956. Did you ever hear the
>   "Flying Saucer" records?

Joe: Oh, where they cut in—they ask the questions and they kinda
. . . So you see that as an influence?

Steinski: Totally. More than an influence, it's a direct line. Yeah.
Absolutely, man. Those guys had pop hits with taking popular
music, cutting it up, and putting it in this context. Totally. Yeah.
Absolutely.[13] (Steinski 2002)

If such influences are rarely seen in scholarly writing about hip-hop,
it is largely because they do not answer the questions that scholars are
interested in: What does hip-hop's popularity say about American culture in the early twenty-first century? How does African American culture
engage with the mass media? How does global capitalism affect artistic
expression?

Although there have been several short works on the role of deejaying
in live performance (White 1996, Allen 1997), there has been very little
substantial work on sampling within a hip-hop context. In fact, to the
best of my knowledge, there have been only three widely published academic works that focus specifically on sample-based musical gestures
(Krims 2000, Walser 1995, Gaunt 1995). All three of these works emerge
from a similar disciplinary perspective: musicology informed by personal
experience with hip-hop music. All three authors provide insightful,
provocative, and—particularly in Walser's case—politically engaged analysis. But because they are musicologists, they focus on the results of sampling rather than the process; they are, essentially, analyzing a text.[14]
Again, each of these works stands on its own, but there is a resound-
ing silence when it comes to other perspectives on hip-hop sampling—
particularly when one considers that hip-hop has been a major form of
American popular music for almost thirty years.

There are two primary reasons for the lack of attention that the non-
vocal aspects of recorded hip-hop have received from academia. First,
the aesthetics of composition are determined by a complex set of ethical
concerns and practical choices that can only be studied from within the
community of hip-hop producers. Most researchers who have written
about hip-hop have not sought or have not gained access to that community. Second, most of the scholars who have studied hip-hop have
emerged from disciplines that are oriented toward the study of texts or
social processes, rather than musical structures. Simply put, it is not the

music that interests them in hip-hop. But such an approach—legitimate on its own terms—does reinforce the notion that the nonverbal aspects of hip-hop are not worthy of attention. For example, Potter, in an otherwise excellent book, dismisses the instrumental foundation of hip-hop almost out of hand, beginning a chapter with the pronouncement that "[w]hatever the role played by samples and breakbeats, for much of hip-hop's core audience, it is without question the *rhymes* that come first" (Potter 1995: 81; emphasis in original). In some sense, this entire study is devoted precisely to questioning this conclusion.[15]

The study begins with a brief history of sampling, questioning some of the assumptions that scholars have made about this history, which have subsequently influenced the general tenor of the scholarship on sampling. Specifically, I have tried to problematize the relationship between general societal factors—culture, politics, and especially economics—and hip-hop music, arguing that individual artists often have more control over the way these issues affect their work than they are given credit for. In other words, I am not so much interested in the conditions themselves as I am interested in the way hip-hoppers, given those conditions, were able to create an activity that was socially, economically, and artistically rewarding. In most cases, my approach can be expressed in three related questions: What are the preexisting social, economic, and cultural conditions? Given those conditions, what did the individual choose to do? Why was the individual's choice accepted by the larger community?

The practice of creating hip-hop music by using digital sampling to create sonic collages evolved from the practice of hip-hop deejaying. The nature and implications of these developments are discussed in chapter 2. Also discussed in that chapter is the way that this progression is largely recapitulated in the lives of individual producers as part of an educational process that intends to inculcate young producers in the hip-hop aesthetic. This process is ongoing throughout a producer's career and may affect many facets of hip-hop expression. In chapter 3, I address hip-hop producers' embrace of sampling by examining their rejection of the use of live instrumentation. I argue that sampling, rather than being the result of musical deprivation, is an aesthetic choice consistent with the history and values of the hip-hop community. Chapter 4 addresses the social and technical benefits of digging in the crates for samples. In addition to providing useful musical material, the practice also functions as a way of manifesting ties to hip-hop deejaying tradition, "paying dues," and educating producers about various forms of music, as well as a form of socialization between producers. Chapter 5 describes the so-called producers' ethics, a set of professional rules that guides the work of hip-hop beatmakers. These rules reinforce a sense of community by providing the parameters within which art can be judged, as well as by preempting disputes between producers. Chapter 6 looks at the aesthetic expectations that guide producers' activities. By critically assessing the producers' own discourse of artistic quality, I attempt to derive the underlying principles that they have created. In doing so I argue that to a great degree these principles reflect a traditional desire among people of African descent to assimilate and deploy cultural material from outside the community while demonstrating a subtle mastery of the context in which it operates. The hip-hop aesthetic is, in a sense, an African-derived managerial philosophy. Chapter 7 discusses the influences that come from outside the producers' community that may affect producers' conduct. Using the sociologist Howard Becker's (1982) notion of an "art world," I look at the immediate material and social forces that help to define the hip-hop world as a collective enterprise.

A significant portion of my discussion concerns the ways in which social, artistic, and ethical concerns work together to construct a sense of relative artistic quality and how this sense of quality circles back to affect individuals' social and artistic praxis.

It is useful to visualize these various levels of subjective quality (as judged by the producers themselves) as concentric circles with the center being the core of, the theoretically "best" approach to, hip-hop sampling. The outermost circle—the decision to use digital sampling rather than live instruments in the first place—reflects the purism of hip-hop producers in defining their genre (chapter 3). Once that decision has been made, the next circle consists of following producers' ethics, which define what may be sampled and how this sampling is to be done (chapter 5). Finally, the most valued status to be claimed by producers—the core—is that of one who, having done these things, is able to produce a creative work (chapter 6). Each circle represents both a level of artistic quality *and* the group of people who have attained that level. The smaller circles are seen as existing within the larger ones, so, for example, all people who adhere to producers' ethics use digital sampling, but not all people who use digital sampling adhere to producers' ethics.[16]

This entire configuration is itself contained within a larger social world, whose concerns deeply and necessarily affect a producer's output, another series of concentric circles.[17] Once again, while it is assumed that members of the inner circles abide by the outer, the reverse is not true. These outer circles include other members of the hip-hop industry, such as MCs, record company representatives, and radio and nightclub deejays, as well as fans. In chapter 8, I argue that this entire structure constitutes what Becker (1982) has called an "art world"—the total social network required to produce and interpret a work of art.

In the epigraph that opens this book, Mr. Supreme relates the common experience of hip-hop producers being questioned about whether or not hip-hop is "really" music. Whenever I speak about hip-hop production, this is almost always the second question I'm asked.[18] As I take pains to point out, it is actually a question about what the word "music" means, and it contains the hidden predicate that music is more valuable than forms of sonic expression that are not music. If one believes that only live instruments can create music and that music is good, then sample-based hip-hop is not good, by definition. The real question, in other words, is, "Can you prove to me that hip-hop is good?" And the appropriate answer, in my opinion, is "No, because it depends on what you personally consider to be valuable; hip-hop is what it is." This is essentially what Mr. Supreme is doing by creating an analogous argument about painting: if you believe that musicians should make their own sounds, then hip-hop is not music, but, by the same token, if you believe that artists should make their own paint, then painting is not art. The conclusion, in both cases, is based on a preexisting and arbitrary assumption.

In fact, the question itself is a trick: it loudly directs one's attention towards hip-hop's formal characteristics, while quietly installing its own prejudices about what music is supposed to be. The process is similar in both form and intent to the concept of the "noble savage" as explicated by Ter Ellingson (2001). By focusing on the question of whether or not savages were noble, the term's inventors were able to reinforce the ideas of "nobility" and "savagery"—both of which were deeply flawed—while simultaneously drawing attention away from them. Similarly, to be drawn into an argument about whether hip-hop lives up to the standards of other cultural forms can only weaken hip-hop's own internal values, and hip-hop producers clearly understand this. For thirty years, in fact, the hip-hop community has steadfastly refused to compromise its aesthetic principles in deference to the majority society.

If hip-hop is revolutionary, then this—even more than its lyrical message—may be where its power truly lies: in the fierce continuity of its artistic vision. And that, ultimately, is what this book is about. Which is why I consider it a statement of both intellectual honesty and political commitment to say that I love hip-hop. I love the crack of a tight snare drum sample, the feel of bass in my chest, and the intensity of a crowded dance floor. "They Reminisce Over You (T.R.O.Y.)" by Pete Rock and C. L. Smooth (1992) is not only a fine example of the sample-based hip-hop aesthetic. It is also one of the most beautifully poignant songs I have ever heard, and it never fails to send chills down my spine. It is these chills that are often lost in academic discussion. It is these chills that motivate hip-hop producers to devote their time and money to sample-based hip-hop. And it is these chills that have drawn me to produce the following study.

"It's about Playing Records"

History

In this chapter, I will discuss some of the developments that have led to current hip-hop sampling practice, beginning with a brief history of hip-hop sampling itself. Having done this, I will discuss the process by which individuals become hip-hop producers. A major influence on both of these processes has been the close historical and social relationship between deejaying (manipulation of turntables in live performance) and producing (use of digital sampling in the studio). Producers see deejaying as an essential element of hip-hop production, to the extent that elements of the practice are often read as symbols of an individual's commitment to hip-hop history and communal identity. Finally, I will address some of the ways in which tropes of masculinity have become encoded in this educational process.

With regard to all of these subjects, I try to stress the ways material reality and specific social pressures have influenced the decisions of individual creators. As I will argue throughout this study, I believe that analyses that focus on more general political and social concerns have tended to understate the agency of the people who have created hip-hop. As journalist and hip-hop pundit Harry Allen notes,

> That's the challenge. And this is a really interesting issue about history . . . to talk about the choices that people make as historical figures. . . . When we talk about history not just [as] a set of triumphal moments, but as decisions people make as they try to

wrestle with obstacles and . . . address fissures and questions and things that are not coming together. I think all people can relate to that. . . . They can relate to the idea of "I've got to do something different to get to someplace different." (Allen 2003)

Accordingly, before addressing the specifics of sampling history, I want to call attention to—and dispute—the scholarly tendency to naturalize hip-hop's emergence as a cultural force. In reading about the music's history, one often gets the impression that given the social, cultural, and economic circumstances in which it arose, hip-hop was inevitable; that if none of hip-hop's innovators had been born, a different group of poor black youth from the Bronx would have developed hip-hop in exactly the same way.

Although he is intentionally overstating his case for literary effect, Robert Farris Thompson exemplifies this approach when he writes that "in the Bronx at least, it seems the young men and women of that much-misunderstood borough *had* to invent hip hop to regain the voice that had been denied them through media indifference or manipulation" (Thompson 1996: 213; emphasis in original). Or, as Jon Michael Spencer puts it,

> The current emergence of rap is a by-product of the *emergency of black*. This emergency still involves the dilemma of the racial "color-line," but it is complicated by the threat of racial genocide: the obliteration of all-black institutions, the political separation of the black elite from the black working class, and the benign decimation of the"ghetto poor," who are perceived as nonproductive and therefore dispensable. . . .
>
> Both the rapper and the engaged scholar seek to provide the black community with a Wisdom [*sic*] that can serve as the critical ingredient for empowering the black community to propel itself toward existential salvation, that can overcome disempowering, genocidal, hell-bent existence. (Spencer 1991, v; emphasis in original)

In short, Thompson and Spencer are saying that hip-hop developed primarily as a form of collective resistance to oppression. While I certainly agree that the dire factors Spencer cites were significant in the lives of the individuals who developed hip-hop, I question whether their existence constitutes a sufficient explanation for the emergence of hip-hop's specific musical characteristics.

In fact, as the historian Robin D. G. Kelley has pointed out, the unquestioned association of oppression with creativity is endemic to writing about African American art, in general:

> [W]hen social scientists explore "expressive" cultural forms or what has been called "popular culture" (such as language, music, and style), most reduce it to expressions of pathology, compensatory behavior, or creative "coping mechanisms" to deal with racism and poverty. While some aspects of black expressive cultures certainly help inner-city residents deal with and even resist ghetto conditions, most of the literature ignores what these cultural forms mean for the practitioners. Few scholars acknowledge that what might also be at stake here are aesthetics, style, and pleasure. (Kelley 1997: 16–17)

Moreover, I would argue that, in addition to the misdirected focus that Kelley criticizes, such analyses may also promote several specific deterministic misconceptions.

The first of these is that a culture can exist outside individual human experience. Hip-hop was not created by African American *culture;* it was created by African American *people,* each of whom had volition, creativity, and choice as to how to proceed. This becomes apparent when one remembers that hip-hop did not emerge fully formed. Like all musical developments, it grew through a series of small innovations that were later retroactively defined as foundational. GrandWizzard Theodore, for example, was not forced by his oppressive environment to invent scratching when he deejayed in the mid-1970s; it was a technique that he discovered by accident, liked, and chose to incorporate into his performances. And if he hadn't, there is little realistic reason to assume that someone else would have. While his sociocultural environment nurtured and embraced his innovation, it did not create it.

In addition to cultural determinism, there is also a great deal of class determinism evident in the scholarly discourse of hip-hop. Although certain elements of hip-hop culture, such as b-boying or b-girling, graffiti writing, and emceeing may well be the products of economic adversity, other aspects, particularly deejaying and producing, are not: they require substantial capital investment. This, in and of itself, is not particularly significant, except to the degree that it contradicts the narratives of those who would characterize hip-hop as the voice of a dispossessed *lumpen-proletariat,* a musical hodge-podge cobbled together from the discarded scraps of the majority culture. David Toop, for example, writes:

> Competition was at the heart of hip hop. Not only did it help dis-place violence and the refuge of destructive drugs like heroin, but it also fostered an attitude of creating from limited materials. Sneak-ers became high fashion; original music was created from turn-tables, a mixer and obscure (highly secret) records; entertainment was provided with the kind of showoff street rap that almost any kid was capable of turning on a rival. (Toop 1991: 15).

Although Toop's examples are certainly accurate historically, one must be careful of letting the very real influence of material circumstance on individuals become inflated into either a motive or an aesthetic for an entire movement. To do so demeans the creativity of the artists involved, suggesting that they had no choice but to create what they did because no other path was open to them. It virtually precludes the possibility that people *chose* hip-hop's constituent elements from a variety of options and thus ignores the cultural values, personal opinions, and artistic pref-erences that led them to make those choices. Toop marvels that "original music" could be created from the "limited materials" of "turntables, a mixer and . . . records." But exactly how are these limited? The idea that an individual could have access to a deejay system and thousands of ob-scure records, but not to a more conventional musical instrument (such as a guitar or a keyboard), is difficult to accept.

New York–based producer Prince Paul, for one, disputes the asser-tion that hip-hop's innovators did not have access to other musical instruments:

> You know, everybody went to a school that had a band. You could take an instrument if you wanted to. Courtesy of your public school system, if you wanted to.
>
> But, man, you playing the clarinet isn't gonna be like, BAM! KAH! Ba-BOOM-BOOM KAH! Everybody in the party [saying]

"Oooohhhhh!" It wasn't that "Yes, yes y'all—y'all—y'all—y'all," with echo chambers. You wasn't gonna get that [with a clarinet]. I mean, yeah, it evolved from whatever the culture is. But it's just an adaptation of whatever else was going on at the time. . . .

It wasn't cats sittin' around like, "*Man.* Times are hard, man. . . . a can of beans up in the refrigerator. Man, I gotta—I gotta—I gotta —do some *hip-hop!* I gotta get me a *turntable!*" It wasn't like that, man.

Ask Kool Herc! He was the first guy out there. I know him, too. We talked plenty of times. A good guy. He's not gonna sit there and be like, "Man. It was just so *hard* for me, man. I just felt like I needed to just play beats back to back. I had to get a rhymer to get on there to make people feel good, 'cause times was just so *hard.*"

Yeah, cats kill me with that. (Prince Paul 2002)

DJ Kool Akiem of the Micranots also questions the notion of poverty as the decisive factor in the development of early hip-hop:

> DJ Kool Akiem: "They were too poor to get instruments." Yeah, right. They were too poor for classes. Somebody came along with a hundred-dollar sampler.
>
> Man, those samplers were [expensive] back then! I mean, you gotta have money, some way, to put your studio together. . . . Producing takes more money than playin' a instrument. You play an instrument, you buy the instrument and then you go to class, you know what I mean?
>
> Joe: Even deejaying costs more money than playing an instrument. . . .
>
> DJ Kool Akiem: I mean deejaying, if you're serious, you're gonna have to spend a thousand dollars on your equipment. But then every record's ten bucks. Then you got speakers and blah, blah, blah.
>
> Even saying that is kinda weird. Obviously, [the academics] just probably didn't think about it. The most important thing to them is, "Oh, the kids are poor," you know what I mean? Not even thinkin' about it. Just like, "Well, that must be it: they're poor!" (DJ Kool Akiem 1999)

As Prince Paul continues, in addition to broad social and economic trends, there were also significant aesthetic, personal, and even romantic factors that came into play when hip-hop was being developed:

> Deejay stuff was more expensive back then than it is *now*. I mean, like, *way* more expensive. So for them to even say that is crazy. [Hip-hop] was cool! It's like: *we liked the music*. Deejaying was cool. . . .
>
> Yeah, there's some socioeconomical issues and everything else that goes on, but that wasn't everybody's, like, *blatant* reason for making the music. There's some other stuff that people don't talk about. Like showing off, you know what I'm saying? There's stuff like girls. Loving the music in general. It's just the feeling that you get when you deejay. Especially back in the days. You can't even describe the whole feeling of how it was, because everything was so new and so fresh. . . . It was all about fun. And it was *a lot* of fun. (Prince Paul 2002)

In 1986, when sampling achieved its initial popularity, the least expensive version of the E-mu SP-12[1] carried a list price of $2,745—well beyond the budget of most inner-city teens (Oppenheimer 1986: 84). And while the current popularity of hip-hop music has led to an increased demand for inexpensive equipment, the Akai MPC 2000 (the most popular digital sampler used by hip-hop producers at the time of this writing) lists for $1,649 (*Musician's Friend Catalog* 2002). The enormousness of the initial investment required of hip-hop producers raises another question as well: how does one develop the capital and infrastructure necessary to make beats? Most of the producers I spoke with worked long hours at mundane jobs, received the equipment as gifts from their parents, or were given used equipment by older siblings or peers who had lost interest in using it. In other words, the reality in most cases is precisely what hip-hop's critics would presumably like to hear: a story of hard-working, close-knit families with a certain amount of disposable income and a willingness to invest that income in their children's artistic pursuits.[2]

Collective History

> The rap DJ evolved from the party DJ, whose ostensible role was merely
> to play pre-recorded music for dance parties; like their audiences, these
> DJs were *consumers* of pop music. Yet by taking these musical sounds,
> packaged for consumption, and remaking them into new sounds
> through scratching, cutting, and sampling, what had been consump-
> tion was transformed into *production*. (Potter 1995: 36)

The basic deejay system consists of two turntables and a mixer that controls the relative and absolute volume of each. Using this equipment, a
new record could be prepared on one turntable while another was still
playing, thus allowing for an uninterrupted flow of music. As has been
extensively documented elsewhere, the central innovation of early hip-
hop was the use of this system with two copies of the same record for
various effects, particularly the isolation of the "break."

As Toop relates,

> Initially, [Kool DJ] Herc was trying out his reggae records but since
> they failed to cut ice he switched to Latin-tinged funk, just playing
> the fragments that were popular with the dancers and ignoring the
> rest of the track. . . .
>
> A conga or bongo solo, a timbales break or simply the drummer
> hammering out the beat—these could be isolated by using two
> copies of the record on twin turntables and, playing the one section
> over and over, flipping the needle back to the start on one while the
> other played through (Toop 1991, 60)

Tricia Rose notes that these breaks soon became the core of a new
aesthetic:

> Samplers allow rap musicians to expand on one of rap's earliest
> and most central musical characteristics: the break beat. Dubbed
> the "best part of a great record" by Grandmaster Flash, one of rap's
> pioneering DJs, the break beat is a section where "the band breaks
> down, the rhythm section is isolated, basically where the bass gui-

tar and drummer take solos." . . . These break beats are points
of rupture in their former contexts, points at which the thematic
elements of a musical piece are suspended and the underlying
rhythms are brought center stage. In the early stages of rap, these
break beats formed the core of rap DJ's mixing strategies. Playing
the turntables like instruments, these DJs extended the most rhythmically compelling elements in a song, creating a new line composed only of the most climactic point in the "original." The effect
is a precursor to the way today's rappers use the "looping" capacity
on digital samplers. (Rose 1994: 74)

The development of elaborate deejaying techniques in the middle and
late 1970s lead to an increased intellectual focus on "the break." Deejays,
who are acutely conscious of audience reaction, now realized that they
could play a good break even if the song it came from was not considered worthy of listeners' energy. Breaks—played in isolation—came to
the fore. Songs, albums, groups, and even genres receded into the background as units of musical significance.

This, in turn, inspired deejays to cast an increasingly wide net when
looking for useful breaks. Since they were only playing a few, often unrecognizable, seconds from each song, they were no longer bound by the
more general constraints of genre or style; All that mattered was a good
break. In fact, many deejays are known to have taken a special delight in
getting audiences to dance to breaks that were taken from genres that
they professed to hate.

Pioneering deejay Afrika Bambaataa made precisely this point to
David Toop in 1984: "I'd throw on 'Sgt. Pepper's Lonely Hearts Club Band'
—just that drum part. One, two, three, BAM—and they'd be screaming
and partying. I'd throw on the Monkees, 'Mary Mary'—just the beat part
where they'd go 'Mary, Mary, where are you going?'—and they'd start
going crazy. I'd say, 'You just danced to the Monkees.' They'd say, 'You
liar. I didn't dance to no Monkees.' I'd like to catch people who cate-
gorise records" (Toop 1984: 66).

The breakbeat focus of the Bronx deejays set in motion a number of
social trends that would give birth to the music now known as hip-hop.
These included the development of a substantial body of knowledge about
the nature and location of breakbeats, an oral tradition and culture to pre-

serve this knowledge, a worldview that valorized the effort necessary to find breaks, and an aesthetic that took all of these concerns into account.

The looping aesthetic in particular (which I discuss more extensively in chapter 6) combined a traditional African American approach to composition with new technology to create a radically new way of making music. As breaks are torn from their original context and repeated, they are reconceived—by performer and listener alike—as circular, even if their original harmonic or melodic purposes were linear. In other words, melodies become riffs. The end of a phrase is juxtaposed with the beginning in such a way that the listener begins to anticipate the return of the beginning as the end approaches. Theme and variation, rather than progressive development, become the order of the day. And, although it would be easy to overstate this aspect, there is clearly a political valence to the act of taking a record that was created according to European musical standards and, through the act of deejaying, physically forcing it to conform to an African American compositional aesthetic.

At some point in the late 1970s, the isolation of the break, along with other effects (such as "scratching," "cutting," and so on), began to be considered a musical form unto itself. In other words, hip-hop became a musical genre rather than a style of musical reproduction when the deejays and their audiences made the collective intellectual shift to perceive it as music. This is often portrayed as a natural evolutionary development, but, as Russell Potter (1995) points out, it requires a substantial philosophical leap, one whose implications could not have been foreseen even by those who were at its forefront. One important force in the shift from hip-hop-as-activity to hip-hop-as-musical-form was the incursion of the music industry, which introduced significant distortions:

> Hip-hop's remaking of consumption as production was the first thing lost in this translation; despite its appropriation of Caz's rhymes, "Rapper's Delight" [the first major rap hit] was first and foremost a thing to be consumed, not a practice in action; its relation to hip-hop actuality was like that of a "Live Aid" t-shirt to a concert: a souvenir, a metonymic token. Hip-hop was something goin' down at 23 Park, 63 Park, or the Back Door on 169th Street; you could no more make a hip-hop record in 1979 than you could make a "basketball game" record or a "subway ride" record. (Potter 1995: 45–46)

Before sampling was invented—in the late 1970s and early 1980s—this decontextualization presented a very specific hurdle for the record industry: although playing a popular funk record at a hip-hop show made sense, playing a popular funk record *on a record* did not. It seemed strange (not to mention illegal) to release recordings that consisted primarily of other records. Early hip-hop labels, such as Sugar Hill, therefore, relied on live bands and drum machines to reproduce the sounds that were heard in Bronx parks and Harlem recreation centers. As Doug Wimbish and Keith LeBlanc (bassist and drummer respectively in the Sugar Hill house band) recalled in 1987, there was a conscious attempt on the part of the record company to capture the essence of these performances:

> Doug Wimbish: The reason you hear tunes [on Sugar Hill raps] and say, "Damn, I heard that tune before" is that you did hear it before. . . .
>
> Keith LeBlanc: Sylvia [Robinson, Sugar Hill president and producer] would be at Harlem World or Disco Fever, and she'd watch who was mixing what four bars off of what record. She'd get that record, and then she'd play us those four bars and have us go in and cut it better. (Leland and Stein 1987: 28)

But in the mid-1980s a new technology developed that was better suited to the needs of hip-hop musicians: digital sampling. In its earliest incarnation, sampling was seen as a strategy for expanding the tonal palette of the keyboard-based synthesizer, as in this definition from a 1986 issue of *Electronic Musician* magazine:

> Sampling is like magnetic tape recording in that both technologies involve the capturing, storing and recreating of audio (sound) waves. In fact, many of the standard terms associated with this technique (e.g. loop, splice, crossfade, etc.) have been borrowed directly from the world of magnetic tape recording. Sampling is the digital equivalent of music concrete, wherein common sounds are manipulated (and sometimes integrated with traditional instruments) to produce musical compositions.
>
> Sampling allows the musician to record sounds from other instruments, nature, or even non-musical sources, and transpose and play them chromatically on a standard piano or organ keyboard.

This new and emerging technology greatly expands the creative horizons of the modern composer. (Tully 1986: 27–30)

Another use, however, soon began to emerge. With the SP-12 in 1986, E-mu Systems introduced the "sampling drum computer" (Oppenheimer 1986: 84). Unlike earlier samplers, which were intended to provide musicians with novel sounds for their keyboards, the SP-12 was created to allow a producer to build rhythm tracks from individual drum sounds that had been previously sampled. In order to facilitate this process, it boasted three separate functions: the ability to digitally record a live drum sound ("sampling"), the ability to manipulate the resultant snippet to the operator's liking, and the ability to precisely organize many samples within a temporal framework ("sequencing"). Hip-hop artists would take the process two steps further. While the new technology was intended to shift the drum machine from synthesized, preloaded drum sounds to more realistic "live" sounds, hip-hop artists were soon using the machine to sample not their own drumming, but the sound of their favorite recorded drummers, such as Clyde Stubblefield from James Brown's band, or Zigaboo Modeliste of the Meters.

It wasn't long, though, before hip-hop producers would go even further. They soon began to use the SP-12 not only to sample drum sounds from old records, but also to sample entire melodies. This technique would not have appealed to musicians from other genres, who wanted the freedom to create their own melodies and had no interest in digital recordings of other people's music. For those trained as hip-hop deejays, however, the ability to play an entire measure—a break, in this case— from an old record was exactly what they were looking for.

The credit for exploiting this possibility is generally given to Queens-based producer Marley Marl. As Chairman Mao writes, "One day during a Captain Rock remix session, Marley accidentally discovered modern drum-sound sampling, thus magically enabling funky drummers from his scratchy record collection to cross decades and sit in on his own productions." (Chairman Mao 1997: 88). The innovation was quickly embraced, and almost immediately ended the era of live instrumentation. In fact, as I will discuss later in this chapter, many current artists characterize hip-hop's brief use of live instruments as merely a deviation, a capitulation to circumstance, rather than a step in hip-hop's evolution.

Hip-hop sampling grew out of the deejays' practice of repeating breaks until they formed a musical cycle of their own. The segments favored by early hip-hop producers tended toward funk and soul breaks, which—even in their original context—were clearly defined. An untrained listener, for example, can easily hear the beginning and end of the break in James Brown's "Funky Drummer" (1969), perhaps the single most-exploited sample in hip-hop music history. The break begins when everything but the drums stops playing and ends eight measures later when the other instruments resume. This conception of the break is consistent with that of the earliest hip-hop deejays; the drums are by far the most important element. In fact, the idea of a break with lackluster drums would actually be contradiction in terms.

But the advent of sampling yielded a significant change: because more than one loop could now be played simultaneously, producers could take their drums and their music from different records. With samplers, any music could be combined with a great drum pattern to make what is essentially a composite break. Moreover, different loops (and "stabs"—short bursts of sound) could be brought in and taken out at different times.[3] This substantially broadened the spectrum of music that could be pressed into service for hip-hop.

Today, the term "break" refers to *any* segment of music (usually four measures or less) that could be sampled and repeated. For example, the song "They Reminisce Over You (T.R.O.Y.)," by Pete Rock and C. L. Smooth (1992) is based on a break from a late-sixties jazz artist. The break in this case, however, is not a moment of intense drum activity but a two-measure excerpt from a saxophone solo. Presumably one who was not already familiar with the hip-hop song would not hear those particular measures as being significant in the context of the original music. In contemporary terms, then, a break is any expanse of music that is *thought of as a break* by a producer. On a conceptual level, this means that the break in the original jazz record was brought into existence retroactively by Pete Rock's use of it. In other words, for the twenty-four years between its release and the day Pete Rock sampled it, the original song contained no break. From that day on, it contained the break from "They Reminisce over You." Producers deal with this apparent breaching of the time-space continuum with typically philosophical detachment. Conventionally, they take the position that the break had always been there, it just took a great producer to hear and exploit it.[4] Record collecting is approached as if potential breaks have been unlooped and hidden randomly throughout the world's music. It is the producer's job to find them. This philosophy is apparent in a contemporary hip-hop magazine's review of a relatively obscure 1971 album, in which the author describes one of the songs as if it had been pieced together from subsequent hip-hop breaks:

> It opens with a solo sax that was re-arranged slightly to become the sax in Artifacts' "Wrong Side of the Tracks." Prince Paul's loop from "Beautiful Night" follows, along with everything but the drums and lyrics of Showbiz and AG's "Hold Ya Head" (sensing a trend?). This bassline also reappeared on Marley Marl's remix of The Lords of the Underground's "Chief Rocka." The cut closes out with the loop from Smif-n-Wessun's "Bucktown" is [sic] immediately followed by the Cella Dwella's classic "Land of the Lost." (Turner 2000: 64)

DJ Jazzy Jay even goes so far as to suggest that the original musicians may not have understood the significance of their own work: "Maybe those records were ahead of their time. Maybe they were made specifically for the rap era; these people didn't even know what they were making at that time. They thought, 'Oh, we want to make a jazz record'" (Leland and Stein 1987: 26).

As digital sampling became the method of choice for hip-hop deejays (who, now that they used sampling, began to call themselves "producers"), their preexisting hunger for rare records became of paramount importance. They developed elaborate distribution systems for records and knowledge about records, yet still went to great lengths to "discover" new breaks before others did. In the mid-1980s, a Bronx-based deejay named Lenny Roberts began to press compilations of rare recordings, each containing a sought-after rhythm break, under the name *Ultimate Breaks and Beats* (Leland and Stein 1987: 27). This development reinforced the producers' resolve to find new breaks that were rarer, and in response Roberts would compile those new breaks on new editions of *Ultimate Breaks and Beats*. As a result of such competition, hip-hop producers soon found themselves with record collections numbering in the tens of thousands as well as a deeply embedded psychological need to find rare records.

At the same time, this process established a canon of records—some of which appeared on *Ultimate Breaks and Beats,* some of which did not —that a producer had to be familiar with, an expectation that still stands to this day. For example, Bob James's 1975 jazz fusion recording "Take Me to the Mardi Gras," though it does not appear on *Ultimate Breaks and Beats,* was a favorite of early hip-hop deejays and producers (most notably, it forms the basis for Run-DMC's "Peter Piper" [1986]). It is so well known, in fact, that few contemporary producers would even consider using it for their own productions.[5] Nevertheless, producers must have the recording in their collections if they want to be taken seriously by others. As I discuss in later chapters, record collecting occupies a role for hip-hop producers similar to that of practice and performing experience for other musicians. Peers would consider a producer who did not own canonical records to be unprepared, in much the same way that jazz musicians would criticize a colleague who did not know the changes to "Stardust."

The *Ultimate Breaks and Beats* series, for its part, eventually grew to twenty-five volumes and spawned hundreds of imitators (see chapters 5 and 6).

> That was big, big, big, big influence to me, you know. I had 'em back in the days in like 1983, 1984, before they were even *Ultimate Breaks,* when they was just Octopus records with the little picture of the Octopus DJ on 'em. . . . That's what they were originally. And they didn't list any of the artists' names or anything, it was just the titles of the songs, no publishing info or nothing. It was just something somebody pressed up out of their house or something. Yeah, they were a big, big influence, man. I mean, I had all of 'em: doubles and triples of everything.
>
> That was the foundation of hip-hop, man, 'cause you listen to all the rap records when they first started sampling, and it was all that *Ultimate Break* stuff. That's the *foundation,* right there. (Stroman 1999)

Although many producers today see such compilations as a violation of producers' ethics (see chapter 5), most make an exception for the *Ultimate Breaks and Beats* collection on the grounds of its historical significance in alerting producers to the value of breaks in the first place: "Those were the ones that started folks looking for breaks and shit, anyway. I don't know too many people that got the original 'Substitution' break, you know? So nine times out of ten, if you hear that shit on a rap record, they got it from *Ultimate Breaks and Beats*" (Samson S. 1999).[6] Of course, not everyone made this exception:

Even [*Ultimate Breaks and Beats*]—I'll tell ya, man—there was a lotta mixed feelings about those, too. . . . You talk to old school cats like Grandmaster Flash, and they'll tell you that was like the worst thing to ever happen to hip-hop 'cause it took all the mystery out of the whole breakbeat game. But it inspired me, man. If it wasn't for them, I don't know if I'd even be in it to the level that I am now. (Stroman 1999)

As the 1980s wore on, the potential of digital sampling to go beyond the mere replication of deejaying techniques led to an increasingly sophisticated aesthetic for hip-hop music. In particular, producers made use of samplers' ability to play numerous samples at the same time (a technique which would have required multiple deejays and turntables), to take very short samples (which would have required very fast deejays) and to assemble these samples in any order, with or without repetition as desired (which could not be done by deejays at all).[7] The creative exploitation of these new techniques, along with parallel advances in emceeing, has led to the late 1980s being called the "golden era" of hip-hop.

One of the most significant forces in this development was the Bomb Squad, a production collective that became known for its work with Public Enemy. Their style—a blend of samples from diverse sources that emphasized chaos and noise—revolutionized hip-hop music. Keith Shocklee, one of the Bomb Squad's masterminds, specifically characterizes their sound as being in contrast to the typical African American fare of the time, supporting my earlier argument that hip-hop was not an organic development:

Public Enemy was never an R&B-based, runnin'-up-the-charts, gettin'-played-all-day-on-the-radio group. It was a street group. It was basically a thrash group, a group that was very much rock 'n' roll oriented. We very seldom used bass lines because the parallel that we wanted to draw was Public Enemy and Led Zeppelin. Public Enemy and the Grateful Dead. We were not polished and clean like any of the R&B groups or even any of our rap counterparts that were doing a lotta love rap. That just wasn't our zone—even though when we were DJs we played all those records. We decided that we wanted to communicate something that was gonna be three dimensional—something that you could look at from many different sides and get information from as well as entertainment. (Chairman Mao 1998: 113–114)

But for most producers, the contribution of Public Enemy and the Bomb Squad lay not so much in their particular approach but in the fact that they had a definable approach in the first place. They were self-consciously breaking new ground in their production style, and that was an inspiration to other producers.

Modern producers cite other historical figures from the late 1980s, such as Ced G of the Ultramagnetic MCs, Kurtis Mantronik, Prince Paul of De La Soul, and the Large Professor as artists whose individualistic styles contributed greatly to contemporary approaches. In fact, this collectively held historical consciousness is clearly one of the things that holds the producers' community together. The veneration of certain lesser-known hip-hop artists, for example, creates a common bond among contemporary producers.[8] One example of this tendency is the respect given to Paul C, a New York–based producer of the late 1980s who passed away before his work became widely known but whose style is heard in the music of those he influenced: "He kinda put it down for Ced G and Extra P [also known as the Large Professor] . . . I think he was one of hip-hop's biggest losses of all time. I think he was destined to be dope. He was gon' be the *man*. He was the best producer that never happened" (DJ Mixx Messiah 1999). Although his name is largely unknown in the broader hip-hop community, Paul C was cited as an influence by virtually every producer I interviewed for this study.

The move by hip-hop deejays into the studio was part of a larger trend throughout the spectrum of popular music toward the increased use of technology in the creation of music. It is no accident that the individuals who create hip-hop music call themselves "producers" rather than composers or musicians. The term "producer" came into vogue in popular music in the 1960s with such individuals as Phil Spector, Brian Wilson, and George Martin. While a recording engineer uses recording equipment to capture a sound on tape, a producer, although performing a materially similar task, is considered to have a larger aesthetic responsibility. A producer chooses the methodology of recording and often the musicians and studio in order to evoke a specific sensibility within the music (Theberge 1997: 192–193). This was a role that could not have be born until the technology existed to support it. When recordings were being made monaurally with two or three microphones, there was little room for individuals to put a personal stamp on the recording process. Although there were certainly creative individuals who developed innovative recording strategies during this era, their work was rarely appreciated beyond a small circle of aficionados, and even then it was noted primarily for its fidelity, rather than for its creativity. As a rule, the intent of recorded music until the 1960s was to reproduce the sound of live performance as accurately as possible (see Beadle 1993, Buskin 1999).

As studio technology developed to the point where musicians could create sounds in the studio that they could not possibly create live (such as playing a guitar solo backwards), the roles were reversed, and the studio recording became the ideal to which live music aspired. Albums such as the Beach Boys' *Pet Sounds* (produced by Brian Wilson) and the Beatles' *Sgt. Pepper's Lonely Hearts Club Band* (produced by George Martin) began to experiment with the artistic possibilities of studio recording. It was at this time that the role of the producer became both feasible and significant (Beadle 1993). In the 1970s, developments in electronic music (particularly the advent of synthesizers and drum machines) made the producer even more important because live musicians were no longer an essential part of the recording process. The roles of composer and musician became integrated into that of the producer. Disco producers such as Giorgio Moroder found they needed only drum machines, synthesizers, and a live vocalist to make hits (Buskin 1999:, 201–205). The development of digital sampling technology in the 1980s continued this trend, bringing past recordings of live musicians back into the electronic mix.

For hip-hop producers the process of creating recorded music has become almost completely estranged from the process of capturing the sound of live performance. Live performance (deejaying aside) does not serve as a significant model for the producers' aesthetic. Conversely, live performances of hip-hop are rarely concerned with reproducing any specific processes from the studio (aside from emceeing); the studio recording is simply played (and sometimes manipulated by a deejay). In fact, one of the major challenges of performing hip-hop on instruments, in the rare cases where this is done, is that many of hip-hop's most typical musical gestures (such as sixteenth notes played on a bass drum) are virtually impossible to reproduce without electronic editing. Sample-based hip-hop is a studio-oriented music.

One effect of this approach is hip-hop's celebration, almost unique in African American music, of the solitary genius. Hip-hop producers hold an image of themselves that recalls nothing so much as European art composers: the isolated artist working to develop his or her music. As producer Mr. Supreme says on his Web site, "It's the shit to be at home at 4:00 in the morning, in your boxers, in front of your sampler, making some *shit,* you know?" (Mr. Supreme, interviewed on www.conceptionrecords.com, accessed 9 July 1999). In a describing his ideal work setting, Mr. Supreme cites three factors, each of which specifically diminishes the possibility of other individuals being present ("at home," "at 4:00 in the morning," and "in your boxers"). This, he suggests, is the best environment in which to create hip-hop music. Hip-hop music confounds many of the generalizations that have historically been made about the communal nature of African American music, especially those that interpret specific musical interactions as reflecting deeper truths about social interactions.

The history of hip-hop sampling, like the history of most musical forms, is a story of dialectical influence. Innovations are accepted only if they conform to a preexisting aesthetic, but once accepted, they subtly change it. Sampling was initially embraced because it allowed deejays to realize their turntable ideas with less work. But the sampler quickly brought hip-hop to places that a turntable could not enter. Nevertheless, a certain consciousness about the significance of the turntable informs sample-based hip-hop even to this day. Moreover, as with any historical narrative, the shape of this story is largely informed by contemporary needs. The narrative that I have recapitulated above is in some sense the origin myth of sample-based hip-hop and serves the needs that such a title implies: it provides a sense of rootedness, group cohesion, and direction for the future. Specifically, this version of hip-hop history foregrounds an evolutionary paradigm that naturally presents current practice as the pinnacle of history. It also notably excludes the influence of disco music on early hip-hop practice (see Fikentscher 2000, Brewster and Broughton 2000).

Individual Histories

The development of individual producers' technical ability often mirrors the development of the form as a whole. This is due primarily to three factors, the first of which is a socioeconomic concern that runs across the spectrum of human activity: one does not invest a substantial amount of money in a pursuit until one is certain that one is serious about it. For instance, Stradivarius violins are beyond the price range of most violinists; even if one could afford it, one would not buy a Stradivarius for a beginning violin student. Similarly, even if they can afford it, few producers purchase state-of-the-art equipment until they are in a position to exploit it to the fullest. As a result, many producers develop their talents on outdated equipment, which is less expensive to purchase and in many cases simpler to operate.

The second factor is a sense that, on a pedagogical level, the most practical educational approach is to recapitulate the form's musical evolution to ensure that each important technique is mastered before moving on to the next one. This approach has a compelling internal logic, if only due to the fact that more complex technologies and techniques tend to develop out of simpler ones, rather than vice versa. Finally, there is a broader belief that an individual working through hip-hop history can develop a deeper understanding of the more abstract philosophical and aesthetic foundations of the form.[9]

For many producers, the educational process began with a single tape deck and the creation of so-called pause tapes: "Basically, it's an early form of sampling, in the most ghetto form possible. What you do is you play a record, and then you pause [the tape], and you play the break, pause it, bring it back, play the break, pause it . . . 'til you have like a continuous loop. And then I'd take another tape and rap over that, put like scratchin' and shit on it. So I started doing it that way" (Samson S. 1999). At some point, many—though not all—acquire a second turntable and a mixer and begin to learn about deejaying. Most producers see learning to deejay and learning to produce as being part of the same process; none of my consultants made a distinction unless I specifically asked them to. Most began by experimenting on their own, and it was only later, after they had achieved some proficiency, that they met other like-minded individuals and began to share information. This pattern has led to certain idiosyncrasies becoming formalized in hip-hop practice:

> Mr. Supreme: Just learned on my own, really. . . . And another
> funny thing is that nobody taught me and when I brought that
> $24 mixer and I came home, I plugged up the turntables. I
> didn't know, but I plugged 'em in backwards. And to me that
> was right, 'cause I didn't know. I just naturally thought number
> one would be on the right side, two would be on the left side . . .
> That's how I plugged 'em in and that's how I taught myself.
> And now a lot of deejays say, "Yeah, you're weird. You go
> backwards."
> Joe: Oh, so you still have to do it that way.
> Mr. Supreme: Yeah, to this day! That's how I learned. I can't go
> the real way. And that's called a "hamster." A lot of deejays are
> called "hamsters," that go backwards . . . I don't know who
> came up with that name or why. (Mr. Supreme 1998a).

In fact, many mixers are now outfitted with a "hamster switch" that automatically reverses the controls so that a backwards deejay can use another deejay's setup without unplugging the turntables to reverse them. So many individual deejays made the same mistake when figuring out how to deejay that their approach, backwards deejaying, is now an accepted practice in the community. This pattern, individual experimentation retroactively legitimized by a professional peer group, can been seen at many points in the development of hip-hop (and, in fact, in most forms of music).

For most, the development of deejaying proficiency was followed by the acquisition of an inexpensive keyboard instrument with a rudimentary sampling function. At this point, the music is powered by youthful enthusiasm, creativity, and a generally high-school-aged peer group that didn't have very high expectations in the first place. Hieroglyphics producer Domino describes his origins as a producer:

I had a partner named Jason at the time. Basically, I was their MC, and we were producing together. . . . I bought this little keyboard, and basically you would push the button and whatever you put into it would be what it sampled. Like, I started off by saying, "I'm dope! I'm dope! I—I—I'm dope! I'm dope!" Didn't have enough insight to do anything with it. Well, he sampled the beat. We used to just like have a continuously drum break and tape it on a tape. And then have another tape player and then record from that tape to another tape player, and add stuff off the sampler—the new things that we had sampled. So by the time you're done, you got like a fifth generation copy. . . . That was the initial way that we sampled. That's how we had the different tracks was by dub, tape to tape. (Domino 1998)

DJ Topspin describes a similar process, which soon evolved into an impossibly byzantine home "studio":

I got a Casio keyboard, a sampling one . . . for Christmas. . . . I thought that was interesting when I first got it. I was like, "Oh, you can sample your voice," and I'd just do that forever and ever. . . . You couldn't really do too much with it, until I looked at the back of it, and there was a input. So you could do something other than your voice. So I went to Radio Shack. . . . I got the thing hooked up. . . . It had the input, and I plugged into the Yorx [stereo] . . . and sampled little bits of stuff. And then I took my Walkman . . . and would sample pieces from a song.

I mean, it was . . . like with a little Y-jack, like you have two head-phone female jacks, and it would be one going into the sampler, one coming out of the Walkman, and vice versa. This big spiderweb concoction. But you could end up playing the Walkman, while hearing you triggering the sampler. . . . The machine was so limited, you could only do like halfs or thirds [of a loop] sometimes, you couldn't get a whole. You'd have to overdub all those pieces. So you'll have like a six-, seven-generation beat. [But] people I was runnin' around with were like "Yeah, that's the *shit,* man!" (DJ Topspin 1999)

Notice that both Domino and DJ Topspin specifically point out how their low expectations facilitated their early development. Both reflect with some amusement that their efforts were acceptable by the standards of their peers.

As they become more emotionally and financially invested in their work, most producers acquire increasingly professional equipment to facilitate it. This raises the issue again of sample-based hip-hop as a non-performative genre. Abstract and aesthetic concerns aside, there is a practical issue here: the hip-hop musician's instrument, the sampler, is a piece of studio equipment. This simple fact totally obliterates conventional distinctions between performing (or practicing) and recording. Everything that is done with a sampler is, by definition, recorded. Moreover, the output of the sampler is almost always transferred to a conventional medium, such as digital audiotape or CD. At the most basic level, the hip-hop producer's "instrument" (sampler/sequencer, mixer, and recording device) is a rudimentary home studio.

Virtually all sample-based hip-hop producers do the majority of their work in such home studios. As Theberge notes, this is typical of contemporary electronic music: "In genres of music that rely heavily on electronically generated sounds, a great deal of pre-production sequencing in the home studio (no matter how modest the quality of the synthesizer set-up) became possible. You could then simply carry the work on diskette to a more professional facility where 'finishing' work could be performed in a reasonably short amount of time" (Theberge 1997: 232).

For many non–hip-hop electronic musicians, the use of a home studio is a matter of convenience and expense rather than of socialization. They tend to make their studio spaces as distinct from their domestic pursuits as possible:

Often ignored . . . is the manner in which the domestic space has been transformed into a production environment. Musicians' magazines often use cliches such as the arrival of the "information age" and Alvin Toffler's (1980) notion of the "electronic Cottage" to explain the existence of the home studio. It seems to me that there is something else quite striking about this particular manifestation of contemporary music-making that is very different from previous uses of music technology in the home; that is, the degree to which the home studio is an isolated form of activity, separate from family life in almost every way.

The home studio is, above all, a private space. Studios tend to be located in bedrooms, dens, or basement rec rooms, far from the main traffic of everyday life. . . . The home studio is thus, by design, a private space within a private dwelling. (Theberge 1997: 234)

For hip-hop artists, however, the integration of the production environment with domestic space is one of its primary benefits. During the time of my research, the Lion's Den, the home studio of the Jasiri Media Group, featured a playpen for the MCs' infant son, and the Pharmacy, Vitamin D's home studio, actually had a bed in it. In fact, as Vitamin D reports, the sense of social ease and domesticity that a home studio can provide is one of its major selling points:

There's really no time-rush thing. You're at the house. . . . People come through unexpectedly and it just adds a whole different energy in the room. So when you're busting [rapping], it's like you kinda get their energy in the track, too. . . . It's how you can keep the spontaneity and stuff going. A lotta times, the best ideas that we've come up with . . . they were spontaneous, they just kinda, "Let's just do this. Let's do it!" you know? You can't do that in a studio. . . .

And you get inspired at different times. You're not always inspired right then, you know? It's like, I might be cleaning up the house, listening to some Miles Davis and hear a cold little riff or something, be like, "Man!" you know? "I gotta sample that right now!" Instead of going in the studio, doing all this. If I become inspired by something right there . . . I'm 'a get to chopping up these pianos, and then lead on from there, I might add these other records and start mixing over it. And it becomes what you hearing on tape. And you can't get that with just going in the studio. (Vitamin D 1998)

And yet the very fact that these home studio spaces have their own names (e.g., "the Lion's Den," "the Pharmacy," "the Basement" [Pete Rock's studio]) suggests that producers actually do see them as being distinct from their general domestic environment. In fact, when referring to the home studio environment in the abstract, producers often refer to it as "the lab," a term which very clearly draws a distinction between work space and living space.[10]

As with any form of music, an important technique of self-education is to listen to other artists in order to learn new techniques:

> Jake One: I try to get into people like that's heads . . . just to know. I'm just curious. You try to break down their method . . . figure it out. (Jake One 1998)

> Joe: So you, like, listen to other producers and break down their formula . . .
> Vitamin D: All producers do that, whether they admit it or not. (Vitamin D 1998)

This does not mean that producers want to imitate each other; the things they listen for tend to be very subtle techniques that nonproducers would most likely not notice. When I asked Negus I if he studied other producers, he was explicit on this point:

> I do. Yup, I do it all the time. Like Timbaland, I'll put him up there, because I like the way he makes beats, in that he samples occasionally, but for the most part his compositions are original. He does use some sounds, but for the most part he doesn't use looped samples. I'm impressed by his music, by his beats. Not that I would necessarily emulate his sound, but . . . I'm impressed with what he's done, in terms of his originality, his creativity. . . . But if

I made a beat that sounded too much like him, I would be like "Man, that sounds too much like Timbaland." I wouldn't be happy with it, because it sounds too much like someone else's style. (Negus I 1998)

And such listening is not limited to hip-hop:

> Joe: Do you listen to other producers to break down their method?
>
> Domino: I listen to *all* music like that. Today I was listening to the Beatles. I was just peepin' how they have things panned [where sounds are placed in the stereo field]. And the ways that they totally change the song, within the song. And how they have a certain type of effect behind the MCs' vocals, or behind the guitar, or whatever.
>
> Whenever I listen to music, I'm not the type of person who really has it as background music. . . . I gotta turn it on, and listen to it, and really listen. . . . That's just how I am. (Domino 1998)

Domino's telling slip—referring to the Beatles' singers as "MCs"—suggests that he is actually listening to the Beatles *as hip-hop music.* While he may appreciate many diverse aspects of the Beatles' music, the elements he cites (how instruments are set off from each other spatially, the structure of the song, the use of various effects) are all specifically applicable to hip-hop production. The producers' aesthetic is such that innovations from other musical forms can be brought in to their own practice.

An important adjunct to the listening process is discussion of hip-hop music with other producers. It is not surprising that this often takes the form of ridiculing absent third parties. As I will discuss in chapter 6, ridicule plays an important role in maintaining the continuity of the hip-hop aesthetic; however, it is also an important pedagogical tool. Hearing another producer berated for something can lead a young producer away from it, before it even becomes an issue in his own music:

> King Otto: I really don't talk with that many producers about mak-

ing beats, per se. We just talk about other people's beats. . . . like make fun of someone else's beat. . . .

Joe: What types of things would you make fun of somebody for doing?

King Otto: There's occasions where maybe somebody sounds like somebody else, 'cause everyone has their own distinct style, but sometimes you'll cross the line and make a [DJ] Premier beat. I know I've done it. Or maybe a Pete Rock beat. 'Cause their sound is so distinct. If you get too close to it you can tell. (King Otto 1998)

This process has a secondary function in that by mutually criticizing other hip-hop artists, producers are implicitly complimenting each other on their knowledge and taste:

I think an interesting dynamic to that, too, is that that type of exchange is something that only happens with people that have relationships with each other where they know that [they both have] a degree of knowledge within music, where that's even the point for bringing the conversation up. It's like, "I know how you know music," so it's like, "What's up with this?"

But it's not just something that you casually do, just every day. You don't sit around and critique, or whatever. But, definitely. That's almost like out of acknowledgement, you know what I'm saying? You respect the other person's opinion, so you wanna see where they're at, with the other music. That's definitely true. MCs do it with MCs. MCs do it to producers. That's the element within the culture where it's like, "Is it fresh, or isn't it?" (Wordsayer 1998)

The producers' educational process is not only practical and historical; it is also deeply ideological. Specifically, it promotes the mythological deejay as the cornerstone of the musical form and, by extension, the community itself: "When you learn as a deejay, you learn what the break is about. That's really like what sampling is about. It's about the break. And it's not really about playing music. It's more of doing what a deejay does" (DJ Kool Akiem 1999).

Academics who have written about sample-based hip-hop have tended to discuss either the meaning of particular samples (Gaunt 1995, Wheeler 1991) or the significance, within a given theoretical framework, of sampling *as a concept* (Costello and Wallace 1990, Lipsitz 1994, Potter 1995, Rose 1994, Walser 1995). While these are both important aspects of sampling's appeal, they have tended to overshadow the specific meanings that sampling as a process carries for those who engage in it. Looking at sampling as a discrete activity that individuals choose to engage in for specific reasons allows us to ask questions about who those individuals are, what their reasons may be, and what their choices can tell us about these questions.

Sample-based hip-hop is produced by a community of like-minded individuals—hip-hop producers—who consider themselves a community and actively work to maintain themselves as such. One of the major tools of this pursuit is the continuous reconstruction of a common history, the cornerstone of which is the heroic figure of the deejay. As a result, broad ideas about the value of community are often transmitted among hip-hop producers as unexamined, common-sense aesthetic notions about deejaying. In fact, the association between deejaying and sampling is so strong that the terms "deejay" and "producer" are often used interchangeably.

When I asked him about this relationship, DJ Kool Akiem constructed a historical argument that associated sampling with deejaying in order to exclude the aforementioned use of live instruments in the late 1970s and early 1980s:[11]

People could say, "Well, Sugar Hill Gang [used live instruments]." Yeah, but see: that's before there were samplers, too. And if they had the sampler, I would like to think that they woulda sampled. That was before there were samplers, and . . . they couldn't just play the record. . . . That's part of the history that people don't really realize: that hip-hop is about the turntables. And cats was rhymin' on turntables. And when they started makin' records . . . they had no choice but to get a band . . . but as soon as there was a sampler, they went back to the root. How it originally was, you know what I mean? (DJ Kool Akiem 1999)

Note that in DJ Kool Akiem's formulation, the use of turntables is organically linked to the use of samplers, and live instruments are outside that direct line. "As soon as there was a sampler," he says, hip-hop musicians were able to return to their original conception, "to the root." There is certainly ample reason to hold this perspective; turntables and samplers *are* similar in that they both utilize other recordings as their means of sound production. But much of the apparent similarity is actually due to the outlook of hip-hop producers themselves; as I discussed earlier, the samplers that they use were never intended to repeat sections of old records.

In other words, I disagree with DJ Kool Akiem when he suggests that hip-hop artists use samplers because they are like turntables. I would argue that, in fact, samplers are like turntables *because* hip-hop artists use them. This is an important distinction because it suggests that DJ Kool Akiem's articulation of a historical narrative that authenticizes sampling by associating it with deejaying is actually part of the same process that caused sampling to be adopted in the first place. Both are results of the hip-hop community's effort to invest a new technology—samplers—with the cultural cachet of an older one—turntables.

This effort is not only a broad theoretical move on the part of the community; it is also manifested in the socialization of individual producers. Virtually all producers, for example, characterize deejaying as an important factor in a producer's education. This implicitly includes the claim that the things that one would learn as a deejay—such as how live audiences react to certain sounds and the way any given melodic phrase would sound if repeated—*ought to* be exploited when sampling. This tendency is buttressed by the implicit acceptance of the aforementioned historical narrative, as well as by explicit statements expressing the value of deejaying to hip-hop production in terms of its historical significance, statements such as "deejays make better producers because the turntables are the foundation of hip-hop."

On the subject of education, most producers take the position that to have a true understanding of the culture, each hip-hop artist should, to some degree, personally reproduce its history: "I think the basis of [production] is deejaying. A lot of people that just get into production, I don't think they have the foundation of what they're doing. It's not really all that direct. I mean, you can learn how to produce. You can make good stuff. But I think you have a better foundation if you're a deejay. Not only 'cause like the history of it, but just some of the mechanics of it" (DJ Kool Akiem 1999). DJ Mixx Messiah agrees: "I think that's a big thing in production, because it's actually the same concept. Because deejaying is pretty much combining sounds and splittin 'em and breakin' 'em down to tracks. And when you hit the [studio] console, for a producer, it's basically just deejaying with more inputs and more outputs, splittin' 'em, you know, more ways. So if you can execute a perfect mix on the turntables, it's almost like you internin' for the console" (DJ Mixx Messiah 1999). Note that this prescription, however, remains very selective—although most producers would agree with DJ Mixx Messiah that a good producer should start out as a deejay, few—if any—would say that a producer should then learn to play bass before moving on to sampling, despite the fact that the use of live instruments was demonstrably a stage in hip-hop's development. Within the contemporary ideology, it is not considered an important stage.

In fact, many producers will argue that the entire production process is, at its foundation, simply a more elaborate form of deejaying:

I think that there's that definite connection because, ultimately, what is sampling today used to be done by the deejays, live. . . . There's a lot of different styles of producing, but . . . one of them was . . . rhyming over breakbeats. Just records. Sample and have it loop. Well, what the deejay's job was, early on—and still is to a lotta people—is to find these breaks and have 'em go back to back to extend the beat, before sampling. So, basically, the concept was done; it's just that it wasn't done with equipment, it was done with a deejay. So they would play this one part of the record, back and forth, back and forth, and then the MC would rhyme over it. So I think it's basically the same thing, in a sense. But now . . . with sampling and stuff you can do more with it, of course. . . .

Let's put it like this: what I do with a sampler, if I had like a twenty-four track [mixing] board, I can have a deejay come in and go, "Make this beat loop." And they can lay that down on one track. And then I can say, "OK, bring in this horn every fourth." Whatever I would sample. And I could have 'em do that . . . and you would be able to pretty much accomplish the same thing. And so I guess it all depends on your outlook, but it's pretty much the same thing. (Domino 1998)

In other words, Domino is suggesting that virtually everything that he does as a producer could conceivably be done by a deejay—it would simply take more time and effort. And this is not merely a philosophical conceit; in some (very rare) cases, production is actually done this way:

I know this cat, before he had a sampler, he did all his production on a four-track [tape recorder]. And he cut everything [with turntables] but you couldn't tell. It sounded like he sampled it 'cause he would either get back to backs or he would keep goin' back and loopin' it over and over again. And . . . he made sure it was precise; if it wasn't precise, he went back and re-recorded it. But, nobody knew—including me, until he told me—that he didn't have a sampler. It was like, "What? You don't have a sampler?!"[12] (DJ Kool Akiem 1999)

Even though most producers today do not use turntables as the primary technology for production, they can still be a valuable secondary tool:

Another thing that I do . . . when I'm making a beat, is that I have a beat running, and I make the main foundation part of it. And then when I find something that sounds like it could go, the first thing I do is I try—and this kind of like goes with the deejay skills—is that I try to line it up. I try to get it on beat, and then try to mix it in with it. So right on the downbeat, I might just cut it in, and just see how it sounds runnin' with it. So I don't have to just go and waste the time of sampling it, and then finding out it's good. Sometimes you can get a gauge of how something might fit by having the beat running with it and then just taking the record and cuttin' it in with it, on beat, and hearing how it sounds. (Domino 1998)

When we discussed the liabilities of producers who did not also deejay, Vitamin D specifically pointed to this technique as being one of the tools they lacked:

Joe: But you feel like [not being able to deejay] kinda limits them
in certain ways, just at least in terms of the things that you
would want to do. . . .

Vitamin D: Nah, I just know it limits them, period. *They* know it
limits them. They're like, "Man, if I could deejay, I'd be able to
mix in a sample and be able to hear what it sounds like and I
could feel it." They can't do that 'cause they don't know how to
mix in the samples. (Vitamin D 1998)

Negus I, who is a producer but not a deejay, supports Vitamin D's
claim on a general level: "It seems like most producers started out as
deejays, but I started out straight producing. . . . I do clearly see the dis-
advantages. Deejays are more familiar with a lot more records and more
music, even though I do listen to a lot of music. But they're more intimate with the actual records and the sound quality of the records. So I
kind of had to fight through that without having that experience as a
deejay" (Negus I 1998).

On a more practical level, as deejay Oliver Wang notes, there are other
reasons why most producers begin their careers as deejays:

It's definitely not a coincidence that most producers start off as
deejays. Because not only were they exposed to music in a very significant sense, they were basically exposed to music a lot, in volume. And also they have access to music, which is always important in sampling. A lot of deejays are also record collectors, which
transitions well to becoming a producer, since you have a source of
sampling to work from. And because deejaying works as a profes-
sion, that can earn you the capital that you would need to become a
producer as well. So I think all those different things kind of work
together. (Wang 1998)

Finally, specific deejaying techniques, especially scratching (the rhythmic use of the sound of a record being pulled back), have become an
essential part of the producers' arsenal. As Samson S. puts it, "There's
nothing better than some good scratching" (Samson S. 1999). While this
is not an insurmountable problem for nondeejaying producers—they can
bring in deejays to do the scratches—producers are more respected if

they can do their own scratches. In our discussion of the producer DJ Premier, DJ Mixx Messiah put a high value on his scratching ability: "He's not like your Roc Raider, Sinista, Q-Bert—you know, 'master of scratch' —but he's a precision scratch technician. His scratches and his cuts matter so much to his songs. It's like the icing on a cake" (DJ Mixx Messiah 1999).

Having experience as a deejay can benefit a producer in many practical ways. From providing specific technical abilities, such as scratching, to facilitating the development of a large record collection, deejaying can lay the groundwork for a successful production career. But the benefits are more than pragmatic. On a more abstract level, the very idea of what a producer should be is deeply beholden to deejaying. As Strath Shepard puts it, "I think the best producers are deejays. The best producers, they just love to deejay" (Shepard 1998). Samson S. takes a more prescriptive approach to the relationship between deejaying and producing: "As far as hip-hop goes, it goes hand in hand. It *can* go hand in hand 'cause a good deejay knows what sounds to use. He knows what the people like. He *should* know what the people wanna hear. He *should* know what'll rock the crowd. He *should* have a ear for music" (Samson S. 1999). Prince Paul expresses a similar opinion:

> Deejaying definitely plays a big part of . . . me producing. At least, knowledge of records and songs and stuff. And kind of knowing the feel and being used to the feel. . . . I apply the same psychology [to deejaying] as when I make records. It's like, you wanna keep the people dancing, keep the people excited, and you have to be able to read the crowd. Like, who's in the crowd. Who knows what. Who knows this. Certain songs are foolproof. Certain beats and certain tempos you have to keep up.
>
> And I apply the same psychology . . . in records that I make. It's like, "Damn, I played this record, everybody got off the floor." . . . Or, "When I did this, somebody cried," or you see like some painful look on some face, like "Oh my god, this's incredible," or maybe it's "Oh *wow*," they start dancing, hands up and stuff. And me kind of seeing crowds when I deejay, or even like playing music. . . . Let's say I played something right now, and I can see your reaction.

And then I play it for a few other people, see their reaction, it kind of gives me a guideline on how things work. (Prince Paul 2002)

This sensibility may be manifested in subtle ways. Producer Pete Rock, for instance, is known for putting brief excerpts (five seconds or less) of rare soul songs on his albums between his own songs. This is generally seen as a challenge to other producers to identify and find these records, a competitive approach that goes back to the early days of hip-hop dee-jaying. DJ Mixx Messiah, however, points out that this practice has an important secondary function that also suggests a deejay-minded approach: "I like his use of interludes in hip-hop. You know, like most hip-hop songs you listen to there's like the high point, the low point, and in between you're waiting for the next cut to come on. Pete Rock keeps you entertained before the next cut actually comes on. . . . That's definitely a deejay thing. You can tell he digs" (DJ Mixx Messiah 1999). In DJ Mixx Messiah's view, Pete Rock creates interludes not only to show off his record collection, but also to keep the listener entertained between songs. A true deejay, in other words, could not let five seconds of silence go by on an album without doing something to remedy it.

Ideas about the relationship between sampling and deejaying are deeply embedded in many aspects of the production discourse. The digital sampler is ideologically associated with an older technology, the turntable, in a manner that is in no way inherent to the technology, but rather is a reflection of the specific social history of the hip-hop community. And people engage with that social history by emphasizing deejaying in their production work.

In any community, history draws borders; that is, in fact, one of its primary functions. Hip-hop is no exception. But one of the least explicit, yet most powerful, boundaries drawn by hip-hop's history-minded educational program is that of gender. To the extent that producers hold in their minds a platonic ideal of the hip-hop producer, they tend to see it as masculine. While this attitude is statistically accurate—there are very few female hip-hop producers—it may also be self-reinforcing. In other words, beyond the lack of role models, the abstract masculinization of the role of the producer requires a potential female producer to follow conceptual and behavioral norms that presume a male constituency. It was not uncommon, for example, for my consultants to refer to producers who violated an ethical requirement (see chapter 5) as "punks" (i.e., effeminate or ineffectual men), an insult that would be nonsensical if applied to a female producer. This coincides with a larger sense that many of the expectations for social interaction in the producers' community are associated with masculine codes of honor. That is to say, it seemed that proper behavior within the producers' community was considered one of the responsibilities of manhood, and that to fail to adhere to them was to be somehow "less than a man." This, of course, leaves women who wish to participate with the choice of being either unfeminine or unethical.[13] To be fair, I have never heard a female producer specifically accused of either of these. But like so many aspects of ideology, such conceptions are manifested in "common-sense" notions about what it means to be a producer. The hip-hop community does not reject the idea of a female producer; it just rarely arises in the first place.

In the last few pages of this chapter I would like to address women's access (or lack thereof) to education in hip-hop production. My intention here is *not* to make a brief formal disquisition on gender in order to justify ignoring it for the rest of the book; rather, I hope that by looking at women's experience in educating themselves about hip-hop production, I can throw into relief the fact that the rest of the chapter—and, in fact, the book—is about men's experience. Ideas about masculinity are internalized as part of the educational process of hip-hop producers, and they continue to manifest themselves throughout a producer's career.[14] These manifestations include a particular concern with honor and ethics, the valorization of fraternal relationships as the building blocks of community, and what Will Straw (1997) has called the "adventurous hunter" approach to record collecting.

The Angel, an experimental hip-hop producer, reports that people often make assumptions about her musical role:

> As a woman, I know that, when people see pictures of me, they assume I'm a singer. Even if I'm sitting surrounded by [electronic] gear, it's still like, "Oh, she sang on something, right?" . . . So the stigma's there. There's no question that, as a woman in the industry, people make those obvious—but wrong—assumptions a lot of

times. It hasn't really stopped me from doing my thing, but that's probably more down to the fact that I won't be stopped. . . . I make my own space. I don't wait to be invited to something; I just get in there and do it. (The Angel 1998)

Kylea, an MC who has done some production, also feels that women may be pressured into more "traditionally" female roles:

It would be nice to see more females producing. . . . Maybe some females feel that that's not a role that they should play, 'cause if you're around people that say, "You stick to writing" or "You stick to singing," but they might wanna produce. But they could be getting pushed back 'cause "It's too much for you." And if you don't have the self-esteem and someone pushes you back, then those words can keep you from being a producer, when you have all the skills you need to be a producer. So, it definitely just depends on your situation, and who you surround yourself with. (Kylea 1998)

In addition to a general sense that hip-hop production is a male endeavor, Rose (1994) has cited two other specific factors that may contribute to the lack of female representation in hip-hop production, both of which were supported by my own research. The first is a general societal norm that tends to steer women away from technological pursuits at an early age: "[W]omen in general are not encouraged in and often actively discouraged from learning about and using mechanical equipment. This takes place informally in socialization and formally in gender-segregated vocational tracking in public school curriculum [sic]. Given rap music's early reliance on stereo equipment, participating in rap music production requires mechanical and technical skills that women are much less likely to have developed" (Rose 1994: 57). In our interview, the Angel raised this issue: "Most people have gotten that start through the technology. And I guess it's almost like boys playing with their trucks and girls playing with their dolls. Most women, I think, shy away from electronics, but that's not to say that *all* do. And I think as time has gone on, more and more women are coming to the forefront as being very hands-on" (the Angel 1998).

The second factor that Rose cites is an educational and mentoring process that is based in one's social circle:

> [B]ecause rap music's approaches to sound reproduction developed informally, the primary means for gathering information is shared local knowledge. As [DJ] Red Alert explained to me, his pre-hip hop interest and familiarity with electronic equipment were sustained by access to his neighbor Otis who owned elaborate stereo equipment configurations. Red Alert says that he spent almost all of his free time at Otis's house, listening, learning, and asking questions. For social, sexual, and cultural reasons young women would be much less likely to be permitted or feel comfortable spending such extended time in a male neighbor's home. (Rose 1994: 57–58)

Deejay Karen Dere also reports that social circumstances are a large part of such decisions:

> I think part of it is like it's a natural evolution when you become a producer, because it's usually like everyone that you're hanging around with is also like trying to buy that sampler, trying to make beats, and that just doesn't happen so much for women. I'm trying to think: when I get together with other women, that are even into hip-hop, what do we do? We're more thinking about the marketing end of stuff, or distribution of stuff, instead of the creative part of it. And I think that's probably just because that's the typical role of women, more so in this industry. The street team coordination, or something that's not so creative. (Dere 1998)

This power of one's social environment to open or close creative doors is also attested to by Kylea's statement above, in which she attributes women's development as producers to "who you surround yourself with."

In this chapter I have tried to emphasize the choices that hip-hop producers make in both their personal histories and the way they stake out a perspective on a shared historical narrative. But in addition to individual and collective narratives, the ideology of hip-hop producers expresses a clear sense of the relationship between the two. Specifically, producers' almost obsessive commitment to deejaying as both a practical and a theoretical model for sample-based hip-hop production reflects a strategy for the integration of collective history into individual lives—and vice versa. The producer embodies hip-hop history through the use of deejaying, in whatever way he sees fit: scratching, looping, digging for rare records, philosophizing. The producer chooses to become part of the collective history every time he makes a beat.

chapter 3

"It Just Doesn't
Sound Authentic"

Live Instrumentation
versus Hip-Hop Purism

Much has been written about the concept of authenticity within the hip-hop world. But due to both the prominence of the MC in hip-hop music and the dominance of lyric-oriented hip-hop scholarship, virtually all discussions of authenticity, explicit or implicit, concern the relationships between lyrics and reality and how the complexities of this relationship might be fruitfully theorized (Allen 1996, Costello & Wallace 1990, Del Barco 1996, Flores 1996, Forman 2002a, Gilroy 1991, Jones 1990, Kelley 1996, Perkins 1996, Potter 1995, Rose 1994, Samuels 1991, Shomari 1995, Wheeler 1991). Other definitions of authenticity and the social structures which may support those definitions have been less fully explored. But the contribution of hip-hop producers (by definition) includes no lyrics and therefore no explicit claims about their social position, so other approaches must be pressed into service.

Adam Krims (2000) has used lyrics and music together to develop a musical "poetics of place," which is then presumed to provide a social context for the artist's lyrical message. Still, though, his remains a primarily analytical, taxonomic approach—its concern, like that of earlier analyses, is more with *what* is represented than with *how* and *why*. Even when scholars focus on sampling specifically, there is still a tendency to focus on the various ways in which the individual samples may reflect the artist's personal background. Tricia Rose, for example, sees sampling as a form of musical pedagogy: "These samples are highlighted, functioning as a challenge to know these sounds, to make connections between the lyrical and musical texts. It affirms black musical history and locates these 'past' sounds in the 'present.' . . . More often than not, rap artists and their DJ's openly revere their soul forebearers" (Rose 1994: 89).

But for many producers, sampling affirms a more diverse musical history. Many of the most popular breakbeats in hip-hop, from its earliest days, have been drawn from white rock artists such as Mountain, Grand Funk Railroad, and Jack Bruce.

As Kodwo Eshun poetically notes, "The Breakbeat is a motion-capture device, a detachable Rhythmengine, a movable rhythmotor that generates cultural velocity. The break is any short captured sound whatsoever. Indifferent to tradition, this functionalism ignores history, allows Hip-Hop to datamine unknown veins of funk, to groove-rob not ancestor-worship" (Eshun 1999: 14). Rock breaks were chosen because, in spite of their origins in the putatively white rock world, they conformed to the *black* aesthetic of hip-hop. But what are black producers trying to say about themselves when they sample white musicians? I argue that the authenticity they seek has less to do with ethnic and political identity than with professional and artistic pride. In this chapter, I suggest that producers have developed an approach to authenticity that is characterized by a sort of aesthetic purism; certain musical gestures are valued for aesthetic reasons, and one's adherence to this aesthetic confers authenticity. In the pages that follow, I will use the hip-hop producers' discourse surrounding the use of live instrumentation as an example of how this process operates.[1] It is also worth reiterating at this point that the approaches and attitudes I will be delineating here are specific to producers of sample-based hip-hop, and may not be held by other members of the hip-hop community.

My use of purism as an organizing principle for this chapter derives directly from the fact that many of the producers I spoke with specifically use that term to characterize their own position. The qualifier "aesthetic," however, is my own addition, and I have included it for two reasons. First, I want to distinguish the purism of hip-hop producers from other essentialist tendencies that have been attributed to hip-hop culture, particularly those of ethnicity and class. I do not deny that such factors have been important to the development of hip-hop music; I am merely arguing that such concerns are of secondary interest to producers in constructing their idea of authenticity, and therefore they will not be directly addressed in this chapter. Second, I use the term "aesthetic" to emphasize the decisive role that abstract ideas of beauty play in the hip-hop discourse, a role that is frequently overlooked by scholars. By focusing on a single aspect of the producers' discourse, concerns about the use of live instrumentation, I will explore the ways in which both aspects of this construct, the aesthetic and the purist, work together to define authenticity for hip-hop producers.

Thomas Porcello's ethnographic survey of non–hip-hop recording engineers' perspectives on sampling defines four themes that run through their discourse:

> First, all the engineers do feel that there are certain uses of sampling which are undeniably unethical, and that sampling should not be a technological free-for-all. Second, there is debate as to where such an ethical boundary should be drawn in practice; the engineers represented here were not in agreement as to when sampling begins to violate the "rights" of the musician. . . . Next, and closely tied to the second point, is a great deal of pragmatic talk about what the engineer needs to do, or should be required to do, in order to avoid prosecution for copyright infringement. . . . The final common thread is a consideration for the fate of the musician. (Porcello 1991: 71)

As Porcello's work demonstrates, the concerns of the non–hip-hop music industry have been primarily ethical and pragmatic. By contrast, I would argue that *none* of the themes Porcello delineates is significant to the discourse of hip-hop sampling.[2] The hip-hop discourse is primarily concerned with aesthetics. Simply put, sampling is not valued because it is convenient, but because it is beautiful.

Virtually all academic writings that have attempted to discuss the beauty of hip-hop sampling have done so within a presumed aesthetic framework that is a natural result of what Jameson (1991) would call the cultural logic of late capitalism. The sampling aesthetic is presented as an example of postmodern pastiche, with all its attendant theoretical implications: juxtaposition of disparate aesthetic systems, blank parody, fragmentation, lack of historicity, and so forth. A related analysis has sample-based hip-hop as a specifically African American response to the fragmented aesthetic of contemporary media culture. Russell Potter writes,

> If Blues is the "classical" music of African-American culture, and Jazz is its "modernism," then hip-hop has a powerful claim to be regarded as their postmodern successor, not so much on account of chronology as on account of what Bakhtin calls "chronotopes" —the linked prismatic synecdoches of cultural history. Hip-hop's central chronotope is the turntable, which Signifies on its ability to "turn the tables" on previous black traditions, making a future out of fragments from the archive of the past, turning consumption into production. With this mode of turning and re-turning, hip-hop's appropriative art (born of sonic collage and pastiche, re-processed via digital technology) is the perfect backdrop for an insistent vernacular poetics that both invokes and alters the history of African-American experiences, as well as black music on a global scale. (Potter 1995: 18)

But I would argue that the extent to which hip-hop expresses a sensibility of fragmentation, whether musical or social, depends on how one listens to it. For hip-hop producers—who *are* highly attuned to the origins of particular samples—the significance tends to lie more in the ingenuity of the way the elements are fused together than in calling attention to the diversity of their origins. In other words, to say that hip-hop is about fragmentation because it is composed of samples is akin to saying that a brick wall is about fragmentation because it is composed of individual bricks. Prince Paul, for example, specifically avoids jarring juxtapositions in his beats: "I always felt like texture is important in music. And, let's say we're sampling something from the 1960s, I couldn't put like Planet Rock laser drums. . . . You know, it doesn't fit. You know, I try to make everything in the same texture" (Prince Paul 2002). I am suggesting an aesthetic that is more concerned with a cohesive organizing principle than the diversity of individual elements that fall into its orbit. And it is worth noting again that I am also describing an approach that is more active than reactive.[3]

More problematic than any specific line of reasoning, though, is many scholars' exclusive reliance on the paradigms of culture studies and literary theory, which implies that the hip-hop community has articulated no aesthetic principles of its own. This is simply not the case. I believe that the main reason that the indigenous discourse is overlooked is that it is not primarily concerned with the issue that most sympathetic re-searchers are interested in: justifying the use of sampling. By this I mean that most scholars seem concerned with demonstrating ways in which sampling, despite its rejection of live instrumentation, is consis-tent with more conventional value systems, whether those be social, po-litical, musical, or otherwise. Hip-hop producers, by contrast, are rarely interested in such moves because for them sampling doesn't require jus-tification on any grounds; it is the foundation of the musical form. If anything, it is the *lack* of samples—the use of live instrumentation—that must be justified. When I asked his feelings about the use of live instru-mentation, producer Jake One addressed many of these issues:

I'm for it. I don't see why not. I really just care how it sounds, I mean the final product. I don't care how it's done. I'm not really "It has to be dusty and blah, blah, blah." I've done live instrument stuff, but I use vintage sounds; I don't use just Casio keyboard and whatnot. . . . But there'll always be *some* sampled element in what I do. I think that's what kinda makes it hip-hop, though, you know? If you're just playing . . . a bunch of instruments and there's no sampled drums, scratches or something, I don't think it's . . . I mean, it's hip-hop, I guess . . . I don't know. (Jake One 1998)

At this point, I asked him what it was, exactly, that might not be hip-hop about using live instruments. He responded, "It just doesn't sound *authentic*. . . . There's something about the way the old records sound when they're put together right. You can't really recapture 'em when you play [live]" (Jake One 1998). In this brief discussion, Jake One, directly or indirectly, touched on no less than five different factors relevant to the producers' discourse on live instrumentation:

1. First of all, like everyone else I spoke with, he understands my question ("What do you think about the use of live instrumentation in hip-hop?") to require a pro or con response. But after making a formal statement of support for live instruments, he proceeds to criti-

cize their use in virtually all cases. Jake One is making a distinction between a *moral* principle—producers should be free to use live instruments—and an *aesthetic* principle—live instruments don't generally sound as good as samples.

2. Furthermore, in saying "I really just care how it sounds. . . . I don't care how it's done," he suggests that, of the two, the most salient principle is the aesthetic rather than the moral or methodological.

3. Further defining the nature of this aesthetic, Jake One presents himself as someone who does not feel that a sound must be "dusty" (containing overt vinyl record noise) in order to be authentic. This implies that there are those in the hip-hop world who do.

4. By the same token, however, he expresses his preference for "vintage" timbres, referring presumably to an analog production aesthetic, which he specifically opposes to a digital, "Casio" sound. Again, his discussion focuses on the *aesthetic* value of the sounds, rather than methodological or moral issues.

5. He continues this line of thinking when he characterizes the "sampled element" as the defining—though not sole—factor of the hip-hop sound. And in response to my request that he be more specific about this, he makes a telling assessment of live instrumentation—"It just doesn't sound authentic"—which he then develops in two ways. The first is with another reference to the timbral value of old records. But the second part of his statement is even more significant: "There's something about the way those old records sound when they're put together *right*" (emphasis added). This suggests that the sampling aesthetic is seen as being, to some degree, inherent in the records themselves; the records *want* to be assembled in a particular way. My sense is that this is due to the compositional elements that come with even the smallest sample, whether those be a sense of harmonic orientation, a rhythmic feel, or a timbral (or even social) "vibe." The less-constrained nature of live instruments—they could play anything—actually makes them *less* valuable because there is no sensibility, no musical clue, for the producer to work with. A sample of a chord played by jazz guitarist Grant Green, for example, can suggest a feel to a producer, and it is

then his task to develop it into a song. A guitar itself, by contrast, suggests nothing.

I believe it is for this reason that many producers think that live instruments should be used only in a supporting capacity: a live instrument does not have the volition to carry a song by itself. I would argue that, for those who have been educated in this aesthetic, a beat created with live instrumentation alone can lack a sense of purpose, urgency, and direction; it has no center. At the same time, it also lacks boundaries. Because musical instruments can play anything, the producer is not constrained by the nature of a particular musical performance on a particular old record. While this could conceivably be seen as liberating, producers are more inclined to see it as cheating. This is where the purist sensibility begins to emerge.

In response to perceptions of aesthetic cheating through the use of live instrumentation, several general rules have developed. The use of live instrumentation is considered legitimate by producers only when three conditions are met: when the live musician understands (or at least capitulates to) a putative "hip-hop aesthetic," when the instruments are used to support musical themes that are already apparent in samples, and when they have the "right" timbre or ambience. The subjective nature of all three of these criteria means that they all must be negotiated in each case. It is also an open question whether the fulfillment of any one criterion is sufficient or whether all three must be met for the use to be legitimate.

Bay Area deejay Karen Dere presents the Roots, a hip-hop group that uses live instruments, as an example of the successful meeting of the first criterion for their acceptable use:

> What I think is cool about [the Roots] is that they all understand the hip-hop aesthetic. And I think oftentimes that jazz musicians, or other musicians, just play to play and they know the standards. Or they're there to totally experiment and do all this crazy improv. It is what hip-hop is about to a certain extent, but you've gotta keep the groove up and keep a certain beat going. And sometimes I think other musicians don't understand that. (Dere 1998)

As Dere points out, musicians who are proficient in another style of music often fail to understand that hip-hop is not aesthetically deficient, but simply operating from a different perspective. As producer Jake One notes, this can create tension in the studio: "Another problem with that is that is a lot of the players don't have a hip-hop background. They'll play it in a way that's technically right, but that's not the way I wanna hear it. And you just have to be forthright and say 'This is how I want it done'" (Jake One 1998).

The second criterion for the acceptable use of live instrumentation, whether they are used in a supportive capacity, is voiced by producer Mr. Supreme:

> I guess it really depends on how you do it. Say you're a real hip-hop producer that samples and uses records. And then you play a bass line under it or follow the loop with a bass line. That's cool, it fattens it up, makes it sound better. It's not really taking away from it, it just adds to it. But if you use like a big horn section, a bunch of guitars and stuff, it's really not hip-hop. It's hip-hop based, because it samples and that comes from hip-hop. It's not hip-hop, it's the way that it sounds. . . . That's my own opinion. (Mr. Supreme 1998a)

Several people I asked about this distinction gave the same example of appropriate use of live instrumentation for support: using a live bass to "fatten up" a sample. In doing so, the producer is using the instrument to emphasize musical figures that are already there, rather than to forge new musical ground. Also, twice in this short statement, Mr. Supreme explicitly equates "real" hip-hop production with the use of samples, highlighting the purist nature of the construction.

A certain purism also informs the third criterion for the use of live instruments, which is that they are acceptable when they have the "right sound." This term includes a host of characteristics that differentiate samples from live instruments, most of which are not consciously considered by producers at any given moment but are deeply ingrained in their sensibility.

Samples, especially those taken from records released in the 1970s, often have distinct timbral qualities that distinguish them from more recent digital recordings. These include the compression and distortion common to analog recording, which is often favorably contrasted with the "crispiness" of digital. When more than one sample is used, there is also a pleasing contrast between the recording environment of different samples; for example, the guitar may be drenched in reverberation while the bass is relatively "dry." Moreover, the attack and release of sounds can be truncated in samples in ways that do not occur naturally. For instance, one can remove the sound of a piano key being struck but retain the sound of it ringing. Similarly, if a short sample is repeated, its timbral elements are reproduced exactly, which may be difficult to accomplish live due to the physical constraints of the instrument or the human body (e.g., sixteenth notes on a guitar all picked with downstrokes). As I discuss in chapter 6, the use of a "looped" (repeated) sample also introduces many new qualities, such as strange melodic and rhythmic discontinuities where the end of the loop meets the beginning. Finally, music with these characteristics may carry a vague associative familiarity (e.g., the kind of distorted, early seventies Detroit funk that was released on the Westbound label, a reggae-like horn section, etc.) that is difficult to recapture with live instrumentation.

Specifics aside, what concerns me here is how the *idea* of a correct sound, particularly one which is based on the characteristics of sampling, functions to limit the use of live instruments. Domino, producer for the Bay Area collective the Hieroglyphics, articulates those limits as follows:

> It all depends on the sound, for me. I like the right sound, so if I can get that—by any means, no matter where it comes from—I'm happy with it. . . . I'm not gonna put down nobody if it's played [live], as long as it sounds good to me. . . . [But] I think there's a lot of people out there that play stuff that doesn't sound . . . like the sounds are either—to me—too new, or just sounds real generic, you know? So the stuff that I did that's live, I kinda want it to sound like it's a sample, in a sense. It may be live, but it's gotta blend in well enough. (Domino 1998)

Like Jake One, Domino adheres to the principle that there is an objectively "right" sound that must be realized for the work to be of value. His statement that he wouldn't speak ill of someone who used live instrumentation to achieve this sound cuts two ways. Clearly, it supports the idea of the aesthetic taking precedence over the method, but at the same time, merely by bringing it up in the first place, Domino subtly suggests that there may, in fact, be grounds for disapproval. In addition, he asserts that live instruments are acceptable only to the degree that they sound like samples, and that in cases where live instruments are used, they must "blend in" with the samples, rather than vice versa. The idea of sampling as an aesthetic ideal may appear jarring to individuals trained in other musical traditions, but it absolutely exemplifies the approach of most hip-hop producers. The press materials for the Roots' album *Things Fall Apart,* for instance, highlight the following statement from the group's manager and executive producer Rich Nichols, concerning their use of live instrumentation: "We spend a huge amount of time trying to make things sound nasty, to get live instruments to bang like they were samples" (Guerasseva 1999).

This effort has not gone unnoticed by sample-based hip-hop artists. Samson S., in praising the Roots, echoes Jake One's measured support for live instrumentation in principle while at the same time specifically maintaining the sampling aesthetic as the ideal:

> I don't have nothin' against live instruments, if it sounds bomb. If it sounds good. That's not my thing, I don't really get caught up in all that. I know some folk'll tell you, "sample, sample." No. As much as I love sampling and sample-oriented shit, it don't stop there. That's not the only type of hip-hop I like. And that's not what hip-hop is *all* about necessarily. Yes, "the deejay" and all that, but, you know . . . I love the Roots! They don't have a peer, though. There ain't too many other live instrument hip-hop groups that sound as good as them. (Samson S. 1999)

A thorough reading of Samson S.'s statement of apparent support for live instrumentation shows it to be highly conditional: "*if* it sounds bomb . . . *if* it sounds good." This becomes even more apparent as he continues:

> Samson S.: But, man, I ain't heard *nobody* make live drums sound good in hip-hop. . . . And I have no idea why fools ain't mikin' their drums properly, or why it don't sound right.
> Joe: Is that what it is? It's just, like, the sound of the drum?
> Samson S.: It's the sound. And maybe, because, I think, we've be-

come accustomed to drums sounding one way, because [of] sampling and shit. So if it doesn't have the sound of records from like '73 or '74, a lot of us get turned off, because we've been conditioned. Myself included.[4] (Samson S. 1999)

Mr. Supreme feels that this shortcoming is not limited to drum sounds: "You can take the same sample and have a band recreate it, and it's not gonna be the same thing. It's just not the same. Things were recorded different back then, and they sounded better, to me. You know? They were warmer. . . . Everything was analog. [Now] everything's digital and it's a little too crispy sounding" (Mr. Supreme 1998a).

While all of the people I spoke with made this argument along similar lines, most (including Mr. Supreme) felt that, in addition to the sound quality of particular samples, there was something equally valuable about the sampling process itself. A good example of the intrinsic benefits of the sampling aesthetic is the case of experimental hip-hop producer the Angel. While she apparently finds the process of sampling old records to be too restrictive (both artistically and financially), this does not require that she turn uncritically to the conventional use of live instruments. Rather, her approach is to hire live musicians, record them in the studio, and then sample that recording and work with the resulting samples to create the finished work. This raises an obvious question, though: Why go to the trouble of sampling? Why not just instruct the musicians to play what you want in the first place? The Angel's response is that there is something in the sampling process itself that cannot be duplicated with live instrumentation:

I work with samples of my own stuff. I create samples. Like, I'll record a whole bunch of stuff and then resample it and mess with it. Either musicians, my playing, my playing keys, my playing other odd instruments, little things that I pick up and mess around with. And program up beats, and just chop up bass drums and snares and bits and pieces and create samples that way. . . . That's always kinda been my trademark of mixing and matching things; having the live instrumentation, but not using it in a conventional way. Because there's a real value to sampling. The reason why people sample is because you get an instant vibe, and an instant sound,

from that original recording that you can't get by recording somebody playing a horn. It's just not the same. I can't describe to you
what that is, but part of it's the ambience, part of it's the atmosphere. Part of it's all the things that are in that sample, that you
wanna EQ [equalize] out, that still give it flavor. That's why I go
through the painstaking, very long-winded process of creating
samples for myself. Because just recording it down straight, it'll
just sound too placid; it won't have any vibe. So there's a real value
to it. (The Angel 1998)

For Oakland-based deejay and journalist Oliver Wang, the aesthetic
value of a sample also goes beyond such timbral issues as record noise
or seventies recording techniques:

In terms of how I feel about live instrumentation, I actually like it a
lot. I think the limitations to it, though, are that loops tend to have
a complexity that it's difficult, logistically speaking, for hip-hop
bands to emulate. For one thing, it's just a matter of getting certain
sound effects, like moogs or synthesizers and stuff. Bands may not
have access to that kind of technology. It's hard to capture the beauty
of a loop when you're playing live. On the flip side, it's hard to capture the beauty of live, when you're looping. So I can see it going
both ways. I don't think hip-hop can afford to have most of its bands
playing live instruments. But I certainly consider that to be real
hip-hop, though. I don't accept the argument that that's something
else. (Wang 1998)

Like the Angel, Wang speaks of the relative merits of live music
versus sampled music in an entirely abstract framework. His analysis
imparts a value to looping that is completely separate from what any particular sample might sound like. Again, this suggests that for hip-hop
aesthetes, there is an intrinsic value to sampling that goes beyond either
convenience or sound quality.

As I suggested earlier, many respected individuals in the hip-hop
world who are not producers—especially MCs—have a far less stringent
standard in this regard. Seattle's MC Kylea, for instance, characterizes
the use of live instrumentation as one of a variety of possible options

that must be kept open in order for hip-hop to progress: "I like [live instrumentation] . . . 'cause it just gives it a broader dimension. When you go back to rules, too, certain people feel that it's not hip-hop if it's not two turntables and a microphone. But it's like, hip-hop, you have to be able to continue to create off of it, in order for it to grow" (Kylea 1998).

Deejay and former label owner Strath Shepard, by contrast, hews to the purist position:

> Hip-hop is based on a deejay. Some groups that would call themselves hip-hop groups, that use live instruments, I wouldn't call that hip-hop. It's rap. They're rapping. But hip-hop is a deejay and an MC. . . . In general, I think of true hip-hop as samples, a deejay, records, beats, digging. I don't think of it as a bass player. I don't care how great they are. . . . I don't know, it's tough to talk about what is or isn't hip-hop. But I think, in general, live instruments, I don't think of that as being the real, *real* hip-hop. I think the focus should be on the deejay.[5] (Shepard 1998)

Seattle deejay and hip-hop producer Vitamin D takes a similar approach. In his formulation, the significant aspect is neither the sound nor the method, but the presence or absence of the deejay:

> I got some live instrumentation in some [of the material I'm working on] now. But I don't think live instrumentation is cool without a deejay being the foundation of what you're doing. Because hip-hop started with the deejay, so that's hip-hop's foundation. So to me it's not hip—I mean, it's still hip-hop, but it's not original-school style. I'm not really against 'em. [But I'm] definitely not just pro-instruments like, "Yeah that's advancing hip-hop," or "That's taking hip-hop to another level." (Vitamin D 1998)

Regarding the question of whether or not music with live instruments constitutes "real hip-hop" or not, Vitamin D makes two interesting points. First, he suggests that this is not an either-or proposition: "It's still hip-hop, but it's not original-school style." Second, after formally professing to not be opposed to their use, he emphasizes that he doesn't believe that the use of live instruments is particularly innovative. This is not an arbitrary comment on Vitamin D's part; the question of whether or not live instrumentation is innovative strikes a nerve within the production community.

Even producers who are not opposed to live instruments in principle resent the notion that the use of live instrumentation constitutes a leap forward in hip-hop production. This is largely due to a sense that most of the individuals who are promoting this view (usually music critics and musicians from other genres) lack an understanding of the aesthetic issues involved. Those who are critical of hip-hop have never been shy about equating a lack of live instrumentation with a lack of musical quality, as the following excerpt from an essay in the *New York Times* illustrates:

> The music business has finally figured out how to do without musicians, those pesky varmints. Today, more and more pop is created not by conventional musicianship but by using samplers, digital editing software and other computerized tools to stitch together prerecorded sounds. From magnates like Sean (Puffy) Combs to innovators like the D.J. and producer Roni Size, pop belongs increasingly to people who don't play instruments and have little or no grasp of even basic harmonic and rhythmic theory.
>
> The issue isn't a mere lack of formal training—pop musicians have always been self-taught; neither Elvis nor the Beatles nor Jimi Hendrix could read music—but a more profound lack of conventional musical skills. As more and more nonmusicians become hit makers, is the skilled pop instrumentalist an endangered species? (Scherman 2001)

Such critics seem to operate from a sense that the use of live instrumentation is self-evidently superior to the use of samples, a view that is often expressed by its corollary, that sampling must be chosen for reasons of expediency. From the perspective of a hip-hop purist, as delineated above, such assertions are both uninformed and insulting in that they overlook the possibility that there may be a legitimate aesthetic reason for preferring samples.

Even apparently sympathetic voices seem to have internalized this equation in subtle ways. Guitar-playing MC and producer Wyclef Jean's *The Carnival,* for instance, is described in *Rolling Stone* magazine as "[a] solo album displaying courage, ambition *and as much musical ability as hip-hop had ever seen. . . ."* (Toure 1998: 38; emphasis added). The idea of relative levels of "musical ability" (as opposed to, for example, more specific rhyming or scratching ability) is one that is almost never invoked in hip-hop. Clearly Wyclef Jean's use of the guitar is the decisive factor in *Rolling Stone*'s assessment.

MC, producer, and graffiti writer Specs, while also not opposed to the use of live instruments, is opposed to the characterization of their use as "innovative":

> I don't like when an entire band is used, necessarily. I mean, it's OK. But . . . a lot of people are doing that, and gettin' pushed up to the forefront as innovators, when they're not, 'cause they didn't start anything. Like if I saw, like, Ultramagnetic MCs [a well-respected group of long standing] with a band or something, then I would say, "OK, they're innovating something." But not people that are just brand new. And, another way, they're not really innovating because all they're doing is playing music. People have already played music in a band before. They've already done that, so they're not really innovating. (Specs 1998)

Specs begins by reiterating the distinction between the use of single instruments in a supporting role and songs where the primary material is provided by live instruments—"an entire band." As he continues, he suggests that innovators should be people who have absorbed the tradition for a long time. His position is apparently that only the most traditional practitioners can be innovative, since they have internalized the aesthetic to the degree that their contributions will necessarily help the entire system to develop. Interestingly, this is a philosophy that I've often heard expressed in reference to South Indian classical music, in which a great musician may be characterized as an innovator *within* the tradition. In any case, Specs's statement suggests once again that hip-hop producers see their work within the context of a valued aesthetic tradition, one that they are not anxious to uproot.

Based on the foregoing discussion, I believe it is possible to make several generalizations about the nature of the hip-hop producers' discourse with regard to live instrumentation. First, the use of sampling is clearly the aesthetic preference of most producers. Even when live instrumentation is used, the ideal that producers are trying to achieve is based on the sound of the sample. The fact that criteria even exist for the appropriate use of live instruments means that their use is seen as requiring extenuating circumstances, which further establishes it as a second choice. This preference is not for the *act* of sampling, but for the *sound* of sampling: It is a matter of aesthetics.

In a broader sense, the fact that a preference exists at all reflects the purism of the hip-hop producers' community. The creation of rules—the wariness about the use of live instrumentation—suggests not only that there is an aesthetic at work here, but that it is worth protecting. And producers are willing to invest an extraordinary amount of time, money, and energy to protect it. A great deal of this capital is expended in the service of "digging in the crates."

chapter 4

Materials and Inspiration

Digging in the Crates

I'm not the hottest crate digger around. I can't remember the names of breaks I used. I'm not like one of them break kids. But I have so many records in my house I don't even like to move, you know? (DJ Kool Akiem 1999)

Sampling—the digital recording and manipulation of sound that forms the foundation of hip-hop production—requires source material. In order to sample, there must be something to sample *from*. For sample-based hip-hop producers, the source is usually vinyl records. In this chapter, I will describe the process of "digging in the crates"—searching for rare records—and discuss its significance to the hip-hop production community. I argue that in addition to its practical value in providing the raw material for sample-based hip-hop, digging serves a number of other purposes for the production community. These may include such functions as manifesting ties to hip-hop deejaying tradition, "paying dues," educating producers about various forms of music, and serving as a form of socialization between producers.

The process of acquiring rare, usually out-of-print, vinyl records for sampling purposes has become a highly developed skill and is referred to by the term "digging in the crates" ("digging" for short). Evoking images of a devoted collector spending hours sorting through milk crates full of records in used record stores, garages, and thrift shops, the term carries with it a sense of valor and symbolizes an unending quest for the next record. Individuals who give themselves to this quest are held in high esteem, and one of the highest compliments that can be given to a hip-hop producer is the phrase "You can tell he digs."

The digging mind-set is one of the things that sets producers apart from other participants in the hip-hop arts. As deejay Karen Dere explains, it can easily approach the level of an obsession:

> My friend Roman, he's from Switzerland. And he took a road trip through the South and pretty much just knocked on people's doors and asked them if they had old records that they wanted to sell. And . . . he came back with just ace records. And that's pretty psychotic, if you think about that in terms of "What would normal people do on vacation?" They went on a quest for records, and that was the whole reason for the trip. If people were having a garage sale, they'd be like, "Do you have records? Does your neighbor have records?" It's a whole 'nother mind set that people have. (Dere 1998)

Jake One, an inveterate digger, describes how he and Mr. Supreme once arrived at a record sale well before dawn, only to find they were not the first ones there: "Me and [Mr. Supreme] in L.A., in February, we went to see Common and the X-Men and there was a swap meet at five in the morning in Pasadena. We went from the club straight there. And there were people [already] out there with flashlights" (Jake One 1998). It is interesting to note that many of the best-known diggers seem to be predisposed to collecting things in general; many also have extensive collections of toys, kung fu videos, action figures, or even, in the case of one of my consultants, Beanie Babies.

As Will Straw points out, male record collectors must work to maintain a balance between the competing tendencies toward hipness and nerdishness which are inherent in the activity:

> Hipness and nerdishness both begin with the mastery of a symbolic field; what the latter lacks is a controlled economy of revelation, a sense of when and how things are to be spoken of. Hipness maintains boundaries to entry by requiring that the possession of knowledge be made to seem less significant than the tactical

sense of how and when it is made public. Cultivation of a corpus (of works, of facts) assumes the air of instinctuality only when it is transformed into a set of gestures enacted across time. The stances of hip require that knowledge and judgment be incorporated into bodily self-presentation, where they settle into the postures of an elusive and enigmatic instinctuality and may therefore be suggested even when they are not made blatantly manifest. (Straw 1997: 9)

Hip-hop production constitutes an ideal venue for developing a tactical sense of when to make knowledge public. In fact, as I will discuss, the constant struggle that producers face between using their work to display their esoteric record knowledge to each other and making beats that appeal to a broad audience that wants to dance is a perfect example of this process.[1]

The "crates" part of the term "digging in the crates" operates on both literal and figurative levels, not unlike the two senses in which MCs use the term "microphone." As Dawn Norfleet writes, "In addition to being an important piece of equipment to rap artists, the mic has also taken on meaning as a symbolic vehicle to demonstrate one's power in a crowd. One reason why the literal and symbolic mic is central to hip-hop themes is because one's skills (verbal agility) demonstrated 'on the microphone' determine whether the performer carries the coveted title of MC, or is merely a 'rapper'" (Norfleet 1997: 123). For producers, it is not the sampler, as might be expected, but the crates that carry the symbolic weight. On the most concrete level, "crates" refers to the fact that inexpensive, odd, or not-yet-priced records are often stored in milk crates on the floor of used record stores; these are precisely the records that producers are interested in. On a similarly literal level, the term "crates" also refers to producers' habit of storing their own records in such crates at home. This is a particularly useful system for producers who are also deejays because they can use the crates to transport records to live shows. On a more figurative level, the crates become a gloss for a producer's record collection, in both quantitative and qualitative senses. Producers, for instance, commonly count their records by crates rather than individual albums (e.g., "How many records do you have?" "About twenty crates."). Similarly, one describes a producer's collection by the records that are represented in their crates (e.g., "How are his crates?" "Good—a lot of jazz."). Producers, in other words, are often judged on the perceived quality of their crates.

The first step for the beginning crate digger is to develop a sensibility about which records might contain material that is useful for sampling purposes. For many, if not most, producers, this process begins with the selective exploitation of their parents' record collections. This has led to a certain core of well-known records, generally those that were popular with urban African American listeners in the 1970s, becoming associated by producers with "mom-and-pop crates." This is one material way in which African American culture has influenced the hip-hop aesthetic. The first and second generation of deejays were afforded access to and familiarity with the recordings of such artists as Bob James, Grover Washington, New Birth, and others whose original listenership was largely confined to urban African American communities. These recordings established the parameters of the hip-hop sensibility; producers who weren't already familiar with them as part of their preexisting cultural background had to make a special effort to learn them.

Once this initial source is exhausted, many producers begin to pursue the original sources of favorite hip-hop songs:

> Most people start out looking for things that they know have been sampled. Basically looking for stuff that other people have used already. . . . Some people don't ever develop past that. . . . But most people, and myself included . . . get to a point where you're not just looking for stuff that people have sampled, but you look for things that *you* might want to sample. Essentially what happens is you look at your crates, and there's certain types of records there. And you just develop a feel for what's good. Even though it's true that a lot of the most corny-looking records have stuff on 'em. You kind of develop a feel for, like, "OK, these people on the cover," or this design, or this era, or this label: I bet it's good. Then you buy the thing, you check it out. . . . and there's stuff on it and you want to sample it. I don't make beats, but I have stacks of stuff that I *would* use. (Shepard 1998)

Because producers are often concerned with the general ambience and production qualities of a record (as opposed to, for example, particular musicians or songs), very general indicators of this "vibe" can be quite useful for the beginning digger: "I think back then it was mostly just looking at the record and whatever was on the cover or what the names of the songs were. That's how we basically found most of the cool stuff" (King Otto 1998).

When King Otto says "the names of the songs," he doesn't mean that he was interested in the particular songs themselves; he is referring to songs that had names that seemed to reflect the aesthetic sensibility he was seeking. Producers may look for song titles that (for example) reflect "down-home" African American culture, celebrate sexuality, utilize an apparent African language, contain references to signs of the zodiac, or (ideally) some combination of all of the above. In a column on digging written for *Grand Royal* magazine, Eric Gladstone is emphatic on this point: "*Go on names alone.* Joe Quarterman's Free Soul, Sho Nuff, Black Nasty—how can you go wrong? And while the word 'funk' in a song is no guarantee of goodness, 'freak' or 'freaky' almost always is" (Gladstone 1995: 32; emphasis in original).

After one has devoted oneself to digging for some time, one begins to develop more specific preferences: "When you're a producer, in the advanced stages, you start getting into, you know, 'Was that Billy Cobham on drums?' . . . So, yeah, you start looking at the personnel. And wondering, 'OK, does this person have a solo album out?' 'Can I get this?' And then it goes on and on. That's the beauty of that thing, for real. Become a little well-versed in music" (Samson S. 1999). Beat digger and producer Phill "Soulman" Stroman sees this development as an organic process: "You start off just diggin' for beats, tryin' to find beats to sample or deejay with. Next thing you know, you're . . . a record collector. You know everything about the musicians, their backgrounds. It just starts happenin', you know?" (Stroman 1999).

Another sign of a more advanced digging sense is the ability to find useful material in unexpected places, records that don't conform to the aforementioned aesthetic sensibility: "Some of the records I have, I just can't believe I have 'em. They're so stupid! But the beats on 'em are just so outrageous! It's crazy. It's like, *what were they thinking?* When they recorded that record, what were they thinking? It could be, like, a senior citizens' band or something, like this little orchestra, and the beat is just crazy—it sounds like hip-hop! I don't get it!" (Mr. Supreme 1998a).[2]

At the same time that producers are learning to distinguish promising cover art from that which is worthless, they are also developing an
increasingly sophisticated sensibility about which specific sounds will
work within their overall musical scheme. As journalist and deejay Oliver
Wang suggests, the growth of such a sensibility is one of the major tasks
set before a producer:

> It's an easy art to learn, just how to work a sampler, how to quan-
> tize stuff. But I think it's extremely difficult to actually develop a
> good ear. For instance, like drums. If you don't want to use the
> same drums that everyone else on the planet's used, there's, like, a
> science to . . . looking on a rock record or jazz record to pick up a
> particular break. You want your snares to sound a certain way. You
> kind of want your low-end kick to sound a certain way, your hi-
> hats. . . . If you listen to beginning demo tapes by producers who
> have just started, you can always pick up when they're using the
> same drum samples as everyone else. Or when they're using purely,
> digitally, like, drum-machine sounds; it just sounds really fake, in a
> way. Nowadays, when producers are so sophisticated, it just stands
> out as being amateurish. (Wang 1998)

The possession of such knowledge is a point of pride among producers and it is not taken lightly:

> There's certain artists that have a certain sound, so, I mean, you'll
> know, "Oh, that's a Bob James–produced record," or something
> like that. You can just tell, even without knowing the actual song.
> You can tell if it's from a certain production company or whatever
> from the seventies. CTI, or a Blue Note record, or whatever, you
> know? As far as records, once you get to a certain point where
> you know a lot of labels, and you can look at a certain record and
> say, "Well, this is gonna have this kind of sound on it." You know
> your producers, your instruments, you know your musicians. You
> become really educated just by default. . . . [Mr. Supreme] will tell
> you record listings. . . . There was a record I pulled at his house
> and he knew, like, the catalog listing and everything. I don't know

if he was joking around, but he knew it, and I was just kinda staring at him. (Jake One 1998)

In a separate interview, I asked Mr. Supreme about this incident. He laughed: "I did! Don't even ask me why I knew! I don't know how I knew! He was across the room. He pulled the record out and he said something. And I said, 'Yeah, that's Groove Merchant number 562.' And he looked at me, he was like, 'You are a nut'" (Mr. Supreme 1998b). While Mr. Supreme's detailed knowledge of his record collection (he has over twenty thousand records) was conveyed to me as a humorous example of the extent of his obsessiveness, he was clearly also proud of that knowledge for its own sake. And there is little question that Jake One, while perhaps considering him "a nut," was also impressed.

Such information is deployed in many ways. For one thing, detailed knowledge of the records that they already have in their possession allows producers to choose new ones that will dovetail nicely:

When you search for just breakbeats, and you know beats, and you have a lot of beats in your head, you can hear something like a little bass line, just even a short one, like two notes or something. You can hear it, and then you can imagine a beat over it. And then you can think, "Man, I can take this and chop these up and play 'em back differently." But the sound is there, the sound is funky. Just hearing stuff and basically piecing it together in your mind. (Mr. Supreme 1998a)

Another valuable dividend of this knowledge is the ability to recognize when another producer uses an original record that one also owns in a new way. This can alert the thoughtful producer to new strategies and techniques: "It depends how well you know these records. . . . There's fools that can chop up something, and I can hear a piece and know what it is. . . . Even a snare, even something as simple as a snare, 'Oh, I know where he got that snare; he got that from . . .'" (Domino 1998).

At the same time, however, such knowledge can lead one to be overly critical of other people's approaches. As Mr. Supreme puts it, "It's kinda like a magician doing a magic trick, and if you know the secret, the trick's not as good" (Mr. Supreme 1998a). Vitamin D feels similarly: "I know if I didn't have as many records as I have, I would appreciate a lot more people's beats, 'cause I wouldn't know what records they were using. Nowadays, I know what everybody's using. It's like 'OK, he's using this. Yeah, I would've did that, too, *but*—'" (Vitamin D 1998).

Among the tricks of the trade that a producer must know is where to dig. Good used records are not found at the major chain record stores. In fact, the most valuable material is often found in the most unlikely places:

> I go everywhere, and you find the best stuff in the weirdest spots. Just places you'd never imagine . . . like a furniture store, a curtain shop. I was in Ballard walking by this surplus . . . military store. And I don't even know why I went in there. I just happened to go in there and they had like five crates of records on the floor. And some good shit! . . . I mean, they're everywhere, you know? (Mr. Supreme 1998a)

> A lot of true country places probably have some nice spots. And a lot of cities that wasn't into a lotta urban music, probably has a lotta urban music just sittin'. You know, maybe somewhere like Salt Lake City. Or Vermont. You're probably gon' find some stuff. (DJ Mixx Messiah 1999)

True digging devotees never miss an opportunity:

> What do I do to get records? Man, I do everything to get a record, man. You name it. A good thing that a lot of people don't know about . . . is you go to like Capitol Hill Mini-Storage. And you ask 'em, "Do you have anything for sale?" 'cause people don't pay their rent, and they'll clear the locker out. And they'll be like, "Yeah, we have a room back here. Everything's a buck in the room." . . .
>
> Family members, aunts, uncles, cousins, friends, girlfriends, even old restaurants that used to have discos, then you go in and talk to them and they still have the records. Just weird places like that.
>
> I guess [that's] what my mom really taught me, 'cause she used

to say "Just ask; you never know unless you ask." So I just started asking everyone for records. (Mr. Supreme 1998a)

Sometimes it gets out of hand, the stuff we're doing. I mean, being nice to people's moms and stuff to get their records. Befriending, you know, elders. I got my girlfriend doing all kinds of work right now on her coworkers. (Jake One 1998)

To be sure, Jake One and Mr. Supreme are considered by their peers to be particularly devoted to the digging process. When I asked Samson S. where he would go to dig for beats, his response was instructive in this regard: "We hit the normal spots. . . . We're not really fanatical about it, like Supreme or nothin' like that" (Samson S. 1999).

In addition to developing promising sources for records and the aesthetic sensibilities necessary to evaluate them, producers also develop digging styles. It is not unusual for producers to carry children's record players (which, unlike adult turntables, tend to be both portable and impact resistant) with them, in order to preview potential acquisitions. While it may unnerve record-store owners to see hip-hop producers listening to, for example, *Sesame Street* records on a Fisher-Price record player, other crate diggers instantly recognize this as a sign of a kindred spirit.

The way producers preview records is similarly recognizable. After searching the entire record store, producers will often assemble a stack of records, each of which they set on the portable record player for several seconds before consigning it to the "buy" or "don't buy" pile. Producers tend to look for visual cues of a break (which can be seen in smaller or larger grooves) and drop the needle at that point for a few seconds. This technique is also used at random points on the record's surface to get a general sense of the album. The clinical speed with which this process is undertaken may seem strange to individuals who may be conversant with more conventional approaches to music listening. But for dedicated beat diggers, it is essential: "You can't go out diggin' without your portable, as far as I'm concerned. Back in the days before I had a turntable, I would just go out. Just take chances on stuff. But now I have a collection of turntables and I'll just take one of them out. And I'll just get a stack of records out at some shop . . . and just start listenin' through stuff" (Stroman 1999).

What they hope to find varies from producer to producer and, in fact, from moment to moment. Sometimes a producer will go out looking for samples of specific instruments:

> [E-Swift] takes on the instruments that are not so obvious in the hip-hop element. 'Cause I remember when he came down here, we went diggin'. It's like every year he accents a different sound, a different instrument: at the time he was looking for tubas. I remember another time, he was looking for harps and violins. And then one time we talked and he was looking for cello in music. . . . He looks for particular instruments. (DJ Mixx Messiah 1999)

> I like to get records with breaks, naturally. Drum sounds. Maybe like bass lines, sometimes you can catch bass lines. . . . I like the Fender Rhodes [electric piano] sound. Horns are kind of played out, but I still like a good horn. . . . Like them ill guitar sounds, I like them 007 James Bond guitars. . . . Oh, I like to sample vocals, like singing. I did this one beat where I sampled Janis Joplin wailing on the chorus. (Samson S. 1999)

In addition to looking for various sounds, producers will investigate various genres for their potential:

> I think that's what separates people, as far as hip-hop junkies and just regular consumer music listeners. People that can spend more than an hour in a record store and still have stuff to look for. "Oh, I gotta go to that section." (Dere 1998)

> When I started, I'd go to a store and I'd go right to the "soul" section. I wouldn't even look at anything else. And I can only imagine what was sitting in those stores that I left there. It's like, now, when I go to a store, I gotta go through the whole store. I go through everything. It's crazy. Just to find a beat, just to find something, 'cause it's all worth it in the end. (Mr. Supreme, 1998a)

Another common technique that producers use is buying records that they don't actually want just to mislead record store owners, who will raise the price of a record once they discover that it has become valuable to hip-hop crate diggers, or other producers who might be watching. In either case, the point is to devalue one's own choices in the eyes of others by purposely choosing a few bad records: "Oh yeah. You always do that. Especially if you go to record shows, you get all these kids that know what you do, and they'll start following you. Even record dealers, 'cause they're figuring, 'Well, if he buys it, it's something. And we can get it and jack the price up.' So you just do that—you just grab something stupid, a Kenny Rogers record or something" (Mr. Supreme 1998a).

Of course hip-hop producers were not the first people to seek rare vinyl; serious record collecting dates back to the beginning of the medium. But many hip-hop producers believe that because of the way they listen to records (and, in many cases, their physical appearance and demeanor), they are not taken seriously by older record collectors. This can be a source of some friction:

> You have to be able to connect with the other record-dealing population, 'cause they don't respect us at all, I know that. And out here [in Seattle], they have no idea what we're doing, still. So I guess that works in our advantage, but it gets on my nerves . . . 'cause a lot of these stores talk about "Don't play that rap in my store." . . . They don't really like to give the credit very much. They're still stuck on the "Floyd and the Stones syndrome," as [Mr. Supreme] calls it. (Jake One 1998)

Lack of respect notwithstanding, the dealers are still willing to take hip-hop producers' money. In fact, as I mentioned earlier, dealers often try to second-guess what the hip-hop buyers are looking for. As Jake One continues, this strategy is rarely successful:

> It used to be, like, "If it had a afro [on the cover], we're gonna charge a bunch of money for it." They just gave up even on that. It's funny, 'cause I'll go into stores around here, and they'll have something for twenty dollars that I see every day. I mean, *every day.* Then, every once in a while, I'll find a record that goes for a lot of money, and it'll be two dollars. Whenever I find something good, it's cheap. Real cheap. Especially out here [in Seattle]. (Jake One 1998)

In addition to purchasing records, producers often trade records with each other. As Vitamin D relates, a producer can develop a high degree of knowledge about what other producers are looking for and can use this knowledge to negotiate mutually beneficial trades. "Jake One comes up to me all the time, 'cause me and him trade records a lot. He be like, 'Man, this is a Vitamin D record, man. This is the only thing I can say. I know you want this record. It's just a Vitamin D record, you know?' Sure enough, I'll listen to it, and he's right" (Vitamin D 1998). This type of public service, however, operates within a fairly strict protocol:

> You have to trade evenly on records. It's weird with records: people will just give you a bunch of records. And if you don't know the rules, you just think, like, "Oh, thanks a lot." But what that really is, is they give you a bunch of records, and if you find something that they need, you have to give it to 'em. . . . You can't abuse that, because it just makes bad relationships. . . . You feel a slight panic when you get stuff from people, because you're like "Oh my god, I have to—," you know? It's like getting something from Don Corleone or something, you gotta pay the thing back. It's not just free. (Shepard 1998)

If they don't abuse the trading relationship, producers can find themselves part of an international trading network:

> The record circles are really . . . it's kind of crazy how small the world is, 'cause everybody knows somebody, a common person. Like, I trade with a couple people out in Toronto, that's mostly who I trade with. And they know the guys in England, and they know so-and-so in Boston, and so-and-so in L.A. Everybody kind of knows of each other. (Jake One 1998)

> Everybody that's up on the beats, as far as records go, we all know each other. It's like "six degrees of separation." Everybody knows everybody through somebody else. I know people all over the world, man. All over the world . . . It's a small world, when it comes to beats. (Stroman 1999)

Finally, many producers can find useful music simply by revisiting old records from their own collection:

> I always gotta go back. There's stuff that we got, say, five years ago with something on it, and it was good for that time period in hip-hop. And then you think, "There's nothing else on that record, it's a

crappy record." Then we go back and listen, and it blows us away, the stuff that's on there, 'cause hip-hop direction constantly changes. Constantly. (Mr. Supreme 1998a)

I always go back and I'm like, "Man, why didn't I hear this before?" I'll just find, like, a whole drum loop on there that I didn't hear before, [or] that I did hear and for some reason didn't want to use it. (King Otto 1998)

Lotta the records that I got and I thought were junk. That might've been back in the days when I was just lookin' for drum beats. But now, it's like, it could be anything on a record. Times change, sounds change, what people are sampling changes. So that record that was wack a few years ago might be the hottest record now. It's just one of those things, man. . . . The record ain't changed, times just have. Your ear has changed. That's another thing, too. Just from listening to more and more records, your taste just becomes a lot broader. You're more receptive to a lot more sounds. (Stroman 1999)

The Significance of Digging

> If you're a sample-oriented producer, [digging is] very important. Some producers live and die by their samples, i.e., Pete Rock and Diamond D, Supreme and Jake One. If that's your thing, if you're a sample-oriented producer, yes. And even if you like to play shit [live], it's still good to have a lot of music to listen to and get influenced. . . . It's very important, though, in hip-hop, since we take music from everything. (Samson S. 1999)

In addition to its most specific value, providing sampling material, digging for vinyl serves numerous other purposes. After all, if getting sound was producers' only concern, there are many easier options available, from purchasing a synthesizer to hiring live musicians to collecting compact discs. Sample-based hip-hop producers, however, rarely exercise these options.

In this section I will deal with four major secondary functions of digging: to feel or display a commitment to hip-hop tradition through the conscious or unconscious reinscription of the value of deejaying (through its association with vinyl records); "paying dues" in a general sense; to educate oneself about different forms of music, both for its own sake and to also to spark one's own creativity; and as a form of socialization, both through digging with other producers and also through talking about digging.

Abstract Commitment to Hip-Hop Tradition

For many producers, the practice of digging in the crates constitutes an almost ritualistic connection to hip-hop history. That is to say, the act of digging itself, apart from any material or social benefits that it may bring, is valued as a central act of hip-hop culture:

> Man, the most times that I just feel a warm gut feeling about hip-hop are like when I'm out in I-don't-know-where. Like, for example, I was in Wyoming in this basement. . . . My brother and my dad and I, we drove for like twelve hours . . . through the night, got to this place. No sleep . . . everything was just messed up. So we walk in this bar at nine in the morning, have a beer, 'cause we were still out from the night before. Then we go in this antique store. I go down in the basement. And it's like, one wall is missing; the whole floor is water. There's just records stacked up on these little pallets. I got this flashlight, and I'm digging through records. I didn't find anything that incredible. I found some records I wanted. But that is, like, *real* to me. I mean, that's kinda crazy and stuff, but that's part of the culture. Going to far lengths to get records. (Shepard 1998)

King Otto characterizes the importance of digging in terms of its relationship to deejaying: "I'd say it's important. It's definitely a part of hip-hop. It goes all the way back to the essence of deejaying: to find something new that people haven't heard. And be the first one to play it, and have people not know what it is, but still like the song. That's why, with hip-hop, you could play just about any kind of record, as long as it was upbeat and danceable, at the time. So it's definitely important" (King Otto 1998).

In addition to the historical value of deejaying to hip-hop culture, there is a visceral power to the act of digging that can be ascribed to more general societal feelings about archaic media:

> I think there's an aura and there's a tradition of it and it's much more exciting to dig through vinyl than it is to flip through CDs. . . . There's an aesthetic of it. You feel like you're doing more work that way. . . . And it has to do with the mystique that vinyl has in our era, [it] maybe seems kind of outdated and archaic, but classy in some ways. . . . Which is, I think, why people like vinyl better. It just feels purer to them. (Wang 1998)

Paying Dues

In addition to the personal enjoyment of digging, it may also serve as a sort of dues-paying process when brought to bear in a social setting. One is simultaneously learning through experience, gathering musical material for later use, and undergoing a rite of passage. Digging is a point of pride for many producers. For example, in 1998 Jake One and Mr. Supreme (as The Conmen) collaboratively created a mix tape entitled *Smooth Criminals on Beatbreaks—Volume 1*, a sampler of original funk and soul songs from which hip-hop songs had sampled.[3] Printed directly on the cassette shell is the legend "All original records—no bootlegs!" disavowing the increasingly common use of breakbeat compilation records by producers and deejays (see chapter 5). For the purchaser of the tape, however, this guarantee has *no practical value whatsoever;* a cassette tape of a bootleg sounds exactly the same as a tape of an original record. But for Jake One and Mr. Supreme, it is clearly important that the listener know of their commitment to searching out original records.

Similarly, the track listing for the song "Holy Calamity (Bear Witness II)" (DJ Shadow's contribution to the 1999 Handsome Boy Modeling School CD by Prince Paul and Dan the Automator) contains the note "For all thre [*sic*] of you that care, DJ Shadow would like to state that all breaks used in this song were taken from the original source vinyl and not bootlegs or reissues. Suckers." A similar sentiment is at work when DJ Mixx Messiah complains about the low quality of contemporary commercial hip-hop; his primary complaint is that few contemporary producers take the time to dig:

The whole difference was when they were creating a lot of stuff, they had time, and they put time into it. Now they thinking more or less about the clubs and the cars, and they not puttin' the time into the track. . . . And they're not digging! The only people digging seems to be the underground or the producers that been putting it down, like Primo [DJ Premier] and Pete Rock. And RZA. You know, them guys—their whole life is about digging. Digging, and working that console. (DJ Mixx Messiah 1999)

For this reason, a producer's digging knowledge is often advertised as a sign of authenticity. The underground hip-hop group People under the Stairs, for example, manifests this knowledge though the design of their record cover, which intentionally evokes CTI, a 1970s jazz fusion label that was home to such musicians as Bob James and Grover Washington Jr.: "Their love for yesteryear's wax is evident on PUTS' own vinyl slice of truly underground hip-hop. . . . The 12-inch label is designed to look like a CTI release, the heavily sampled imprint. 'We didn't want to be too esoteric with the label association,' says Thes. 'We were gonna go with Milestone or Prestige, but we decided to keep it simple. Every beatdigger knows about CTI'" (Sour 1999: 76). Moreover, when I asked Mr. Supreme to expound on the difference between himself and more commercially oriented producers, he specifically refused to belittle the creativity and effort of commercial producers. The difference, he said, is that he digs: "There's work and thought behind it, 'cause it's basically put together the same way everything else is. What's different is what they use. It's the difference between using a Diana Ross record, that you could go out to any thrift store right now and buy, or using some Filipino soul band from Switzerland that no one's heard of and that's just funky as hell" (Mr. Supreme 1998a).

Beni B, founder of the Bay Area Hip-Hop Coalition, is widely viewed as a leading crate digger. While he promotes the many educational benefits of digging, he is also unusually candid about its social purpose within a competitive, male-dominated community: "Well, you know, too, man, it's also a pissing contest, too. Let's not kid ourselves, it's a pissing contest. It's like 'OK, so you got this, you got that. Blah, blah, blah'" (Beni B 2002).

Education about Music

A third function of digging is to educate producers about styles of music with which they may not be familiar, as Domino pointed out when I asked him to describe the relative importance of digging to hip-hop production:

> Very important. I think it's not for just beats. I'm really a big fan of different types of music. . . . There's so much good music that never really blew up to the point that it would ever be [reissued] on CDs today. So I've got turned on to stuff that I normally wouldn't have got turned on to, if it wasn't for trying to dig for samples. Since it's part of making tracks, at least for me, hip-hop–wise, it's kind of like an extra bonus. (Domino 1998)

This benefit can accrue with regard to not only genres, but also more specific strategies and approaches to music making. In this light, digging for records is seen as an educational process, as the following exchange with Negus I attests:

> Negus I: I think that [knowing a lot of records] is important, because it's gonna give you a lot more to draw upon, but it's [also] gonna open up your mind to different ideas of what you can do. Even combining different eras of music. And knowing that there's been some different kinds of things going on earlier, that you might not have known about. Like even in the bebop era, or the free jazz era. The kinds of things that were going on then are just as experimental, or even more, than any kind of crazy things that people put together now. . . . Like how Premier puts together sounds in a way that's unique, and it's kind of off the wall. But there were people in the free jazz era that were doing things just as off the wall as that, with live instrumentation. . . . They were breaking out of a formatted type of musical style already. And I think he probably got a lot of influence from some of those old records, just in terms of not being formatted in traditional scales and musical progressions.
>
> Joe: So just not even in terms of specific musical sounds or samples or anything, but just ideas about music.
>
> Negus I: I think overall ideas and perceptions of music. Things

you can do, or can't do, or supposed to do, or not supposed to do. (Negus I 1998)

Samson S. goes even further, arguing that the knowledge gained from digging is beneficial to producers not just for its influence on their work, but for its own sake as well:

Gotta know some music, man. And that's where the crates and shit come in. That helped me out. I mean, I wouldn't have known about . . . Three Dog Night or some shit if it wasn't for just having records. . . . I didn't grow up on that; I grew up on Al Green and Marvin Gaye and that type of shit. So I didn't hear Three Dog Night in my home. I started hearing that stuff later, when I started sampling. . . . That's the good thing about being a sample-oriented producer, because you get that education. Like I said, if it wasn't for this shit, a lot of us wouldn't be able to sit and have intelligent conversations about . . . Joni Mitchell or jazz and things like that, but because of hip-hop, we've learnt these things. So that's the good thing about it. 'Cause a lot of us, we get these records and we sample 'em, and, like, occasionally, we'll actually put the record on and listen to it! And, believe it or not, some of us actually listen and like these records! (Samson S. 1999)

Beni B. takes this argument a step further again, suggesting that the digging outlook—the use of active learning to define general sensibilities and specific musical knowledge—can be productively applied to other areas of life as well:

Joe: What was it in hip-hop that made you want to dig?
Beni B: Just the spectrum of music. And just knowing that "OK, where did this come from?" "OK, where did that come from?" It's like taking a history class and you're sitting in class and your instructor's telling you "Columbus discovered the Americas." OK, but who came before Columbus? Why was he there? So you can have answers, but who's really asking the questions? And that's what it's about, man. It's about asking the questions. (Beni B. 2002)

Digging as Socialization

Finally, digging in the crates serves as an important form of socialization for hip-hop producers. Not surprisingly, producers who are friends, such as Jake One and Mr. Supreme, spend a lot of time either digging together or talking about digging. In addition, when producers travel to other cities, it is common practice for local producers to introduce them to prime digging spots: "That's cool, 'cause it's like a exchange of information. 'Cause you're getting to find a record store. They're probably finding out what kind of stuff you're looking for. You're from another place, you probably have a different insight to certain things" (DJ Kool Akiem 1999). In addition to its educational benefits for both parties, the practice also reinforces the social bonds between producers in different areas, social bonds which remain in effect after the traveler returns home. The close-knit nature of the production community contributes to an atmosphere of collegiality.

In the following conversation, for instance, Jake One speaks about his lack of buying power and how this requires him to put more effort into digging. In order to make the distinction between his own social circle and "producers with more money," he gives an example of the other style of digging. But, somewhat paradoxically, his knowledge of how more moneyed producers dig is based on his own experience digging with them. This is not necessarily a contradiction; Jake One's distinction is simply finer than it appears at first glance. Even distinctions between producers from different cities with different styles are based on the assumption that they are ultimately part of the same social circle.

> Jake One: Obviously, the producers with more money run together, 'cause they can go spend all the money. Then there's like the lower-echelon people like me and my little cohorts. And we're into dollar shopping.
> Joe: There's that story about Mr. Walt [of the Beatminerz] buying a whole record store in Louisiana, or something. . . .
> Jake One: Yeah, we're not buying any record stores. I think the most I ever bought in a store was a crate [approximately seventy-five to one hundred records]. And I'd like to have bought more, but I couldn't, you know? . . . I went to Chicago this summer,

and I bought a bunch there. We hung out with No I.D., who's Common's producer. This guy was dropping, like, a thousand dollars in every store! I just couldn't even believe it. I was just in shock. I was like, "I gotta get paid; I wanna do that." (Jake One 1998)

At this writing, hip-hop production is undergoing an evolution in digging. As I mentioned at the beginning of this chapter, the idea of digging is intimately related to the idea of the break: producers are digging for breaks. In recent years, though, three factors have conspired to make this a less attractive proposition. The first is a growing sense that sampling a break and repeating it (also known as "looping") does not show enough artistic creativity on the part of a producer. Many producers hunger for a more personal form of expression, which they feel can be found by sampling smaller musical segments and rearranging them (see chapter 6). This practice still requires records, but the sensibility behind their acquisition may be different:

I used to really try to find the coolest records I could find. That was, say, early nineties and late eighties. . . . But I started realizing that I wasn't really looping too much, so I wasn't really needing the cool records, 'cause I could just use little pieces of other things. So I'll buy whatever kind of record I can find that looks interesting: twenties piano records or violin training records. *Sesame Street* records . . . I mean, I still like finding good records. And classic breaks and stuff like that. But I don't put as much time into it as, like, [Mr. Supreme] and Jake and those guys. (King Otto 1998)

The second factor is an increasing consciousness on the part of music publishing companies about sample clearance. It is fairly easy to recognize a two-measure section of a popular song, and hip-hop artists can therefore expect to pay the original copyright holders for every break-length sample they use. From a financial standpoint, this rapidly reaches the point of diminishing returns. I will deal with this issue more extensively in chapter 7.

Finally, there is a sense among many producers that the finite supply of old soul and funk music has been fully mined, that "all of the good breaks have been found":

I think it used to be [important]. Because this is such a young process. Sampling has only been around, really the way it is now, for
ten . . . or fifteen years. So it went through a stage where finding all
these old breaks and things was something that was exciting. But
now it's kinda got played out. And I think a lot of producers are
kind of bored doing it, because it's no fun. It's more fun to make
your own. We got past that. So now almost all the old breaks and
old songs have been found. So you kinda have to take it somewhere
else. (Negus I 1998)

Now I don't really feel like [having rare records is] what makes a
producer. Maybe that's an extra bonus. But I wouldn't dis anybody
'cause they [didn't] . . . Now it's a situation where it's whatever you
can do with it. I think that now it's harder to find a loop and make a
beat out of just a loop. (Domino 1998)

Mr. Supreme, however, disputes this assertion:

Like [Jake One] said, there's things that's drying up, 'cause everyone used everything. [But] I can easily pull out a thousand records
that no one's touched that are incredible. And *I* haven't even used
'em! And the reason is because I know the record, and it's just that
record to me. You know what I mean? And I just put it on the shelf.
And people will come over, and I'll play 'em stuff. And they're like,
"Are you crazy? Why haven't you used that? Let *me* use it!" . . . So
there is tons of stuff that no one's even touched on. I mean *tons*.
(Mr. Supreme 1998a)

In addition to break-related issues, there is the increasingly common
practice of "online digging"—usually facilitated by eBay. Though most
producers were initially resistant to the use of the Internet for digging purposes, more are embracing it every day and altering their digging philosophies accordingly. One very common approach among producers is
to continue their digging practices in the physical world as before with
the addition of purchasing extra copies of good records with the intent to
sell them online.

Even producers who are particularly committed to digging in the
crates are careful to emphasize that digging is only one of a number of
important skills that a good producer must possess:

People have this big misconception about, "whoever got the illest crates got the best beats." . . . It's important to me, but I think it gets way overvalued a lot of times, because people forget to listen to the records they have. Or they just don't do anything with the records. Thing is, a lot of my favorite producers use records that I have and they've used them while I still have 'em, and *I* didn't think to do it, so. . . . I think the more records you get, I mean obviously you're gonna have a better chance of making a good beat, but it kind of makes you lose focus. . . . It's your ear, I guess, more than anything. (Jake One 1998)

Samson S. agrees: "I know some producers out there that got a *grip* of records. *Hella*. And when you listen to their beats, it doesn't matter. *Their talent does come into play*. I mean, you could have every record ever made in the world, and a sampler. But if that's all you have?" (Samson S. 1999). In fact, a week after our first interview, Mr. Supreme asked me to interview him again, specifically to make this point: "It doesn't matter how many records you have; it's how you flip 'em, you know? So what if you have a thousand dope records? If you're not getting' busy with 'em . . . Anybody with money can be a record collector. I just wanted to make that clear, that there was cats that I know that don't have a whole lot of records, that are *nice* [extremely talented]" (Mr. Supreme 1998b). Having a substantial record collection is a necessary precondition to making good beats, but it is not the only condition. But while the records themselves may provide only the raw material for hip-hop production, the *act of searching for records* provides much more.

Digging in the crates provides a material focus for a variety of social interactions among producers. These may include everything from community building to the development of a personal reputation to aesthetic and ethical education. The substantial amount of effort that producers put toward digging attests to the continued significance of all of these things within the world of hip-hop production. In fact, it is precisely the social, symbolic, and aesthetic values of digging in the crates that allows it to remain a central focus for hip-hop producers even as its practical value diminishes.

Sampling Ethics

> Joe: It's one of those things, that there seem to be . . . I don't know if
> "rules" is the right word. . . .
> Vitamin D: Yeah.
> Joe: But there are certain things. . . .
> Vitamin D: They're rules! It's all following *rules*. (Vitamin D 1998)

One major influence on the artistic practice of hip-hop producers is their general adherence to a defined set of professional ethics. In this chapter, I will explore the major themes of this ethical system, in order to set the stage for questions regarding the producers' philosophical outlook and aesthetic approach. I will argue that at base these ethics tend to equate creativity with moral value. From that axiom, a variety of rules have been derived, disseminated, and enforced within the producers' community.

It is important to note at the outset that what is at issue here is the validity of various *strategies* toward sampling; producers' ethics are not concerned with whether sampling *itself* is appropriate or not. As I discussed in chapter 4, hip-hop producers, among themselves, feel no need to justify sampling; it is the foundation of the musical system. This may be why the so-called producers' ethics have largely been overlooked by the academic community—they simply do not bear on the questions that most scholars have been interested in. But they do shed light on many issues that are important to this study, including the way a community's social norms may be reflected in its specific musical choices, how an ethical system may be used to create and maintain social boundaries, and how music can mediate between the interests of individuals and their community.

Furthermore, it must be said that many of these rules hold little significance for the larger hip-hop community. If a producer violates them, it
will often only be apparent to other producers. At the same time, high
ethical standards are largely valued only within the production world.
But, as will become clear in the following pages, concern for one's reputation among other producers is often enough to enforce a sense of ethical obligation. The community of hip-hop producers is small enough that
the threat of ridicule among one's peers can be a substantial sanction.
Similarly, a sense of ethical obligation serves to demonstrate producers'
concern for their peers' opinions. In a spoken interlude on their 1998 album *Moment of Truth,* for instance, Gang Starr's DJ Premier berates other
hip-hop artists for "lettin' the industry control the rules of the hip-hop
world that *we* made." In doing so, he is implicitly arguing that this hip-
hop world can be distinguished and protected from the "industry" by its
control of a set of rules. In other words, producers' ethics are one of the
primary factors that allow hip-hop musicians to see their work as an endeavor that is separate from commerce: as art.

Section headings in this chapter reflect my own attempt to express
each ethical principle in its most generally applicable form; the rules
were not necessarily stated to me in these terms by any one consultant.
Furthermore, I want to make it clear that by distilling the various ethical
issues into a prescriptive form at the beginning of each section, it is not
my intention to endorse that particular approach to the ethic in question.
I have taken this step merely to delineate the ethics in their most generic
terms before discussing the complexities that inevitably underlie them.
Similarly, such an approach may appear to impose a systemicity on the
rules that does not actually emerge from the community. While the
following pages will clearly demonstrate that these ethics are highly con-
tested, it is essential to their function that they not be seen as the construction of particular individuals. I would suggest, therefore, that regardless of how unsystematic the enforcement of the rules may be in
practice, the systemicity of the rules *as a matter of principle* is of the ut-
most importance to producers.

Although the development of an individual producer's particular ethical sensibility is often based on his own participant-observation, its very
existence in the first place is founded on the assumption that the ethics

have an internal systemicity that exists independently of the observer: "I guess where the ethics came from, to me, is just because I figured out what other people were doin' and just kinda did what they did. And then found the system in it" (DJ Kool Akiem 1999).

Ethical debates tend toward the theological, which is to say that despite many disagreements, the rules themselves are seen as being timeless and unchanging. As deejay Strath Shepard comments: "I don't know how those things come about, exactly. And you just know 'em. I mean, I don't know who told me those rules. But everyone just kinda knows" (Shepard 1998). Though many specific rules probably date back to the earliest days of hip-hop, it is difficult to say with certainty when the idea of an overarching ethical system first developed. My sense, though, is that it developed in the late eighties or early nineties. One piece of evidence for this hypothesis is that many of what would now be considered to be fairly strict rules were routinely violated in the mid-eighties. For example, it is considered a violation to sample a recording that has already been used by another producer without substantially changing it. But the Rap Sample FAQ, an online compendium of sample sources, lists almost two hundred songs that sampled from James Brown's "Funky Drummer," virtually all from the middle to late eighties—and the actual number is probably closer to several thousand (http://www.members.accessus.net/~xombi/intro.html, accessed 23 August 2002). And when I raised this issue with Steinski, a producer who first came to prominence in the early 1980s, it resulted in the following exchange:

> Joe: A lot of people only sample from vinyl, as a matter of principle. A lot of people won't sample from a compilation, because they feel like the work has already been done, you should be digging for your own records, and things like that. . . . Obviously, you don't feel strongly about those things. . . .
> Steinski: Yeah. In the interview you can say "made face."
> (Steinski 2002)

Today, the rules exist in the background, and are rarely discussed unless violated:

If I hear somebody do something that's unethical, I'll just make a note of it. It's not all that often that I do hear that. . . . I've talked to people and heard tracks, and I'm like, "What are you doing? You sampled that offa Lord Finesse. You sampled that beat. That's wack [objectively bad]." I've gotten into arguments over stuff like that. . . . [But] the cats that I talk to mostly are in my same school of ethics, really. We don't really talk about that all that much. (DJ Kool Akiem 1999)

Ethical arguments among producers usually make use of one of two strategies. They will either appeal to other rules that supersede the one in question or argue for specific exceptions to a rule without technically violating it. Such practices, in a backhanded way, serve to demonstrate the symbolic power of the rules; if the rules were not endowed with symbolic significance, individuals would simply ignore them, rather than develop elaborate philosophical rationalizations. Moreover, even producers who have no intention of actually using the exemptions they've created still enjoy developing these arguments on an abstract level.

For the purist, the ethics are one of the major tools for preserving the essence of hip-hop, even to the degree that producers in search of greater purity will actually create new rules for themselves. As producer Vitamin D put it, "I'm trying to keep it as close to the foundation as I can keep it. . . . And this is just a philosophy that I came up with later on, 'cause before I was using drum machines, break records, and whatever —I didn't care—just 'cause it was new to me. But I feel that in order to have growth, your standards have to grow, so I'm kind of raising up my standards" (Vitamin D 1998). Note that Vitamin D's explicit goal in raising his standards is to "keep it . . . close to the foundation." In his formulation, increasingly stringent practice, such as rejecting drum machines and break records (also known as "compilations"), brings him closer to the "foundation" of hip-hop. The new rules are seen as implicit in past hip-hop practice.

For those of a less purist bent, the rules are valued almost for their own sake; the more rules producers can take on without compromising the quality of the finished product, the greater their skill is considered to be. From this perspective, following the rules is seen as a challenge whose rewards come mainly in the social realm. As producer Samson S. describes it, "Some producers have ethics and some don't. So it's a ethical thing, basically. If you wanna feel like this is your creation, and you hooked it up, and you wanna be proud of your shit, have other producers like, 'Whoo!', you're not gonna get that respect without ethics" (Samson S. 1999). For those who hold this philosophy, then, the ethics serve to define the boundaries of originality.

None of these perspectives are in any way exclusive. In fact, more than one approach comes into play in most situations. The common thread that unites them is their sense that the rules themselves can define the essence of hip-hop. But following the rules—demonstrating one's dedication to the form on a philosophical level—does not necessarily mean that one will produce music that will be accepted by the production community; there are other aesthetic and social variables as well. Vitamin D, for example, is explicit about the distinction between music that he feels violates a "hip-hop principle," and music that he personally does not care for: "There's some things that are wack, and there's some stuff that I'm just not feelin'. But it's not wack. I'm just not feelin' it. There's a difference. A lot of stuff, I'm not feeling. [But] it doesn't go against any of the hip-hop principles that everybody else knows" (Vitamin D 1998). The ideal song, of course, will be both ethically correct *and* pleasing to listen to. Such judgments and the distinctions they entail are much easier to make in the abstract than in actual practice. In many—if not most —cases, ethics are intertwined with aesthetics or practical concerns. For instances where the two seem reasonably separable, I will address the aesthetic aspect in chapter 6. But in some cases, ethical and aesthetic issues are so closely tied together that it would be misleading to separate them; in such cases, both aspects will be explored here.

"No Biting": One Can't Sample Material That Has Been Recently Used by Someone Else

The most basic ethic is to be original, often expressed in simple terms as "No biting." Discussion of this rule requires that I introduce four terms that frequently arise in production-oriented conversations: "biting," "flipping," "chopping," and "looping." My intention here is to present these meanings in their most skeletal forms in hopes that their various connotations will become apparent in the discussion to come.

"Biting" is a term that is used throughout the hip-hop world, and it refers pejoratively to the appropriation of intellectual material from other hip-hop artists. Generally speaking, it *does not* apply to the appropriation of material from outside the hip-hop community. Again, this supports the general idea of ethics as being responsive to community needs—the concerns of outsiders are not at issue. "Flipping" refers to creatively and substantially altering material in any way. This term tends to be limited to the producing community, although one can also "flip" lyrics, by, for instance, taking a common phrase and using it ironically. The idea is that one is adding value through the creativity of one's alterations. "Chopping" and "looping" are technical terms that are specific to the production arena. "Chopping," as its name suggests, refers to altering a sampled phrase by dividing it into smaller segments and reconfiguring them in a different order. "Looping," by contrast, refers to sampling a longer phrase (one or more measures) and repeating it with little or no alteration.

DJ Kool Akiem defines biting:

> To me it means, one, I'm not gonna just take a loop that somebody else did—if that's all they did, just loop it—I'm not gonna come and do the same thing without doing something to it to make it better. . . . Also, I'm not gonna take two elements of something that somebody else took. Like, if somebody samples this James Brown piece and then they put the "Substitution" [drum break] on top of that? I won't do that. To me, that's biting. (DJ Kool Akiem 1999)

Samson S. explains the social repercussions for violating this rule: "You can't knowingly do that. I mean, you can if you want, but you ain't gonna get no credit. Everybody gonna be like, 'Oh, you bit such-and-such.' So why even put yourself through that?" (Samson S. 1999).

There are three generally recognized exceptions to the "No biting" rule: if one flips the sample, if one is specifically parodying the other known usage, or if the bite is unintentional.[1] Vitamin D. is in the mainstream of producers when he states that he would not use the same sample as another hip-hop artist "unless I'm just one hundred percent flippin' it impossibly" (Vitamin D. 1998).[2] Taken in conjunction with DJ Kool Akiem's and Samson S.'s earlier comments, it is clear that this is basically a matter of creativity deployed in a manner similar to its use in other forms of music. To do the same thing someone else does is not creative, but taking a new approach to familiar material is. Strath Shepard is emphatic about the boundaries of the exception: "Drums can get reused, but samples can't get reused. I don't think they should be reused. That's a rule. . . . Unless you chop it up. But I'm saying: you have to chop it up really good. And do something totally different with it. . . . Samples shouldn't be used more than once unless they are really flipped" (Shepard 1998).

As producer Negus I explains, the creativity may be valued either on its own terms or in relation to another use of the same sample, that is, as parody, which is the second exception:

> It would have to be an obvious thing that I was doing. Like, "I'm obviously using this sound that is already out right now, or it's just been out, but look how I'm doing it. Look, I'm changing it." So it wouldn't be like a underslide, like "Oh, I'm using a sound that I wonder if people are gonna notice that it's the same sound." No. I would make it obvious that, yeah, that is the same sound, but look what I did with it. Or commenting on the other song, almost. (Negus I 1998)

One frequently cited example of this practice is the track "Ya Playin' Yaself," produced by DJ Premier in 1995 and featuring Jeru Tha Damaja: "There was one instance where I really noticed it was a response. The Junior M.A.F.I.A., the 'Player's Anthem.' Premier and Jeru came with a song called 'Ya Playin' Yaself.' They used the same bass sound, and he flipped it around, and they changed the title. I thought that was quite clever. And he made it into something totally different. But it was the same elements, two totally different songs" (Jake One 1998).

In figure 1, I present the essential bass line from each song. I have numbered each note of "Player's Anthem" sequentially. For "Ya Playin' Yaself," each note has retained its corresponding number, so that the figure shows how DJ Premier chopped and rearranged the riff. DJ Premier's reorganization of the sample retains enough of the original bass line to be recognizable, yet changes its melodic contour and rhythmic emphasis. The lyrics of "Ya Playin' Yaself" support its interpretation as a response to "Players Anthem." The Junior M.A.F.I.A. song is a celebration of materialism, and the response is a criticism of such attitudes,

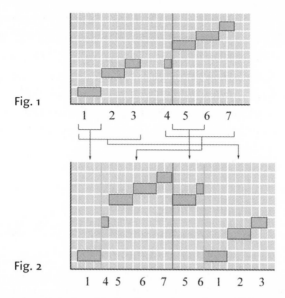

Fig. 1

Fig. 2

Fig. 1. Chopping. Relationship between primary bass riff from "Player's Anthem" by Junior M.A.F.I.A. and primary bass riff from "Ya Playin' Yaself" by Jeru the Damaja, Fig. 2.

deconstructing the original lyrics in a manner parallel to the way DJ Premier's beat recasts the original bass line. "You're a 'player,'" Jeru rhymes, "but only because you be playin' yourself."

Finally, the same song may be sampled coincidentally, as Seattle MC Wordsayer (who works with Negus I) notes:

> The thing that trips me out is how you can have producers in the same time, but in different places—like thousands of miles apart—taking those same elements from the same song. Using them in different ways, but using that same song, or that same album, around the same time, around the world. That's a trip, and that happens a lot. You hear somebody has a beat that's out, and you have the same elements that you're working on, or have worked on, at the same time. (Wordsayer 1998)

This raises the question of whether any given instance constitutes a coincidence or a bite, and more to the point, how such a determination would be made within the hip-hop community. To some degree, circumstantial evidence comes into play, such as which song was released first or how widely circulated each song was (i.e., whether producers are likely to have even heard the song that they are accused of biting). But in my experience, the decision is largely based on the reputation of the individual being accused. Producers of high repute are virtually never accused of biting, even in circumstances where others might be criticized. A producer who has demonstrated ethics in the past is more likely to be given the benefit of the doubt in a questionable case.

Essentially, then, the prohibition against biting reflects an approach to creativity that is similar to that employed in other forms of popular music, with one difference. Since the music is sampled, originality cannot be the ethical "default category." That is to say, in other forms of music, one is assumed to be creating original work, unless there is evidence to the contrary. In hip-hop, by contrast, one must always be prepared to defend one's creativity, and this requires standards. The producers' ethics in general and the "No biting" rule in particular help to promote those standards.

Records Are the Only Legitimate Source for Sampled Material

> I don't even have too many CDs. I don't like anything about CDs.
> I'm definitely a vinyl man. (Stroman 1999)

There is a sense among many producers that vinyl records are the only legitimate source for sampled material. This sensibility is, in many ways, a point of intersection for several otherwise unrelated concerns. On a philosophical level, the rule is closely tied to the practice of digging in the crates, as discussed in chapter 4, and represents an intellectual commitment to the deejaying tradition as the foundation of hip-hop. Aesthetic issues may also come into play, with the analog sound quality of records being preferred over the digital qualities of compact discs. Practical concerns also arise, insofar as records are more convenient to sample from, in certain ways, than other recording formats. Furthermore, the specific musical material that producers are interested in is often available only on vinyl. Finally, a practical connection between deejaying and producing is also a factor: producers who are also deejays tend to already have records available. Although, strictly speaking, these are not all ethical factors, each will be dealt with in this section because they all work to reinforce what is seen as ethical behavior.

Many aspects of hip-hop deejaying practice, such as digging in the crates, have become central to the ideology of hip-hop generally, even for those who are not deejays themselves. On some level, most hip-hoppers hold some deejay-oriented philosophical positions, not only because they love deejaying for its own sake, but also because deejaying positions itself as traditional, and they are committed, on a more abstract level, to the *idea* of tradition. Oliver Wang is particularly candid about this fact:

> I might critique the kind of overly purist perspective on "vinyl only," but I still agree with it. Like, I've never bought something on CD because it had breaks on it. And if I could do it, I'd always find it on vinyl. And the thing is, I've actually thought about it, and I don't know why I do it, except that it's just the tradition I learned. Because, I gotta say, CDs are more convenient. And if it is about the music, I'd rather listen to the music, instead of just isolating a break every time. In which case I'd rather have it on CD, because I can take it with me in the car, et cetera, et cetera. But when I dig, I only dig in vinyl. (Wang 1998)

Producer Specs sees digging for vinyl as a process of paying dues and expresses some distaste toward those who are spared that process by the increasing availability of CD reissues of classic records: "It just seems too easy. . . . Because you don't have to go out shopping for CDs. You don't have to dig through CDs because they're remastering everything on 'em. You don't have to search. You have to search for records. . . . So it cuts down the whole searching aspect. Like, most any good deejay or producer is gonna have to do some work. And now you don't" (Specs 1998).

Strath Shepard positions digging for vinyl as an expression of a philosophical commitment to hip-hop culture:

> It's like Zorro said in [the 1983 hip-hop film] *Wild Style*: it's like, "painting on canvas: that's not graffiti. You have to go out and rack up; you have to take the flak from everyone." You have to take the

flak from the record dealers, you have to wake up in the morning and get your hands dirty. You have to be willing to go through some crazy shit to get your records. And with a CD, it's like you could just go to Blockbuster and buy that thing. Part of the culture is just digging. (Shepard 1998)

Another issue is the sound of the vinyl medium itself. While this was important in principle to many of my consultants, for many others, the value is purely situational; that is, they value the sound of records when they are looking for that particular sound. In this regard, the sound of vinyl becomes like any other aspect of a potential sample. Domino, for example, sees both the pros and cons in the use of vinyl, stating that "I like grittiness, but a lot of the pops and stuff, I'm not into" (Domino 1998). For Negus I, whether or not to use a record is a decision that must be made on a case-by-case basis: "An Al Green CD and Al Green record: it's no different to me. If I want some of that character from the vinyl, I'll use it. But if I don't need that, and I just want a clean sound I hear on that, I'll take the CD" (Negus I 1998). DJ Kool Akiem characterizes this as an issue of aesthetics and practicality, with few ethical underpinnings:

I don't really sample off of CDs. Unless I have a certain reason, like I wanted something really clear that I have on vinyl, that I found . . . [but] it's too messed up, or something like that. Actually, I can't really remember sampling offa any CDs. If that's the only format that that comes in, that I could find, I might. But I don't see . . . ethically, anything wrong with it. I mean, it's a format. [But] I don't sample offa tape, 'cause it sounds crappy. (DJ Kool Akiem 1999)[3]

Such aesthetic determinations, while they may be left to the tastes of individual producers, are rarely value free, and this one is no exception. The Angel, for instance, characterizes the exclusive emphasis on vinyl as "snobbery":

I never had a particular snobbery about whether or not I got things from vinyl, because I could get something clean off of a CD and add vinyl noise to it. It's not about how you do it, it's about how you put it together. You know what I mean? It's how much ingenuity do you infuse into the process to get to where you want to be. There's so many different ways of achieving what you need in the process, that it's not really a problem. But I know some people [are] very, very, strict about that; I personally think it's ridiculous. . . . There *is* a different sound to vinyl compression. [But] if you need it, you can do that these days. You can process things in that way and you can get it to sound that way. (The Angel 1998)

Aesthetic issues aside, records may simply be valued for their practicality. Producers are interested in "breaks"—segments of several seconds each that may be located anywhere on a recording. A producer can search a record in mere moments, simply by dropping the needle at various points. This cannot be done with a compact disc or cassette:

I think it's just easier to do it with records. It's just easier to manipulate, you can listen to it a lot faster, go through stuff quicker. You know, you could listen to little niches in the song a lot quicker, as opposed to having to deal with a CD player. Or a tape player, even worse. To me, there's no connection to those two different things. It just seems hard to even conceive of me sampling from some CDs. (Domino 1998)

In addition to general convenience, Domino continues, there is a more specific benefit to sampling records: "I know for a lot of people that got samplers that don't have as much sampling time, they sample on 45 [rpm], which means you can get more out of your time. And you can't do that if you had a CD player" (Domino 1998). That is, many samplers have a limited amount of memory, or "sampling time." A producer can maximize this time by speeding up a 33 rpm record to 45 rpm (thus making the sample half as long), sampling it, and then slowing the sample back down to the original speed. The result may be of slightly lower quality, but it uses far less memory.

For Samson S., this—more than aesthetics or tradition—is the reason for using records: "I don't have anything against [sampling from CDs]. We haven't done it yet; it takes too much sampling time. See, on the vinyl, you can just speed it up and sample it. It's practical reasons. And plus most of the stuff you wanna sample is on vinyl anyway" (Samson S. 1999). Another reason for relying on vinyl, as Samson S. points out, is that it is the only format in which most of the valued music is available. As Domino puts it, "There's not too much on a CD that's appealing to me, the kind of stuff that I look for" (Domino 1998).

Finally, there are more general issues of practicality as well. Many producers may simply not have CDs available, as my conversation with producer King Otto confirms:

> King Otto: I probably wouldn't sample off a CD. But I've sampled off tape before, only a couple times, because I didn't have the record. But I would pretty much stick with records, as a rule. . . .
>
> Joe: It's interesting, I noticed you said you "probably" wouldn't sample off a CD, as if it's just never come up before.
>
> King Otto: Well, I don't have any CDs. [But] I wouldn't sample off CDs, I don't think.
>
> Joe: And that's just for the sound?
>
> King Otto: The sound, and maybe the ethic thing of it. (King Otto 1998)

This is a particular issue for producers who are also deejays; they use records for their other pursuits. All other things being equal, it still is far more efficient to simply buy the record, which, in addition to being a source of samples, can be played in a club or on the radio in its original form (hip-hop deejays prefer vinyl over other media because many of hip-hop's foundational deejaying techniques, such as scratching, can only be performed with vinyl records, although the electronics industry is working hard to create CD players that can emulate the feel of a turntable).

> Negus I: That only makes sense. Because why would you spend your money on a CD, when you could spend that money to buy the same thing on a record? And as a deejay you could use it.
>
> Joe: Especially if it's your *job* to be a deejay.
>
> Negus I: Yeah, 'cause a lot of it come down to economics and finances. (Negus I 1998)

One Cannot Sample from Other Hip-Hop Records

As far as, like, for your music? Oh *hell* no! (Samson S. 1999)

Nah. Hell nah. That's like crazy wrong. And cats be doin' that! That's just ridiculous, man. Totally ridiculous. (DJ Kool Akiem 1999)

The value of "digging in the crates" is again manifested in this rule. One shouldn't sample from another hip-hop record because one would be exploiting the effort of the original producer who dug for the sound. As King Otto puts it, "It doesn't take any work to sample from a rap record, basically. Because it's already there for you, it can be sampled" (King Otto 1998). The rationale behind this rule is so self-evident to producers that it only becomes an issue in three rather narrow areas: sampling individual drum hits, sampling vocal expressions as a tribute to the original MC, and briefly sampling the instrumental track for purposes of parody or homage.

In our conversation, Jake One describes how the first practice, sampling drums, works:

> Jake One: People . . . sample drums off of hip-hop records. You know, somebody leaves the kick open or something. . . .
> Joe: When you say, "leaves the kick open," you mean there's just the drum sound with nothing on top of it. . . .
> Jake One: Yeah. You can take it and put it in your beat, you know?
> Joe: So do people purposely *not* do that [leave drums open], so that [other] people won't . . .
> Jake One: I don't know. . . . Q-Tip used to always leave drums open. I remember the Mobb Deep single "Give Up the Goods," he had a kick and a snare on there. The snare is too recognizable, though. See, you wanna be able to take something that nobody knows. . . . What was that other record? "The World is Yours" remix? He left kicks and snares open with that. . . . "One Love," people take drums off of "One Love." Premier, I noticed, doesn't leave drums open. Like if you have an instrumental, he'll have a voice echoing through it. . . .
> Joe: Do you think he does that on purpose?
> Jake One: I think so. Cause if the only dropout in the song, he hap-

pens to throw an extra delay on it in an instrumental mix, it sounds kind of weird. . . . It's crazy. . . . I think about this stuff way too much. Way too much. (Jake One 1998)

In noting that he thinks about these issues "way too much," Jake One is, at least in part, referring to the fact that he was immediately able to call to mind several examples of hip-hop songs which contained moments where a drum was played in isolation, including one on which there was only a single potentially usable drum hit in the entire song. This is typical of the way hip-hop producers listen to music. In fact, it is perhaps the most significant aspect of this particular prohibition: in order to invoke the rule in the first place, a listener must be able to identify the recorded origins of a *single strike of a drum*.[4]

Later in our conversation, Jake (now joined by Strath Shepard) makes reference to this fact and notes the sanctions that can expected for a violation:

> Jake One: You'll get ridiculed! I'll ridicule someone if I hear 'em use the "One Love" drums, or something like that.
> Strath: He probably did that [left it open] on purpose, actually, because that drum is so . . .
> Jake One: Yeah, it's so distinct.
> Strath: And no one knows what it is.
> Joe: So do you think he did that just as a challenge to people?
> Strath: Yeah. Like, "I'll know if you take my drum." (Jake One 1998)

The use of ridicule as a viable sanction suggests a relatively unified and small community, regardless of the physical distance involved. The idea that producers in New York might be concerned that a producer in Seattle is laughing at them speaks volumes.

Mr. Supreme discusses sampling from hip-hop records in the plaintive tone of one who feels that his own work has been devalued by the lowering of ethical standards: "I don't think it's appropriate to take the instrumental of a rap record and use it. But I'm sure people would argue with me. They'll say, 'Well, what's the difference if we took that or Bobby Azzam from Switzerland?' Well, to me, there *is* a difference, you know? There's a difference" (Mr. Supreme 1998).

The producer Specs, though he admits committing this particular breach of etiquette in a certain case, has a similarly visceral reaction to this particular rule: "That's a weird one because I've actually done that before, because I don't have an 808 [a Roland TR-808 drum machine]. And there's a certain record, Brooklyn Alliance, that has this 808 kick that I always sampled. . . . But not music, though. I would never sample something that was already sampled from somebody else. That just seems like some weird type of incest or something. Just kind of strange. I would definitely say that was a rule" (Specs 1998). Specs's reasons for not sampling from other hip-hop records suggest that, as with Mr. Supreme, the practice is actually emotionally uncomfortable: it's "kind of strange" and "like some weird type of incest." At the same time, though, he makes an exception for drum sounds, as does DJ Kool Akiem:[5] "Nah. Possibly if it's like a 808 boom maybe, or something like that. That's just no big deal, but I wouldn't sample something that somebody else sampled" (DJ Kool Akiem 1999).

Like Specs and DJ Kool Akiem, King Otto exempts drum sounds from the rule, but holds fast when it comes to nondrum sounds: "I'd say that's a rule. I think everyone has, once or twice. Like a kick [drum]. I've taken a kick off a record before. I took some drums off a Tribe Called Quest record once, when nothing was playing but the drums, so that you couldn't really tell that I got it off there. But, other than that, I wouldn't do it. I wouldn't condone it" (King Otto 1998). King Otto specifically states that not only would he not do this himself, but he would also not condone the practice for others. This supports the idea of it being a rule, rather than a personal preference.

The use of vocal samples from other hip-hop songs is more problematic. For some, the resistance to their use exists primarily in the realm of emotion. As Mr. Supreme says, "It just kinda makes me mad. . . . I don't know why, it just does" (Mr. Supreme 1998a). For others, it's a matter of aesthetics more than ethics: "Yeah, I agree [that it's bad to sample vocals]. But I'm not totally against it. As long as it ain't like, 'Punks jump! Puh-Puh-Puh!' you know, like in them drum and bass records. . . . That gets to be corny. But if you strategically place it in a song, it don't matter. To me, at least" (Samson S. 1999). Perhaps the most intriguing take on this rule came from Vitamin D. He argued that it was permissible to use vocals from other hip-hop records, but only if they were placed there in

real time by a deejay playing the original record on a turntable—it was
not permissible to insert the vocals with a sampler:

> Let's say I wanted to take [a] Greg Nice [vocal] and put that in the
> chorus. . . . I have to cut it in if it's gonna be in the song. I can't
> sample it in; a lotta people will just sample it in. . . . I have to cut it
> with the turntables, I can't sample it in. . . . [When people sample
> vocals], I be like, "Hey, what are you doing, man? You're taking away,
> man!" (Vitamin D 1998)

DJ Topspin agrees, at least in principle:

> Yeah. I mean, yeah, you should cut it in. He's a very hardcore dee-
> jay, and I believe that, too. I mean, I don't have a *problem* if it's sam-
> pled. I have more in my life than to have a problem with what
> somebody does on a record. . . . [But] if you're doing nothin' but
> sampling a vocal and just hittin' it, then that says that you have no
> deejay skills or desire to showcase them. Really . . . you should
> scratch them in if you can. Anybody can learn a machine and load
> 'em into a machine. (DJ Topspin 1999)

When I asked Negus I about this restriction, he theorized that it was
based on Vitamin D's dual identity as a producer and a deejay:

> I think . . . that's because . . . He may think that using vocal sam-
> ples is kind of cheesy, unless you actually do it as a deejay . . .
> 'cause he's a producer *and* a deejay. And I think he may feel that
> sampling somebody's vocals and laying it on your track is kind of
> cheesy, as a producer. *So he does it as a deejay.* . . . But I know D has
> a lot of those rules. (Negus I 1998)

This supports the social nature of these rules; the appropriateness of
using vocal samples from other hip-hop records depends upon the identity of the individual in question, and the tradition that individual claims
to represent. The sampling of rap vocals, in Vitamin D's view, is a violation of the professional ethics of the producer, but not of the deejay.
In addition, Negus I's comment that Vitamin D was a particularly rule-
oriented producer (a contention supported both by Vitamin D himself
and by other producers who know him) illustrates that it is not uncommon for producers to have rules that only apply to themselves.

DJ Kool Akiem, however, does not accept the distinction: "Nah. I don't agree with that. I mean, I could see why that rule would exist, but I don't agree with it. Because . . . Well, put it like this: say you don't want the scratch on it, you just want the cut? How're you gon' know? What's the difference gon' be? If you cut it in, or you sample it in, you ain't gonna know [the difference]" (DJ Kool Akiem 1999). DJ Kool Akiem's approach is based on the sound that ultimately emerges rather than the method with which it was created. To "scratch" the vocal sample into the recording is to emphasize the sound of the vocal being moved back and forth on a turntable—something that cannot be done with a sampler. But to "cut" the vocal sample in is to use only the sound itself. This would sound the same whether it was done with a turntable or a sampler. And if you can't hear the difference in the final product, DJ Kool Akiem argues, then there's no basis for claiming an ethical violation. This approach to ethics has a practical value; in most cases, the only evidence of how something was created is how it sounds on the final record.

The final exception to the rule against sampling other hip-hop records is the use of brief sections for the purposes of parody or reference. When I asked him about sampling from other hip-hop records, DJ Kool Akiem was emphatically opposed to the practice, except in this case: "You have to have, like, a certain specific reason. And I can't hardly see nothin' except for when Ice Cube did 'Jackin' For Beats.'[6] That's like the only possible way I could see. . . . You know what I'm sayin', it's like a novelty thing" (DJ Kool Akiem 1999). DJ Topspin agrees: "Me, personally, DJ Topspin in Seattle, I'm not gonna sample anybody else's record that came out a year ago for any other purpose instead of a quick reference" (DJ Topspin 1999).

Not everyone is opposed to sampling from hip-hop records. Domino, for example, feels that recent events may have conspired to make digging-related ethics obsolete. Note, however, that before he explains his philosophical acceptance of the practice, he is careful to state that he personally doesn't—*ever*—sample from hip-hop records:

> I don't ever . . . do that. [But] I don't think it's a big deal. . . . I know a lotta people that you could tell they sampled a known sample from, like, a Tribe record, as opposed to getting it from the original. I think that, back a couple of years ago, I woulda been like, "Oh

that's wack," 'cause I think to a lot of producers, part of the art was finding the record. But now, with the popularity of these breakbeat records. . . . that put out all the hard to find records, anyway—in abundance . . . it's the same thing [as sampling from hip-hop records]. (Domino 1998)

As this example illustrates, producers often construct legalistic exceptions to production ethics, even when they have no intention of actually using the exceptions they create. This was an attitude that I encountered regularly during my research, and it shows the abstract enjoyment that can be derived from working with the ethical system.

The rule against sampling from hip-hop records emphasizes the value of hard work and creativity. Sampling from a hip-hop record, producers argue, does not demonstrate either of these qualities because the record has already been discovered, presented, and optimized for a hip-hop aesthetic.

One Can't Sample Records One Respects

Another rule I have: I don't sample records that I respect. I don't know, but that's the only way I can really put it. The reason why I haven't sampled some of the records down here is just 'cause I got too much respect for it, man. The record still bugs me out, to the point where I don't know how I'd flip it, you know? I get that when I listen to Miles Davis. . . . He just trips me out. I be like, "Man!" Can't really mess with that. That's a sacred type thing. (Vitamin D 1998)

To a large degree it's like: unless you can add something, or flip it in a totally amazing way, leave it alone. Like, there's some artists, I just kind of feel like, "Don't mess with Stevie Wonder or Marvin Gaye stuff." (Dere 1998)

There are records that are just there. They're fresh already. And you taking it isn't gonna make you a better producer. I mean, there's records I've used, I'm, "I can't sample this. This guy's tight! You just gotta sit back and listen to this." 'Cause you can mess up a good record. . . . A nice song, until you loop it and say how fresh you are over it. It's like, there's some records that can be left alone. . . . Something that you

> can't really mess with, just because it's so pure, it's like putting it into a hip-hop context can be difficult and almost detrimental to the record itself. (DJ Topspin 1999)

This rule rests on three pillars: that sampling may be disrespectful to a great artist, that some music is so good that sampling does not improve it, and that sampling something that was already good is not sufficiently challenging. The first and second of these are telling in that sampling is not seen as being disrespectful to artists in general, only to particularly esteemed ones. The third pillar supports the idea that ego gratification and fun are a part of hip-hop in production; listeners are presumed to make an assessment of the degree of difficulty when they judge the accomplishments of other producers.

Not everyone agrees with this rule, however:

> Nah. . . . If I respect a record, I'm samplin' the hell out of it! Now, I mean, I ain't gonna force it. If there's a record I like a lot, but I can't find nothin' on it. . . . But, nah, I don't have that rule. (Samson S. 1999)

> Nah. I don't agree with that. I mean there's some fantastic stuff that I have high praise for. But I'll still sample it. To me, it's the highest praise to sample it. (DJ Kool Akiem 1999)

While Negus I agrees with Samson S. and DJ Kool Akiem, his take on this issue shows that the underlying concern of individuals on both sides of the issue is essentially the same—how one can best exercise one's creativity: "I would definitely use a part of a song that I loved, because it has that spirit in it. And I would like to get some of that spirit. But I would have to put as much of my spirit into changing that sound and doing something to it, to make it worthwhile. I wouldn't wanna just use the [melody] and put a beat over it" (Negus I 1998).

One Can't Sample from Reissues or Compilation Recordings of Songs with Good Beats

Midway through their 1998 album, *Moment of Truth,* Gang Starr's DJ Premier abruptly stops the music, in order to deliver the following rejoinder to unnamed individuals in the hip-hop community that he feels have violated ethical principles:

> What's the deal with you break-record cats that's puttin' out all the original records that we sample from, and *snitchin'* by puttin' us on the back of it, sayin' that we use stuff? You *know* how that go! Stop doing that! Y'all are violatin', straight up and down! Word up, man; I'm sick of this shit. Y'all muhfuckas really don't know what this hip-hop's all about. So while y'all keep on fakin' the funk, we gonna keep on walkin' through the darkness, carryin' our torches. Underground will live forever, baby! We just like roaches: never dyin', always livin'. And on that note, let's get back to the program. . . .

The general tone of DJ Premier's polemic is consistent with the conception of professional ethics that I am proposing. Both his use of the term "violating" and his argument that "you *know* how that go" (i.e., ignorance is no excuse) suggest a world in which all who participate are expected to abide by the professional ethics of the producer. In this case, DJ Premier is specifically referring to the use of so-called breakbeat compilations.

It was not long after sampling began in the mid-1980s that Lenny Roberts's *Ultimate Breaks and Beats* compilations popularized the practice of deejays and record collectors assembling rare jazz, funk, and soul singles into anthologies, thus reducing the need for producers and deejays to dig for original recordings. Since that time, hundreds of such anthologies have been released—usually unlicensed, often unlabeled, almost always on vinyl—and they have become something of a sore point for producers who do dig for beats: "[They] get scorned, 'cause you spent so much time looking for records and you got these fools samplin' off hip-hop records and compilations. . . . Your time isn't well spent, you know? It's like they're just making a mockery of your searches. . . . And it's obvious, you know, sometimes when somebody uses a certain drum sound, and you know they don't have that record" (Jake One 1998).

Other producers agree:

> People are putting out breakbeat records and stuff and that's not really cool . . . 'cause it makes it super-easy. All these kids in the suburbs can sound like they're just the greatest producer in the world.

They got all these breaks that everyone else has. So it's just weird. I don't think it should be that easy. It's not meant to be easy, you know? (Specs 1998)

People can be a producer and don't have to really search and find the good records. Before, it was kinda like you were as good as the records that you found. . . . The better records that you found, the better you would be. (Domino 1998)

Simply stated, compilations are seen as a shortcut. They save the producer much of the effort that was previously necessary to make a beat. While the producers' statements demonstrate that this is resented for that reason alone, Beni B adds two other complaints: the first is that taking the easier path denies the producer the musical education that he could have gained from digging, and the second is that by not "putting in the work," one is taking unfair advantage of the knowledge developed by an earlier generation of producers and deejays and thereby exploiting hip-hop itself.

> Beni B: The thing to understand about reissues is that reissues
>   are just that: they're reissues. They're not an education, OK?
>   They're not an education. Some people are of the belief that
>   "OK, I can go out and I can buy all these reissues." But you
>   know what? Let's face it: again, it's not an education.
> Joe: So you mean you have to do more work than that.
> Beni B: Yup. You gotta put in the work, baby. And a lot of times,
>   you know, cats are not trying to put in. . . . Some people put
>   in the effort, other people don't. And you have to be willing to
>   put in that work. And if you don't put it in, you always wind up
>   short-changing it. You just can't do that. . . . You have to respect
>   it, man. And a lot of people, it's like they *claim* they respect it,
>   but, let's face it, they really don't. Everything has a past. And
>   everything has a beginning. And so you gotta . . . have respect
>   for that. (Beni B 2002)

Many producers—while acknowledging the annoyance of seeing others have easy access to records that they had to invest a great deal of time, money, or effort to acquire—still do not feel that this rises to the level of an ethical violation:

I'm not against compilations, personally. Sometimes it really burns me up, though, when I see stuff that I spent a whole lotta money for, that people didn't really know about; now all of a sudden everybody on the block has it for, like, nine dollars. That kinda burns me up. But I've gotten a lot of stuff that I couldn't find elsewhere on compilations, too. So it's a double-edged sword. Take the good with the bad; that's all there is to it. (Stroman 1999)

Samson S. sees digging for original records as a function of ethics, which are themselves a function of ego. One holds oneself to a higher ethical standard out of pride: "I understand [sampling from compilations], but my ethics won't allow me to do it . . . only because, like I said, it's all ego and being proud of your shit. Being like 'Yeah, I found this'" (Samson S. 1999).

A similar approach may be at work for Domino:

In the end of the day, when it comes out, no one's gonna know the difference. I think that's kinda like a producer pet peeve. That's kind of like part of the fun. Like you can say, "Look, I got all these songs! I got the originals, I got this, I got that!" It's almost, in a sense, no different than pullin' out the John Coltrane *Blue Trane* original. And then a kid comes and pulls out the reissue, on vinyl. You know what I'm sayin'? If you put on the records, you'd hear the same shit. In fact, the new one would probably sound better! But ultimately, when you listen to it, it's the same thing. But . . . certain people, like collectors, would say, "No. The original's the one." So it all depends on what you're getting out of it, your outlook. (Domino 1998)

This formulation likely accounts for the apparently paradoxical philosophy espoused by most producers when they explicitly grant legitimacy to compilations while simultaneously making an emphatic point of their own strict avoidance of them: "I don't have no rule against it. [But] I don't really do it. I could see where I would, if I just couldn't get something. That's, again, it's 'Who's gonna know?' It could be like a compilation, or it's a re-pressing, or them breakbeat records. What's the difference? Everybody sampled offa them *Ultimate Breakbeats* back in the eighties. I can't think of no artist that didn't" (DJ Kool Akiem 1999).

Prince Paul takes this argument one step further; he feels that his ethical sensibility actually works against his creativity.

> You have these records now, especially the new ones—not like Super Disco Breaks and the other ones in the early days, the Ultimate Beat Breaks and stuff—but the ones now that they have everybody's sample—"They used this, they used that"—and it has it all on one record? That was a *crime* back in the days! It's more like, I came from the era when you found records that nobody had, or you got the original. To me that's cheating: "Oh, I got all these beats on one record." And, unfortunately, I kind of keep that with me to this very day. But I'm breaking out of that. It's something like . . . an internal fight inside me: like, "It's not right." 'Cause it's a moral sense. Sometimes what you're stating is not a technical sense, it's just a morality thing. It's like staying true to whatever you think is real. . . . I have, like I said, these old-school ethics, but then I'm not blocking myself from learning. That's the important thing. (Prince Paul 2002)

Harkening back to Vitamin D's rule about not sampling vocals from other hip-hop records, some producers make a situational distinction for the use of compilations. DJ Topspin, for example, feels that compilations are acceptable for live deejaying purposes but should not be sampled on recordings: "If you're spinnin' 'em somewhere, that's cool. You know, you can't have every record. No matter how much searching you do, you can't have every piece of vinyl. So I appreciate compilations that have tight songs, to play 'em. But as far as me making a song from it? Nah. 'Cause someone else did the footwork to get it in your possession. And that's half the fun: coming out with something you either made or found or manipulated yourself" (DJ Topspin 1999). Even people who use compilations can still think it's wrong: "I used to buy 'em, back in the days. To have records with just drum loops on 'em. It would be popular loops, and it would just go for like three minutes, or whatever. And back then, I'd be known to sample some of that stuff. I always felt like I was cheating. And I still kinda feel like it's cheating if you sample from a reissued record, or one of those breakbeat records" (King Otto 1998).

It is important to remember that the ethical issue here has nothing to

Compilation records a/k/a breakbeat records, from the collection of the author. Photo by author.

do with the fact that the record is unlicensed and the original artists are being deprived of royalties. The ethical problem for producers is that those who use compilations are not doing the work of digging for their own beats. This is significant because it is an example of how ethics can run parallel to a legal concept and yet be based on an entirely different set of concerns. Oliver Wang's perspective on this issue is an incisive one:

> The interesting thing . . . is that artists don't get paid off of used records. So, for instance, let's use Bob James, a lot of people sample Bob James. If you find a copy of *Two*, which has "Mardi Gras," which is the break that everyone knows, right? Collectors will sell that [for] upwards of twenty dollars, which is actually woefully overpriced for that. But it's not like Bob James makes any profit off of that. Versus if someone puts "Mardi Gras" on a legitimate compilation, which are much more frequent nowadays. Most compilations these days, permission has been granted. In theory, the artist is actually getting paid off the compilation. Versus if you're digging

in a used record store for stuff, the artist is never gonna see a penny of that. . . . So then the question becomes who's more important: the artist you're sampling from, or the deejay that you're working with? I mean, that's kind of a side issue; you still shouldn't sample from compilations, 'cause it's lazy.[7] (Wang 1998)

For most hip-hop producers the answer to Wang's question is simple: without question the deejay, the producer, is more important. But this is also an example of the kind of legalistic theorizing I mentioned earlier: after Wang lays out his argument, he declares it moot. The use of compilations is considered inappropriate regardless of whether or not the original artist is paid, for all the reasons my consultants cited.

The problematic relationship between producers' ethics and legality is also brought to light in yet another way with compilations. On some more recent compilations, the labels contain information not only about the original song, but also about hip-hop songs that have sampled it. This is viewed as an ethical violation for two reasons. The first is that it gives away privileged information that should rightfully be acquired through diligent digging or at least through word of mouth. The second is that it puts the cited hip-hop producer at legal risk: many of the samples have not been legally cleared, particularly if they were, for example, only one or two notes from a saxophone solo. Although such a sample would probably not require the producer to pay publishing rights to the original composer, it would still technically require a payment to the record company for use of the master recording (see chapter 8). This is what DJ Premier refers to as "snitching."

As Domino explains, with regard to DJ Premier's statement on *Moment of Truth,* which began this section:

On Biggie's second album, he has a song called "Ten Crack Commandments" that Premier produced. And, basically, it's like a drum and then he's scratching in [a two-note pattern], and all he doin' is scratchin', and it's just he's scratching in a little sound. Well, not too long ago, I was looking at these break records. . . . I played the record, and it was like—you hear it—but it was like, *wow,* you know what I mean? Someone who found that record *peeped* it. Even though it was such a little piece, they put it on the back of a record, and so now everyone knows. And probably the guy who made the [original] song probably wouldn't even have recognized that that was his record, unless he reads . . . this breakbeat record that someone came out with. And so that's what they were talking about. (Domino 1998)

I have heard three exceptions to the "no compilations" rule, all of which are in dispute: if one only samples drums, if one "does the work" to dig for the original record, and if one only samples from the original *Ultimate Breaks and Beats* compilation.

For Negus I, the use of drums from breakbeat records is an issue of creativity, analogous to the "No biting" rule:

I know that's a big no-no. I've taken drum sounds from breakbeat records, but not looped the break, as it is on the record. I've just chopped up the snare and the kick, or take a high-hat off it. And I usually do that when I'm getting frustrated, 'cause drum sounds are hard to find. And when I'm getting frustrated, I'll just take a couple drum sounds off of a breakbeat record, just so I don't get frustrated and turn my machine off and do something else, because I can't find any drum sounds. I'll just do that just to keep the process going. . . . That's a whole thing too: even if you do use sounds, like drum sounds, from a breakbeat record, if you can flip 'em up in a way that nobody's done it before? True, you're using the sounds . . . but you are doing something that's creative . . . so if you use it like that, I think you won't be in violation as much. (Negus I 1998)

Strath Shepard agrees that sampling drums isn't a serious violation: "I'm kinda undecided about sampling off of bootlegs. I definitely don't think you should sample loops off bootlegs. Your music should not be from bootlegs. Because someone else essentially found it before you, and if they didn't use it, they could have used it. So I don't think you should sample the music part, but drums are a little different. You could sample drums off bootlegs" (Shepard 1998).

The second exception is sometimes made on the basis of the producer's level of effort in digging for records. This refers to the essence of the complaint about compilations in the first place: that one hasn't done the work. Theoretically, producers can posit situations in which the work *was* done, but for some practical reason, one is deprived of the original record. This may be acceptable. The following conversation with Mr. Supreme illustrates how such an argument may be constructed.

> Mr. Supreme: I'm kind of mad that the comps come out. It kinda ruins it. We've spent all these years trying to be fresh, and dig, and find all this shit. And then some asshole puts it out for the whole world to use. It kinda hurts you, you know? . . . But at the same time, who cares? . . . If it's good, it's good. Why not? If you can make a good record, why not?
>
> Joe: Yeah, but you're *saying* that, 'cause you're . . . open minded. But you don't actually *do* that [sample from compilations], though. You know what I mean?
>
> Mr. Supreme: [laughs] No, you're right! I don't do that . . . [but] we really created this hip-hop shit. Like Premier said, we did create this shit. So for some jackass to try to sell me a beat for fifty dollars that he wouldn't give a fuck about. . . . If it wasn't for us it would be a one-dollar record! So how's he gonna try to sell it to us for fifty dollars? It's like "So forget you, I'll go buy the bootleg for eight bucks up the street!" But at the same time, [buying compilations is] kinda wrong, you know? Its gotten out of hand, that's what it's come down to, is that it's gotten out of hand. But, yeah, like you say . . . I don't do it. There are rules; I try to be open minded, but there's just some things I don't do. (Mr. Supreme 1998a)

Mr. Supreme begins with a strong statement of general opposition to compilations before suggesting that the value of a good sample may, in some cases, outweigh the "No compilations" rule. At this point I call to his attention the fact that despite his theoretical acceptance of that exception, he still regards the rule as binding on himself personally. He responds by developing a different exception to the "No compilations" rule: why should producers be forced to pay inflated record prices, when they were the ones who created the demand in the first place? He presents himself, hypothetically, as someone who has a choice between the original record and a compilation; this implicitly requires that he have done the appropriate digging (otherwise he wouldn't have the option of choosing the original). Thus the exception is drawn: *Assuming one has done the work*, it would be acceptable to avoid paying the inflated price to a record collector by buying the compilation. (Notice, however, that although Mr. Supreme develops two different rationales for violating the compilations rule, he, like several other producers I interviewed, ends his statement by saying he still wouldn't do it.)

This approach—that compilations are justifiable if one does the work—is not unique to Mr. Supreme; Phill Stroman maintains a similar position:

> Maybe if I was a person who didn't have any records, maybe I'd have a little complex about it. But I *got* records. I don't have nothin' to prove to anybody. . . . I got credentials, as far as diggin'; I'm not some kid who just picked something up from the store down the corner. I mean, I dig. I put in my work, you know? I paid the dues. So, yeah, I'll take something from a compilation, what the hell. (Stroman 1999)

Finally, Samson S. articulates an exception that is particularly interesting. He distinguishes between the original series—*Ultimate Breaks and Beats*—and other, more recent compilations. In his formulation, apparently, *Ultimate Breaks and Beats* has been around long enough that it has, in some sense, become an original recording.

> Joe: Sampling from compilations.
> Samson S.: Oh, like them breakbeat records? Man, we've *all* did it! And I don't care what nobody say! People can talk about rules and shit, [but] everybody done sampled offa them *Ultimate Break and Beat* records. I mean, that's why they made 'em back in the days—for that. But . . . you don't wanna do no beat sampling goddamn *Q-Bert Marshmellow Breaks* [a more recent compilation] or nothin' like that. . . . Just go get the old school *Ultimate Breaks and Beats*. . . . You can use those, that's not really forbidden. But all these new breakbeat records coming out, it's not wise to do that. You should just go out and get your own shit. (Samson S. 1999)

DJ Kool Akiem's response to this assertion demonstrates the rhetorical complexity that invariably ensues when these discussions begin. He addresses Samson's exemption from the perspective of one who doesn't agree with the original rule to begin with. In essence, his intent is to demonstrate the hypothetical weakness of the exception (which he, in reality, agrees with) in order to show that the boundaries of the rule itself are untenable: "I can kinda understand. The reason is because everybody sampled off of them. So that's not a good enough reason, 'cause your rule should still stand fast. Just 'cause everybody else did it, that don't make it OK. Say you take another one of them compilation sets, everybody started sampling it, would it be OK then? When it wasn't before? So that's why I don't have no problems with compilations" (DJ Kool Akiem 1999).

One Can't Sample More Than One Part of a Given Record

> I have another rule: "Thou shall not sample two sounds from the same record." Unless it's a continuous loop, like if you're choppin' something. . . . But don't fuckin' jack a bass line from the record, horns from that same record, Fender Rhodes. . . . We call that cheating. (Samson S. 1999)

The association of ethical righteousness with creativity is manifested in this rule. Essentially, the rule argues that it is not creative to combine things that already go together. This is a point of pride with many producers:

> I wouldn't do that either. One thing that's real wack to me is, in the same cut, using samples from two different cuts on the same [original] album. Or even the same artist, I wouldn't do that. Unless it's maybe just a drum, you know. Something real small, maybe. But I wouldn't do that. I guess the reason why for that is because it . . . feels like cheatin' a little bit. Or too easy, because you're blending two sounds that are almost the same. . . . Part of the artistry is to combine elements that wouldn't be combined normally. You know, that's one aspect of the artistry. I wouldn't put two samples of the same artist on the same cut, at all. Ever. Won't do that at all. And I almost wouldn't sample—like for a album—I wouldn't sample the

same artist twice, either. You know, maybe something real small or something, but definitely not two loops, 'cause then you might as well just be makin' *his* album. (DJ Kool Akiem 1999)

DJ Topspin explicitly characterizes this as a matter of personal pride: "As far as the producers' ethic is concerned, it's all in what you want to do and what you feel *proud* of doing. I wouldn't feel proud taking more than one thing from the same record and putting it on the same beat" (DJ Topspin 1999).

It is significant that when producers are judged to be breaking a hip-hop rule, they are often accused of "taking away." The phrase is telling; it assumes hip-hop is a collective enterprise, and it suggests that when producers violate rules, they are not only failing to contribute to the collective project, but actually undoing what has already been accomplished by others.

This, I submit, is due to the values that the producers' ethics encode: material effort or hard work, and intellectual effort or creativity. The value of material effort is manifested in the emphasis on vinyl records over other media and the rejection of compilations and other hip-hop records as sample sources. Producers are expected to put in a certain amount of effort to obtain their samples. To circumvent this expectation is unethical.

The value of intellectual effort can been seen in producers' reluctance to indulge is such creative shortcuts as sampling records that are already great and sampling more than one part of a particular record. This value is also the underlying rationale for the more general "No biting" rule: one is expected to inject a certain amount of creativity into the process.

When producers make unethical beats, they are implicitly suggesting that hard work and creativity are not important. They are *taking these things away* from the practice of hip-hop production:

KRS-ONE once said to me that every wack record sets hip-hop back five years. He may have been speaking in a hyperbolic sense, but there he was expressing an idea based on the interconnectivity to which you allude. . . . Maybe it has to do with the fact that musical ideas are so viral. They're so easily transferred and they're like colds. You can really pass them along easily. You can get them easily and pass them along easily. . . . It's like if you had a rare gas and you were supposed to protect it. And then one day somebody just walked around and picked the bottle up and opened it. It's hard to get that gas back. It's hard to bring that rare thing back. And when you do something that's bad, these ideas have a way of spreading and becoming part of the body. And so people really look at that as very severe. It's not like building blocks where you can pick them up, they're all discrete. . . . Ideas are hard to locate and hard to stop. (Allen 2003)

In contrast, to express oneself *within* the traditional boundaries honors the form as a whole and elevates the individual producer. Deejay Strath Shepard, for instance, defends the producer DJ Shadow, essentially making the argument that regardless of how his music *sounds,* it is hip-hop if it follows the ethics of hip-hop: "A lot of people argue about whether DJ Shadow is hip-hop or not. Because he claims real hip-hop, to the fullest. But then, you get the album, you listen to it, and most people are like, 'Well, that's not hip-hop.' But I consider it hip-hop, because of the way it's made. It's made with records and sampling and a deejay. So . . . to me, if he wants to call it hip-hop, he can call it hip-hop" (Shepard 1998). What Shepard is suggesting is that an artist may maintain an allegiance to the hip-hop producers' community through his adherence to ethical practice, and that such dedication may carry more weight than the actual sound of the music.

That said, the ethics are merely the price of admission; a producer must have ethics in order to be respected, but the mere adherence to traditional ethics alone does not guarantee the praise of other producers. The acceptance of one's musical peers requires a keen grasp of a more abstract and malleable set of standards, of what might be termed "aesthetic expectations"—collective ideas about what sounds good. Prince Paul is rather blunt about the distinction:

There's a lot of underground records that people [are] like, "I'm so true to hip-hop," that's *crappy.* It doesn't matter how you make the record, or what style you use. It matters if it's good. That's the bottom line, man. 'Cause I can go to Fat Beats [a New York record store that sells underground hip-hop] now—not to name names—but a lot of kids like, "Yo, we're from the *true* school, we only perform in underground clubs and we make no money 'cause we keepin' it real. And we got X amount of people while we perform. We got a breakdancer and a graffiti artist and we wear only shell toes." And you listen to the record, and it's *garbage!* It's flat-out garbage. You know, it's like, "Yo, that has nothing to do with the quality of your music." (Prince Paul 2002)

The quality of a producer's music is judged by standards that are far more subjective and abstract, and it is to those standards that I now turn.

chapter 6

Elements of Style

Aesthetics of Hip-Hop
Composition

I think that hip-hop was really just like kind of a crystallization of
other forces in African American culture generally. Things around oral-
ity and pattern and rhythm and . . . all kinds of musical ideals that
kind of made it likely. Technology. Changes in the availability of technology. But probably a whole set of, kind of, directions.

    It seems to me that I've often heard people—and usually white
people—say [that] when they first heard hip-hop, it was like: "Wow—
what is *that*?" And for me, it was like "Oh. OK. Great." It just was just
something that seemed fitting. (Allen 2003)

In the preceding four chapters, I discussed the necessary preconditions
for a producer to create a sample-based hip-hop beat: developing a general sense of hip-hop's technique, form, and musical values (chapter 2),
making the decision to use digital sampling rather than other means
(chapter 3), gathering material and ideas through digging in the crates
(chapter 4), and identifying oneself with the producers' community by
adhering to producers' ethics (chapter 5). In this chapter, I will address
the aesthetic principles that guide the creation of a beat. As in chapter 3,
I use the term "aesthetic" simply to refer to abstract ideas of beauty.

    The aesthetic elements I will discuss can be distinguished from the
ethics discussed in chapter 5 by the fact that they have no moral overtones; they are merely opinions about what sounds good. As a result, there
are no aesthetic requirements, only aesthetic preferences. Making a poor
aesthetic choice does not call one's legitimacy as a producer into ques-

tion, only one's taste. This distinction is true in all cases because it is definitional; when an aesthetic choice begins to take on moral implications, it becomes part of the system of ethics.

For sample-based hip-hop producers, aesthetic concerns manifest themselves at four levels: the underlying structure of hip-hop beat, the internal characteristics of individual samples, the relationships that samples take on when juxtaposed, and shared assumptions and contextual cues that imbue any given choice with significance. I have made these distinctions for the sake of analytical clarity, but in practice these categories have a dynamic relationship with each other. Each may affect the others, and any specific concern may have influence in two or more categories (for example, the rhythmic pattern of a drum sample, which is an internal characteristic, will profoundly affect its relationship to other samples in the same song).

Underlying Structure of a Hip-Hop Beat

Virtually all hip-hop music is based on a cyclic form. As I discussed in chapter 2, this form is derived from the approach of early hip-hop deejays, who used turntables to repeat drum breaks from funk and soul records. When sampling became the tool of choice in the mid-eighties, the process became more complex as these drum loops were augmented with nonpercussive musical material. Soon both percussion and melody were being pieced together from ever-smaller samples, often a single note or drum beat. But the formal characteristics remained the same— the loop continued to reign. Regardless of the technique used to realize it, the producer's ideal is to create a repeating figure that can be altered through the addition or subtraction of various elements at different times.

The looping feature on early samplers was originally intended to extend the potential length of notes played on keyboard controllers without taxing the sampler's memory. For instance, if one wanted to play a continuous four-second clarinet tone on F-sharp, the sampler might simply repeat a one-second clarinet sample four times. But hip-hop artists saw in this function the potential to reproduce the work of early deejays who repeated the breaks of popular songs.

While the transition from the use of turntables and live instruments to the use of looping samplers in the mid-1980s is almost universally viewed within hip-hop as a natural evolution, it is important to note that there were many other options open to deejays at the time, none of which were seriously considered. These include continuing to use turntables as the exclusive source of musical sound, using live instrumentation to improvise musical material that was not derivative of preexisting breaks, and using samplers to create noncyclical musical figures. The fact that none of these options was chosen suggests two things about the artists' outlook: that they wished to preserve what they viewed as the essential feature of hip-hop music, the break, and that despite this purist tendency, they were not entirely satisfied with the options that the turntable offered them. This raises an obvious question, perhaps the central question of hip-hop music: what is it about looping as a strategy that can engender such purist commitment from its fans without making them feel constrained?

On the most basic level, looping automatically recasts any musical material it touches, insofar as the end of a phrase is repeatedly juxtaposed with its beginning in a way that was not intended by the original musician. After only a few repetitions, this juxtaposition, along with the largely arbitrary musical patterns it creates, begins to take on an air of inevitability. It begins to gather a compositional weight that far exceeds its original significance:

> Sometimes, I'll put a loop on and let it play for, like, two or three days. I've done it before. When you do something like that, you get to hear all different parts and pieces and elements of it that you never really heard before. . . . It probably sounds strange to a lotta people, but you get to hear stuff that the musician didn't try to put in there. You know what I mean? It's just in there. (DJ Kool Akiem 1999)

While this may sound like a very abstract and mystical statement, the process to which it refers is fairly concrete. The things "that the musician didn't try to put in there" are musical relationships and emphases that are created by the new context. Imagine, for instance, a sample that contains a single chord change plucked from a jazz recording. When it is looped, the end of the second chord will lead directly back into the beginning of the first, creating a harmonic relationship—a new chord change—that was never intended by the original composer. In a very real sense, this relationship is created by the sampling producer, and it is this process to which DJ Kool Akiem refers.

While looping may not change the *sound* of the music—its rhythm, melody, harmony, or timbre—it changes the entire sensibility within which this sound is interpreted. Melodies become riffs. As the end of a phrase approaches, the listener begins to anticipate its beginning. In the best beats, in fact, a virtual call-and-response develops in which a break actually answers *itself*—the end of the break establishes a tension that is resolved by the return of its own beginning.[1] Looping—creating a cycle out of linearly conceived melody—imparts a new compositional logic to preexisting material and once-random juxtapositions. Moreover, in cases where the original recording was not in an African-influenced genre, it serves to "Africanize" musical material by reorganizing melodic material in accordance with specific African preferences such as cyclic motion, call and response, repetition and variation, and "groove."

This and other sampling strategies, which I will discuss shortly, allow a producer substantial space for creative control and manipulation while maintaining most of the characteristics of the original recording. An analogy that I often use to describe this concept is that of an origami master folding a print of the *Mona Lisa* into some elaborate shape. A critic could argue that nothing has been accomplished; the surface of the paper remains an unaltered image of da Vinci's masterpiece. But the surface is not where the meaning lies, and that is precisely the point.

The ambiguity inherent in looping has another benefit, one that has long been recognized in African American culture: it allows individuals to demonstrate intellectual power while simultaneously obscuring the nature and extent of their agency, a practice that has been extensively theorized as "signifyin(g)" by Henry Louis Gates Jr. (1988), among others. Since sampling relieves producers of responsibility for the particular notes, looping is an ideal form of signifyin(g). It allows producers to use other people's music to convey their own compositional ideas.

Theorists of popular music have historically tended to read repetition as the hallmark of mass production (cf. Adorno 1990; Attali 1996: 128–130). But hip-hop in general—and the sampled loop in particular—is a logic of musical repetition *as* artistic differentiation; the producer's creativity lies in the ability to harness repetition itself. As James Snead has observed, "European culture does not allow 'a succession of accidents and surprises' but instead maintains the illusions of progression and control at all costs. Black culture, in the 'cut,' builds 'accidents' into its *coverage*, almost as if to control their unpredictability. Itself a kind of cultural *coverage*, this magic of the 'cut' attempts to confront accident and rupture not by covering them over but by making room for them inside the system itself" (Snead 1984: 67; emphasis in original). In the case of hip-hop, the "almost" in this quotation can be safely ignored: controlling the unpredictability of random musical gestures is the explicit and acknowledged goal. This again is what DJ Kool Akiem is referring to when he speaks of the looping process allowing a producer to hear musical figures that "the musician didn't try to put in there." At the same time, the loop provides a format within which all aspects of the beat, from the drums to the vocals, can begin to take shape: "Usually you start with the drums. It's like I always say: that's the backbone and the heart of it. If you can have a real nice beat—just the drums—almost anything you put under it's gonna sound good. 'Cause the beat is there, you know? It's flowin' and it's there"[2] (Mr. Supreme 1998a).

The creation of an underlying rhythmic structure for a hip-hop song is one of the most subtle and important tasks set before a producer. Most producers refer to this phase of the production process as "locking up" a beat, a phrase that connotes a number of different elements coming into a self-sustaining, almost predestined, relationship with each other. Moreover, the term puts the emphasis on the *process* of creating electronic music rather than the product. The "locking" to which the phrase refers is an activity in the present tense, not a quality that exists in the abstract; that is, there is no concept of relative "locked-up-ness" that can be used to judge one beat against another; a beat is either locked up or it is not. And if it is not, then it is not really a beat, because—by definition —the process of its creation has not been completed.

Such present-tense rhythmic relationships (often referred to as "grooves") have historically been analyzed as artifacts of live performance interactions (cf. Keil and Feld 1994, 1995; Dudley 1996; Monson 1996; Progler 1995). For example, Ingrid Monson notes that "[t]he basic rhythmic *hookup*, or synchronization between the drummer and the bass player, in this sense is a function of how well the walking bass line locks or is in the pocket with the ride cymbal rhythm. A drummer's preference for working with particular bass players is often a function of how easily and naturally this hookup occurs" (Monson 1996: 56; emphasis in original).

In the case of hip-hop, however, a groove is the work of one individual —the producer—who juxtaposes recordings of other musicians from various genres and is not working in real time. To what extent are previous theoretical conceits applicable here? Is it possible for groove to be the work of a single musician or composer? And, if so, do such grooves have the same social significance as communally created live music? Hip-hop is not completely unprecedented in this regard: the interlocking texture created by the two hands of a ragtime pianist, for instance, offers an example of a groove created by an individual. But perhaps the more intriguing question concerns the extent to which groove is compatible with deferred gratification, the extent to which production is performance. In other words, to what degree—and in what sense—is it "groovy" to lock up a beat that will only be heard in recorded form at a much later date?

The value of groove to the production process is demonstrated by the number of tools that producers consciously utilize to address it. Perhaps the most important of these is the "quantize" function, invented by electronic engineer Roger Linn and introduced in his Linn LM-1 drum machine (which did not sample) (Horwitz 1999: 150). Quantization automatically moves samples to the nearest appropriate beat within a scheme that the producer chooses. For instance, if the producer chooses a framework of straight sixteenth notes in a particular tempo, the quantize function will set the beginning of every sample to the nearest sixteenth note. While this has the benefit of precision, it could, in fact, make the sequence overly precise or mechanical sounding.

Furthermore, since one is working with samples of live musicians, the rhythms *within* the samples themselves may not be precise. In such cases, Domino points out, quantization could actually make the drums sound incorrect:

As far as quantizing goes, I've never really tripped as much on that when I made drums, just because I had a sequencer that was able to move things. So I didn't want to quantize because I wanted to put everything exactly where I want it. And I think quantizing is good at putting things on [the beat] exactly, but sometimes it gets to the point to where you want a drum to hit somewhat differently. Especially if you're trying to lock up drums with a certain type of sample where it was a live drummer, so it's not exact. The quantize can actually make your drums off. So I wouldn't use the quantize, I would just hit the snare and adjust it if it needed adjusting. (Domino 1998)

While one might conclude, in light of Domino's statement, that the microrhythmic precision of quantization is not valued by producers, that would be something of an oversimplification. In fact, producers actively seek a balance between sounding mechanically precise and overly loose. Straying too far in either direction can earn the condemnation of other producers; for example, many are critical of the production work of RZA, the producer for New York's Wu-Tang Clan, precisely because he *does not* use the quantize function: "I think it's crazy, 'cause I just don't see why you'd do that. And it sounds sloppy. I mean, some of it's really bad. Really, it sounds like he sat by his sampler and went like that [slaps table]. Just put his hand on some of the keys. And whatever the sounds came out is what came out. But people love it. . . . If I did that? Man, people would think I was crazy" (Mr. Supreme 1998a).

Samson S. agrees with this assessment: "Awww, man, his beats is sloppy. . . . But that was part of his appeal, initially . . . 'cause you like, 'Oh yeah, he just don't give a fuck.' . . . But after a while, you know, it got tiring. He'll still do a dope beat or two every now and then. But, yeah, he doesn't quantize his beats properly. And he knows that" (Samson S. 1999).

It is interesting that Prince Paul, who has worked extensively with RZA, confirms both of these assessments but maintains that RZA's violation of the norms of hip-hop production is not a weakness, but a strength:

I seen him, like, do a whole track and put a snare in *manually*. I mean, it was like sequenced stuff and it's already looped and ready. He's like "Kack! Kack! Kack!" [imitates hitting a sample pad] . . . through the whole track! Different velocities: some harder, some lighter. And I'm like, "What is he *doing*?"

But it sounds so good! And he kind of brought me back to knowing the bottom line is: it's what sounds good. It's not what technically looks right. (Prince Paul 2002)

Adding to the rhythmic complexity, as Domino suggested earlier, is
the fact that producers are often working with samples that are neither
complete rhythmic cycles nor individual percussion noises. Often a single sample will contain a brief (two- or three-beat) rhythm. Part of the
producer's task is to assemble these fragments into a larger rhythmic sequence that has a consistent feel:

There's lots of breaks that I appreciate and enjoy, and I have those,
too. But all I need is a little one-and-a-half-count [one-and-a-half-
beat segment] of anything, and I think of it in "How can I make
that into a sixteen-count, something that sounds live?" And it's all
in how you think of it. How you chop it. You can rearrange anything to make it sound fresh. . . . Just changing the structure of a
beat. . . .
  When you learn how to chop it up, you can think of it in a
different time signature, where you say, "That would be good for
this one-and-a-half-count." You can piece four one-and-a-half-counts
and have a six-count beat.[3] (DJ Topspin 1999)

Moreover, in creating a rhythmic structure, the producer must not
only be aware of the horizontal rhythmic variation of a particular drum,
but also the vertical inconsistencies that invariably appear when a large
ensemble is playing together on the recording to be sampled from:

In sampled music, there's never just one sound. In a sample,
there's all kinds of different sounds, because you're sampling from
a record with maybe eight or nine different people playing instrumentation. Even if they're not all playing at the same time, at least
three or four of them are gonna be playing. Whether it's a small hi-
hat or something else.
  I think a lot of times, people who are producers who haven't
sampled music, when they first start, they'll put on a record and

. . . might hear a horn and wanna sample that. But won't necessarily realize that there's like a key[board] tone underneath that, and a little hi-hat, and other sounds. They'll just hear the horn. You kinda have to train yourself to hear everything that's going on within that . . . three-second span, 'cause there's always a lot of different layers going on, and you have to listen for all that. . . .

For example, I might hear a key[board] tone . . . or a chord, and wanna use that. But I have to pay attention to whether there's a little hi-hat going on, because, if I sample that, I'm gonna have my . . . own drum track. And that hi-hat in that key[board] tone can throw the whole drum track off because it won't be on time. And I have to pay attention to that. (Negus I 1998)

As far is the rhythm is concerned, the producer needs to find and sequence drum patterns that don't conflict with each other or the other elements of the beat. Only after avoiding that pitfall can the producer begin the process of creatively structuring a rhythmic pattern that is aesthetically valuable.

With regard to rhythmic sequences, the producers are playing a complex balancing game, attempting to create a groove within a very narrow window of acceptability. As with live music, the distinctions are often so subtle that they are beyond conscious thought: "I think most producers seem to have an innate sense of what's right, even if they can't articulate it. I don't think I could articulate it. But I'll sit and fuck around with placing a sample or stretching it or doing something like that, until it's like 'OK, that's good—that feels right to me.' And that feeling, well OK, that's kind of what makes my stuff" (Stein 2002). As Negus I continues, the value of a groove is often felt in the body through the oft-cited "head-nodding" of listeners or through dance: "Even though I don't dance so much anymore, I think it also helps to be a dancer, to dance a lot. . . . If you dance a lot, you know what's gonna move you to dance. And so, when you're making a beat, that's gonna help you a lot. As opposed to something that *sounds* good, something that *feels* good is really important" (Negus I 1998).

Producers must balance the requirement of precision—which is also a practical necessity for deejaying (see chapter 8)—with the requirement that the rhythm be conducive to dancing (a quality often characterized by hip-hop heads as having "bounce"). The beat must neither be too mechanical nor too "sloppy."

The significance of hip-hop's rhythmic structure should not be underestimated. In fact, as Domino argues, many producers see the rhythm as the essence of hip-hop: "When you really think about it, what makes it hip-hop is the drums. In the end, that's really what makes a song hip-hop to me. Anything else that you put over it can be . . . different types of things. But I think that the element that makes it hip-hop, it comes back to the type of beat that's under it. And I think that if you have that, then you got hip-hop" (Domino 1998).

Internal Characteristics of Individual Samples

The timbre and other qualities of potential samples are a particular concern for hip-hop producers. Nowhere is this interest more manifest than in the selection of drum sounds. In fact, hip-hop producers often comment on the apparent lack of concern for drum timbres among musicians in other genres:

> When I go to a music store and talk to someone that sells equipment, they'll argue with me. And say, "Man, this is the greatest machine." Of course, they're a salesman. But they'll tell me, "You can't beat this machine. It has a hundred snare sounds in it. A hundred kick drums." Yeah, but they all sound like shit! They all sound electronic!
>
> And he's like, "You rap guys crack me up. You wanna spend all this money and get top-of-the-line equipment and then sample a record. A crunchy, dirty record." Well, yeah, of course we do, 'cause those are the dope sounds. They don't really understand that. We do it for a reason, and that's what makes the records fresh. (Mr. Supreme 1998)

The aesthetic delight that producers take in finding a good sample is comparable to that of a wine connoisseur savoring a fine vintage. There is a sense of almost epicurean passion when Mr. Supreme describes a good drum sample: "To me, personally, I just love to hear a cracking snare, you know? A sharp, punchy, cracking snare" (Mr. Supreme 1998b).

Such obsessive attention to percussive detail is not lost on other producers or, in many cases, astute fans. As Oliver Wang noted earlier, inattention to the details of drum sounds is often heard by the careful listener as being "amateurish" (Wang 1998). In fact, deejay and journalist Karen Dere feels that it is even possible to make genre distinctions based on the quality of the drum samples used:

> I think people don't focus enough on hi-hat sounds . . . or snare sounds. . . . I think that's what kind of draws a huge distinction between a lot of—I don't want to characterize it, necessarily, as "gangsta rap"—but people who are more street-oriented. . . . They don't focus on obsessing about a certain snare sound. . . . They'll just use the stock sound, like off some CD or something, and they don't care, because they're just out there to try to push stuff out on the market. (Dere 1998)

As the following conversation with King Otto demonstrates, producers who *are* concerned with their drum sounds are often willing to go to great lengths in order to isolate a single usable percussion sample. After digging in the crates to find the record in the first place, one must still search the record itself for the ideal sound. This process often includes the use of tonal filters to isolate the drum sample from other, unwanted, sounds:

> King Otto: You can find a snare in the middle of a song, and it might have a bass line or something behind it. But you can filter out the bass line, and then you've got a snare. Same thing with a kick [bass drum] or a high hat. Kicks are the hardest.
> Joe: Why is that?
> King Otto: If you find a kick in the middle of a song and it's got something with it, it's harder to [isolate] low-end stuff. If there's a horn over the top of it, the horn's gonna stay there. Unless you take all the highs out, and then you don't really have a kick anymore, you just have like a muffled little "boomp."

> Joe: I see what you're saying: it's easier to filter out low stuff. And because the kick is low, you can't put a low filter on it. . . .
>
> King Otto: Right. Like if there's a high frequency running over the top of a hi-hat that you find, it's not gonna sound that bad if you leave it in there. It might actually embellish the song. Which it might do in the kick, but more times than not, it just doesn't sound good. You wanna have a clear kick. In my opinion. (King Otto 1998)

As far as timbre is concerned, the producer's first task is to find drum sounds with an acceptable timbre that is not overshadowed by other instruments. Having done this, they must organize them into a pattern that is not only rhythmically consistent, but also *timbrally* consistent. The drum part of a typical hip-hop song, after all, may use a snare drum sample from a 1970s rock record, a hi-hat sample from a 1950s jazz record, and a kick from a 1980s drum machine. The ability to make such juxtapositions sound natural is the hallmark of a good producer. As DJ Topspin observes: "There's . . . an art to finding records that harmonize with each other, naturally. . . . Finding stuff . . . that are from opposite ends of the world, that come together on the same beat and compliment each other. . . . Putting stuff together: it's composition, to me. I may be thinking about this too hard or making too much of it, but I think it's composition" (DJ Topspin 1999).

While such anachronic collages would seem to hold a great deal of interpretive promise for semioticians, producers are not particularly concerned with using samples to make social, political, or historical points. In fact, symbolic meaning (as opposed to pragmatic value within the musical system) is almost universally overstated by scholars as a motive for sampling (e.g., Potter 1995, Rose 1994, Costello and Wallace 1990).[4] Generally speaking, producers value the meaning of a particular sample not primarily for its own sake, but more as a venue for ambiguity and manipulation. While producers do occasionally exploit the symbolic value of an original song (either as parody or tribute), the practice is generally viewed as gimmicky. This is largely the result of a practical factor: in order for the meaning of the song to be apparent to an audience, they must be familiar with the original record. And a producer that too often samples songs that a broad audience would know is considered to be pandering (or worse, to not have rare records in his crates).[5]

When I asked Samson S. if he would sample a song because of what it represented to him, he was unequivocal in his response: "Not based on that fact alone. I don't care how much the record meant to me, if it's not poppin'. . . . I go on just straight sound, man. You know, 'Do I like it?,' 'Does it sound good to me?,' that type of deal. I don't really get all up into this mystical shit" (Samson S. 1999).

Of course the distinction between "straight sound" and meaning is a complex one, and no decision can be made entirely on the basis of one factor to the exclusion of the other. The questions "Do I like it?" and "Does it sound good to me?" are not matters of objective reality, but are conditioned by a lifetime of music listening in various social settings. And the use of sampling itself is largely based on the significance that the vinyl medium holds for producers. But this is a far more abstract and general sensibility that the one often attributed to hip-hop musicians. In short, I would argue that while the general aesthetic sensibility, or "vibe," of a particular sample is of great importance to a producer, the specific cultural context from which it emerged is not.

One instance in which the complexity of the sound-meaning distinction becomes apparent can be found in samples of recordings that are seen as having little intrinsic value in their original form: "corny" records. Most hip-hop scholars have interpreted producers' embrace of corny records as an example of irony or sarcasm, as when Mark Costello and David Foster Wallace spend five pages interpreting DJ Jazzy Jeff's sampling of the "I Dream of Jeannie" theme as a wry commentary on the situation comedy's treatment of 1960s sexual mores and technophilia (Costello and Wallace 1990: 60–65).

Another good example of this tendency among scholars can be found in Elizabeth Wheeler's analysis of De La Soul's "Say No Go," for which producer Prince Paul used a sample of the song "I Can't Go For That," by the white pop duo Hall and Oates:

> The mixes of De La Soul epitomize the art of ironic sampling. As the basis for "Say No Go," the story of a crack baby, producer Prince Paul takes the cheesiest pop song imaginable: "I Can't Go

for That" by the "blue-eyed soul" duo Hall and Oates. De La Soul pick out the incidental line "Don't even think about it, say no go," and transform it into the centerpiece of their version. The phrase "say no go" leaves the context of an insipid love story and lands in the ghetto, where babies addicted to crack cocaine are born every day. . . .

"Say No Go" also contains the blank pastiche that links hip-hop most closely with postmodernism. Ultimately, you cannot tell what De La Soul think of Hall and Oates; they use "I Can't Go For That" not only ironically but neutrally. Out of the corny, Prince Paul salvages the hip: one compelling seven-note riff and one soulful twist of Daryl Hall's voice. (Wheeler 1991: 200)

But I would argue that such analyses miss the forest for the trees. You *can* tell what De La Soul think of Hall and Oates: they think they sound good. Whether they are considered "corny" or "hip" is largely irrelevant. When I presented Wheeler's analysis to Prince Paul, his response confirmed this interpretation:

> Prince Paul: Wow. That's pretty deep. But I think the bottom line is just: that was a good song! . . . We didn't consciously think of "Hall and Oates," "Resurrecting," you know, "Postmodern." We was just like, "Wow. Remember that song? That's hot!"
> Joe: See, that's part of it, too. . . . she *assumes* that you think that song is corny. . . . I thought that there was a lot behind making an assumption like that. Like, "Oh, well somebody like Prince Paul couldn't actually *like* that song, because . . ."
> Prince Paul: Nah, that was a hot song! (Prince Paul 2002)

Of course, Prince Paul's perspective on his work is not the only valid one. But I have personally heard the original Hall and Oates song played in a hip-hop club to an enthusiastic reception. If irony is a phenomenon of interpretation, and neither Prince Paul nor his audience interprets the sample as being ironic, who exactly does? Moreover, as producer Samson S. points out, adopting an ironic approach could have serious repercussions for a producer's reputation: "I'd sample something wacky, somethin' people wouldn't expect: maybe some Neil Sedaka or something. You know, that's fun. But that can backfire on you, too. . . . Folks be thinkin' you serious, and be like, 'Man, that shit is *wack!*'" (Samson S. 1999). Implicit in this comment is that ironic intent is *not* the default presumption of hip-hop listeners ("folks be thinkin' you serious"); if something does not sound good, regardless of the producer's symbolic goals, it will be rejected. In other words, while humor and irony do exist in hip-hop production, they are not used to a greater extent than in any other form of music. Irony aside, the reality of producers' intent in sampling corny records falls into two general categories: (1) some records may have sincerely valuable elements, regardless of their overall corniness; and (2) making a good hip-hop beat out of a corny record shows one's skills as a producer (highlighting the processual aspects of hip-hop production).

For Samson S. the value of corny records is primarily a practical one: no matter how bad the original record is, it may still contain useful sounds and should therefore not be overlooked as a potential source: "Even on corny records like Neil Sedaka, or [Englebert] Humperdinck, or whatever, I've found, like, little bits and pieces on them records, too. You can use damn near anything, even if it's just a hi-hat." (Samson S. 1999).

For Specs, the use of such samples is an opportunity to display one's skills as a producer. The ability to make an aesthetically pleasing beat out of displeasing samples is seen as one of the hallmarks of an accomplished beat maker:

> I had to stop sampling [jazz records] for a while, because it was too easy . . . to get a certain vibe. . . . So I had to stop that for a long time. I started sampling the corniest records that I could possibly find. Anything. Anything that was really wack: Neil Sedaka, anything. That helped me a lot, too. I created all types of beats that I pretty much love and it was just the wackest records around. And I think that's important to do, too. Because too many kids are just grabbing up something and taking the first lick they hear. Then they get kind of known for it. It's just too easy. Too many artists be able to make careers off the same vibes and stuff. There's a limit to that. There should be. (Specs 1998)

The value of corny records is a combination of the inherent value of their sound, the challenge it provides to the producer, and—to a far lesser degree—humor or irony. Creating a beat from a corny record is more about an interpretive process than an ironic product. Again, I feel that overt parody, while present, has been overstated by other scholars, who are committed to a view of hip-hop production as being primarily about ironic recontextualization. The same holds true for other samples. While a very general symbolic or practical value—a vibe—is a central factor in producers' decisions about which samples to choose and how to treat them, any specific meaning that may be ascribed to a sound segment is largely beside the point. Although the internal qualities of a given sample are certainly important for their own sakes, they are also judged on how they interact with each other.

Relationship between Samples within Structure

Sampling allows producers to take musical performances from a variety of recorded contexts and organize them into a new relationship with each other. It is this relationship that represents the producers' art, and it is this relationship that reveals the producers' aesthetic goals. And given the cultural context from which hip-hop emerged, it is no surprise that these goals would reflect African American sensibilities, particularly an affinity for collage.

The West African cultural predisposition for collage and diverse textures in music (often organized through rhythm) is well documented (Arom 1985, Chernoff 1979, Merriam 1982, among others). In African American music, Olly Wilson has characterized this tendency as a "heterogeneous sound ideal": "By this term, I mean that there exists a common approach to music making in which a kaleidoscopic range of dramatically contrasting qualities of sound (timbre) is sought after in both vocal and instrumental music. The desirable musical sound texture is one that contains a combination of diverse timbres" (Wilson 1992: 329).

Wilson's take is significant in that it treats timbral diversity as an abstract aesthetic preference, rather than simply the natural result of some other factor (such as the mapping of social roles onto music), or happenstance. In addition, sample-based producers have many options available to express their aesthetic preferences that are not open to musicians who use live instruments. These include the ability to juxtapose the ambient qualities of different recording environments, to repeat individual notes exactly (in terms of dynamics, attack, and so on), and to organize sounds into patterns that would be difficult or impossible to perform live due to the physical demands of an acoustic instrument.

Perhaps the best example of the producers' approach to the relationship between samples is the high value that they place on "chopping" them. This term refers to the practice of dividing a long sample into smaller pieces and then rearranging those pieces in a different order to create a new melody. In other words, chopping actually takes a continuous musical performance and makes it *sound* like a collage. In the years since sampling began, in fact, chopping has largely displaced other forms of collage in sample-based hip-hop.[6]

The idea that this is a conscious approach to composition (as opposed to a technological shortcut) is supported by its increasing adoption into other forms of African American music that do not sample. One instance of this phenomenon is the song "Girlfriend," which appears on the 2001 album *Songs in A Minor* by R&B singer Alicia Keys. The song is based on a disjunctive and off-kilter chopped piano loop from the 1995 hip-hop single "Brooklyn Zoo" by Old Dirty Bastard. It is significnt that Keys's version is not sampled; she learned the strange chord changes and rhythms from the record, then performed them herself on the piano, imitating the chopped sound.

It is in the relationship between the samples that the process of composition begins to exert a decisive influence as producers experiment with different patterns and approaches to organization. It is no accident that producers characterize their home studios as "labs." In making their studios into laboratories, producers are making themselves into research scientists: "Like the particle physicists who break open atoms, hoping to later dig out their most elementary particles, dope DJs break open breaks, searching for the answer to hip-hop's most basic, yet unanswered question: how small is a piece of funk?" (Allen 1988: 11).

The image resonates with producers' methodology: individual experimentation with the intention of "discovering" worthwhile musical combinations. This approach sees musical figures as preexisting structures to be plucked out of the ether by the devoted producer, much in the same way as Michelangelo is said to have viewed his sculptures as being implicit in the stone, his role being merely to chip away extraneous material.

The hip-hop sampling aesthetic that producers learn is based on the deejay's discovery of new breakbeats and new combinations thereof. For DJ Kool Akiem, making beats is a process of exploration informed only by a preexisting aesthetic; he is looking for things that sound good together:

> A lot of times, I'm not really looking for a specific sound. The way I make beats, I'm not like, "Oh, I need a horn on here." And then go lookin'; "I know what horn I want." And go find that horn. I throw down something, and then I just go through a lotta records and kinda feel out, "Well, this might sound good with that." . . . I mean, occasionally, I guess I'm going for something specific. But usually I'm just randomly throwin' stuff on there, kinda feelin' it out. Tryin' to, you know, "Ooh, if I chop it here, it'll sound like that." (DJ Kool Akiem 1999)

Mr. Supreme also favors an unstructured approach:

> Mr. Supreme: Sometimes, I'll know exactly what I'm gonna do. I'm gonna use such-and-such drums with this. Sometimes, I'll just grab a stack of records, and come in, sit at the sampler, and start putting stuff together. And kinda mess with it like that. So it's a little of both.
>
> Joe: And I'm assuming both of those work equally well, otherwise you would have started to do one or the other.
>
> Mr. Supreme: Yeah, and it's crazy, 'cause you might go in with no ideas, a stack of records, and make something dope in five minutes. It's probably one of your better beats. Or really work on something for a month, and it's good, but it's not one of your better things. It's just how it goes. (Mr. Supreme 1998a)

Steinski has a similar outlook: "I never come to a project with 'Here's the thing I would like to express.' Or very much thought, period. It's totally visceral. And I just come in with a bunch of elements that I want to screw with or a technique I want to try. Or a new outboard plug-in that I wanna mess with and it kind of goes from there" (Stein 2002).

The producers' methodology has much in common with the experimental approach of collage artists who work in other media, particularly visual media. When African American collage artist Romare Bearden describes his approach to his work, for example, he could easily be discussing hip-hop:

> You have to begin somewhere . . . so you put something down. Then you put something else with it, and then you see how that works, and maybe you try something else and so on, and the picture grows in that way. One thing leads to another, and you take the options as they come, or as you are able to perceive them as you proceed. . . .
>
> Once you get going . . . all sorts of things begin to open up. Sometimes something just falls into place, like piano keys that every now and then just seem to be right where your fingers happen to come down. But there are also all those times you have to keep trying something over and over, and then when you finally get it right you wonder what took you so long. And of course there are also times when you have to give it up and try something else—which sometimes turns out just great as the beginning of another, totally different picture. By the way, this sort of thing is much more likely to have to do with how something fits into the design or ornamental structure of the painting than with its suitability as subject matter.[7] (Melberg and Bloch 1980: 17–18)

It is interesting to note also that Bearden specifically states that the larger design or structure is more important than the significance of the individual item (or sample). This is a sentiment that is echoed repeatedly by producers.

Interpretive Context

The specific choices that producers make are judged within a larger interpretive context that is maintained through social interaction in the producer's community. This is analogous to the context in which verbal speech acts are interpreted, particularly the self-consciously performative African American forms that are most closely related to hip-hop, such as toasting and verbal dueling:

> Because verbal dueling treads a fine line between play and real aggression, it is a kind of linguistic activity which requires strict ad-

herence to sociolinguistic rules. To correctly decode the message, a hearer must be finely tuned to values which he observes in relation to all other components of the speech act. To do so he must rely on his conscious or unconscious knowledge of the sociolinguistic rules attached to this usage. *Meaning, often assumed by linguists to be signaled entirely through code features, is actually dependent upon a consideration of other components of a speech act. . . .*

It is this focus in black culture—the necessity of applying sociolinguistic rules, in addition to the frequent appeal to shared background knowledge for correct semantic interpretation—that accounts for some of the unique character and flavor of black speech. (Mitchell-Kernan 1999: 323; emphasis added)

The aesthetic principles of hip-hop provide a similar framework for the understanding of beat construction. The distinction becomes apparent in one of my conversations with Mr. Supreme, in which we argue the point:

> Mr. Supreme: There are no rules in hip-hop. That's what so unique about it. You don't have to have a chorus, you don't have to have a bridge, you know? You don't even have to have a melody if you don't want to. There are no rules, but that's what makes it fresh. It's different.
>
> Joe: But you gotta have a snare. . . .
>
> Mr. Supreme: I know! I could go crazy for those snares! Yeah, you have to have a snare. No! Actually, you could have a bass line, someone freestylin' over it. (Mr. Supreme 1998a)

Mr. Supreme is arguing that there are no morally enforceable requirements for how a hip-hop composition should be organized, citing the lack of such conventional formal elements as a chorus, bridge, or melody. In response, I mention the nearly universal use of "a snare," distinctive snare drum samples that emphasize important beats (usually the second and fourth beat of a hip-hop composition in common time). But Mr. Supreme had not forgotten about snares. As he argues, they are not, in fact, required—they are simply a universal preference. Put another way, the rule of including a snare has no moral overtones; it exists primarily to aid others in their interpretation of the producer's work.

This is demonstrated by the highly specific exception Mr. Supreme proposes, in which an MC "freestyles" (rhymes in an informal style) over a drumless bass line. In a subsequent conversation, he could cite only a single recorded example of this occurring, and the appeal of that song was specifically based on its violation of the listener's expectations: "You're waiting for the beat to kick in, and it never does" (Mr. Supreme 1998b). In other words, the producer is toying with listeners' expectations about how a hip-hop beat should sound. The meaning, as Claudia Mitchell-Kernan would say, is not signaled by the "code features" of the beat, but by an "appeal to shared background knowledge." Although the "snare" is not ethically required, it is conventionally expected.[8] It is an aesthetic norm, but not an ethical rule.

The aesthetic norms of hip-hop production are maintained through a variety of means, but none is more telling than the criticism of other producers, as the critiques of RZA's approach to rhythm cited earlier in this chapter demonstrate. In addition to their avowed purpose— defending the value of rhythmic precision among producers—these critiques also support the image of a producer as a composer of art music; they make a distinction between popular acclaim ("People love it") and the expectations of a more knowledgeable elite ("He doesn't quantize his beats properly"). In other words, while producers may criticize RZA's rhythmic consistency, they are clearly aware that this problem is of little or no concern to the majority of hip-hop fans. In fact, RZA is one of the most popular and well-respected producers in the history of hip-hop.[9]

In the eyes of the producers, a proper appreciation of hip-hop beats requires that one be educated in its aesthetic:

> King Otto: I like to make stuff that people can't really name [the sample]. Can't really say, "Oh, that's so-and-so." Sometimes, though. I like to use popular stuff, sometimes, and then make it sound different.
>
> Joe: When you say "stuff that people can't really name," do you mean people in general, or other producers?
>
> King Otto: I mean other producers. That's really the people I think about when I'm making something, is other producers. Or rappers, and so forth. I'm not concerned with the general public, I think. (King Otto 1998)

Phil Stroman expresses a similar sense that producers hear hip-hop differently than fans do: "The general listening public don't know nothin' about none of that. All they know is: is your record hot or is your record not hot? That's kinda like one of those little things within the digging community. . . . The average person would have no idea what's going on. They hear the beat and think either 'I like that beat,' or 'I don't'" (Stroman 1999). Samson S. also makes a distinction between hip-hop production for general audiences and beats that require a some education to appreciate: "I like to do beats that other producers [appreciate] . . . 'cause there's some beats out there that the average person might like . . . but you gotta really do beats and know what's going on to *really* understand how Premier chops up certain things, or Pete Rock. . . . For the most part, producers like that are respected among other producers" (Samson S. 1999).

Producers are faced with a substantial challenge: they must impress each other with their creativity and the rarity of their samples without losing the affection of fans who have no interest at all in the esoterica of hip-hop production. The conflict between maintaining the respect of a small purist community and pursuing the kind of economic success that can only be obtained through broad popular appeal is hardly unique to hip-hop. One sees similar struggles in musical communities from the bebop purists of the 1950s to the folk revival of the 1960s to the guardians of straight-edge punk rock in the 1980s. Prince Paul, for one, is acutely aware of these pressures:

> Prince Paul: I have to really think about it like this: the average
>   kid who's listening to it . . . really don't care where half the stuff
>   came from. The bottom line is that it sounds good. And a lot
>   of times I have to go with that mentality of: it sounds good. Not
>   necessarily like, "Man, if Cut Chemist hears this, he's gonna
>   know!" and, "If I chop this, Premier's gonna—" you know, I
>   don't think of that. I'll put other things in there to bug 'em out,
>   to keep 'em coming to me. But overall I put that out of my
>   mind. At least, I try to.
> Joe: So that's interesting, you're kind of saying two things at the
>   same time. You're saying you don't want to do that, but you actually *are* doing it—you can't help yourself. . . .

Prince Paul: Yeah, yeah. Because it goes whatever sounds good, man.

Joe: But you are still, in the back of your mind, thinking what Premier will think if he hears the beat or whatever.

Prince Paul: Yeah, yeah. You can't help it, you know. It's you looking at your peers—your musical peers. A lot of times, you wanna bug them out, but then again you wanna have an equal amount of success as well. It's not cool to bug 'em out then, man, you can't pay your light bill. Or your fans at large are like, "Man, that was crap." (Prince Paul 2002)

A number of people have written about how hip-hop sampling—because it uses old sound recordings—represents an engagement with musical history in various ways (Rose 1994, Gaunt 1995, Potter 1995). It is true that hip-hop producers comment on, play with, flip, remake, and relive history. But it is not so much the history of a community or even of a musical form that producers are interested in, but the history of sound recordings.

As DJ Kool Akiem straightforwardly puts it, "It's not about playing music; it's about playing *records*. . . . To me, sampling is playing records more precisely" (DJ Kool Akiem 1999). Although the genre, artist, and original social context of a sample are important, hip-hop producers are much more concerned with the label the song was released on, other songs that appeared on the same album, the album's cover, and the associations that it carries within the producers' community. This is reflected to some degree in the ethics I discussed in chapter 5—producers see a substantial difference between sampling a song from the original album and sampling the same song from a reissue. And producers can almost always name the deejay that first used a particular record for either deejaying or sampling purposes. In a magazine interview, for example, both DJ Jazzy Jay and the interviewer seem to actually cede a kind of moral ownership of certain records to the deejays who first popularized them among the hip-hop audience:

PB: Was Magic Disco Machine yours, because you seemed to cut that a lot?

JJ: No, that is credited to Kool Herc, I used to go to Kool Herc parties and listen to that all the time. (P. Brothers 2002: 9)

In most cases, when a producer samples a song, the record on which it appears quickly becomes well known in the producers' community. Other producers will often buy the record if they don't already have it. It is then a small step to sample another part of the same record. In chapter 2 I quoted a review of the reissue of a record that had been sampled in a number of hip-hop songs. If asked why they sampled it, most producers would most likely give both vague aesthetic rationales (it has the "right sound") and practical ones (the song in question has only three instruments and no drums, thus giving the producer a great deal of flexibility to combine the sample with other instruments and rhythms). But an underlying condition for both of these assessments is the status of the record itself. Because the album was not popular when it was released, the vast majority of hip-hop producers presumably learned of it—as I did—through some variation of the following scenario: They were out digging for records with a friend who pulled it out, handed it to them, and said, "Do you have this? [Producer's name] used it for [name of song]," citing one of the songs that sampled it. They purchased the record, brought it home, and listened to it, and were struck by a *different* section of the record, which no one else had sampled yet. For producers, this entire process—in some sense, a part of the record's history—is encoded in the use of such samples.

An unusually overt example of this philosophy can be found in a cover version of the song "Daylight" that appears on the 2001 album *Angles without Edges* by Yesterday's New Quintet (a pseudonym of the producer Madlib). The original version of the song was recorded in 1977 by RAMP[10] on their album *Come into My Knowledge*. It is best known among producers because a two-bar sample of its melody provided the basis for the classic hip-hop song "Bonita Applebaum" by A Tribe Called Quest on their 1990 album *People's Instinctive Travels and the Paths of Rhythm*.

As a result of being sampled, the previously obscure RAMP album became highly prized by hip-hop producers, sometimes selling for hundreds of dollars, until it was reissued on vinyl in the late 1990s. On the Yesterday's New Quintet album, Madlib constructs a cover version of "Daylight" from samples of *other* songs (augmented by his own keyboard work). Moreover, the rhythm of Madlib's drum track is not based on the rhythm of the original version of "Daylight," but on the drum loop that A Tribe Called Quest combined it with to make "Bonita Applebaum," taken from the blues-rock band Little Feat. In short, Madlib's version of "Daylight" is a virtuoso demonstration of production technique and knowledge, referencing the social and economic history of a commodity (the RAMP album), its use in the hip-hop community ("Bonita Applebaum"), and Madlib's own relationship to both.

Another major issue of interpretive context concerns the ambiguity inherent in sample-based hip-hop. A hip-hop beat consists of a number of real-time collective performances (original recordings), which are digitally sampled and arranged into a cyclic structure (the beat) by a single author (the producer). In order to appreciate the music, a listener must hear both the original interactions and how they have been organized into new relationships with each other. Sample-based hip-hop music, therefore, is simultaneously live and not-live. The vision is both communal (that of the original ensembles) and individual (that of the hip-hop producer). And the formal structure may reflect both linear development (in the original composition) and cyclic structure (in its hip-hop utilization). I argue that the aesthetic goal of a hip-hop producer is not to resolve these ambiguities, but—quite the contrary—to preserve, master, and celebrate them. In this regard, hip-hop production is like juggling: the number of pins and the patterns they describe in the air are not significant for their own sake, but as indicators of the juggler's skill in manipulating them. This veneration of processual mastery is deeply embedded in hip-hop's rhythm, melody, and structure—in fact, anywhere ambiguity is to be found.

There are many reasons why African American culture would foreground ambiguity. These reasons generally fall into three categories: African-derived cultural values, social strategies that reflect the particular needs of African American people, and interpretive approaches that combine the two. All have been discussed extensively elsewhere, and I will only recapitulate them briefly here.

In order to operate effectively in American society, African American people tend to be conversant with both African American and European American cultures, languages, and symbolic systems. As a result, these individuals would naturally tend to be attuned to the multiplicity of interpretations that may be drawn from any given interaction (social, musical, or otherwise), not to mention the value of being able to control those interpretations.

A more pragmatic reason for the valuing of ambiguity is the idea of code, that certain forms of communication must be shielded. Ambiguity is a factor in this process because the best codes are those that do not even appear to be transmitting information at all; they have a secondary meaning that serves to draw attention away from the code's central message. In order to effectively accomplish this, the speaker must be able to control both texts simultaneously: a meaningless or unconvincing cover text is of little value. When scholars hear "The Signifying Monkey," a traditional toast that epitomizes the use of double meanings, they tend to focus on the monkey's use of multileveled rhetoric to harm the lion; this is, in fact, the primary theme of the poem (see Gates 1988). But at the same time, the monkey's power derives specifically from the fact that the lion takes his words completely at face value. If the monkey's ambiguity were obvious, his words would lose much of their effect.

Perhaps the best examples of this principle can be found in the African American spirituals of the antebellum era, many of the coded meanings of which are only now becoming apparent to non–African Americans. In order to serve their function, the spirituals had to be credible as religious songs; a song that simply told fugitives to wade in the water in order to throw pursuing hounds off their scents would certainly be repressed, were the water not presented as symbolic of a Christian baptism. More important for my purposes, it is likely that for many enslaved African Americans, the song really *was* about baptism as much as it was about fleeing slavery. The value of such ambiguity was reinforced by the stakes: the loss of either interpretation could cost real human lives.

Finally, there is a second-order factor, which is that engaging in any of these processes trains individuals to think about and become comfortable with them. Working in a highly heterogeneous artistic form, whatever it may be, requires the ability to hold many things in one's mind simultaneously. Thus exposure to music (or any other pursuit) that upholds one of these traditions would help develop a particular appreciation for ambiguity in others (Kyra D. Gaunt, telephone conversation with author, 17 June 1999).

One way in which African American traditions are brought to bear on contemporary ambiguity is the rhetorical strategy that Gates (1988) has called "signifyin(g)." Signifyin(g) is a complex phenomenon with many facets. For my purposes, I wish to emphasize signifyin(g) as a process in which an individual demonstrates a mastery of ambiguity for an audience that has a particular appreciation of such gestures. In other words, for hip-hop production, signifyin(g) has two important aspects: (1) it is primarily a process, rather than a quality, and (2) it is a social activity—it is meaningless without an audience.

The term "signifyin'," without the *g*, is a traditional one in African American culture. In her groundbreaking work, *Talkin and Testifyin*, Geneva Smitherman describes signifyin' as a rhetorical strategy that may be used for both education and entertainment: "[S]ignification has the following characteristics: indirection, circumlocution; metaphorical-imagistic (but images rooted in the everyday, real world); humorous, ironic; rhythmic fluency and sound; teachy but not preachy; directed at person or persons usually present in the situational context (siggers do not talk behind yo back); punning, play on words; introduction of the semantically or logically unexpected" (Smitherman 1977: 121).

Mitchell-Kernan points out that, aside from its social serviceability, there is a distinctly artistic aspect to signifying as well:

> Signifiying . . . is clearly thought of as a kind of art—a clever way of conveying messages. In fact, it does not lose its artistic merit even when it is malicious. It takes some skill to construct messages with multi-level meanings, and it sometimes takes equal expertise to unravel the puzzle presented in all of its many implications. Just as in certain circles the clever punster derives satisfaction and is rewarded by his hearers for constructing a multi-sided pun, the signifier is also rewarded for his cleverness.[11] (Mitchell-Kernan 1999: 317)

Gates has developed the term "signifyin(g)," with a parenthetical *g*, in order to highlight the relationship between the traditional African American practice of "signifyin'" and the semiotic practice of "signifying." In Gates's view, signifyin(g) constitutes not only a rhetorical strategy but also a framework within which rhetorical strategies may be evaluated (Gates 1988: x). Not surprisingly, it is a framework that values the aforementioned characteristics, particularly multiple meanings and recontextualization. This idea of evaluation emphasizes the fact that the practice necessarily operates in a social context.

Writing about hip-hop, Russell Potter has argued that, "the practice of *Signifyin(g)*, which Gates demonstrates compellingly lies at the heart of much vernacular African-American language and art, is a theorized practice which is fundamentally ironic, fundamentally *postmodern*. Signifyin(g), briefly put, is both the trope of pastiche and a pastiche of tropes and its most central trope is that of the sly exchange of the literal for the figurative, and hip-hop is its most profound and lively incarnation" (Potter 1995: 18). While such practices are relatively easy to find in the verbal aspects of hip-hop music, scholars have stood on somewhat shakier ground when it comes to the instrumental aspects. All too often, hip-hop's readily apparent collage structure leads to simplistic conclusions about the ways in which signifyin(g) functions in hip-hop composition. Moving Gates's definition of signifyin(g) from text-based literary studies to musical analysis tends to put the focus more on the structural relationships between individual musical elements (and, to a lesser extent, the contexts from which they are drawn) than on the procedure that put them there in the first place.

It is tempting, particularly in view of the conceptual similarities between hip-hop production and the composition of European art music, to see the compositional activity as secondary to the work that it produces. But to do so would be to overlook the most central aspect of the aesthetic system: the process. And signifyin(g) is, first and foremost, a process.

One important venue for the hip-hop signifyin(g) process is "flipping," the substantial alteration of intellectual material. I discussed this practice in the previous chapter as an ethical responsibility, but here I wish to explore its aesthetic value:

> Negus I: If you're gonna use something that's obviously recognizable, do something to it. To where maybe people can't even figure out how you got that melody out of that sample. How did you take it off the record and get that melody?
>
> Joe: So it's like you're almost working with the fact that it's recognizable.
>
> Negus I: Yeah, exactly. (Negus I 1998)

For Samson S., there is a distinctly social value to the practice:

> Like I said, it goes back to showing off your skills again. The best
> thing is to take something everybody knows. Like, for instance,
> this producer Bean One . . . Man, he took the beginning of "Off
> The Wall," the Michael Jackson song, and *flipped* it! I was: "Awww,
> *man!*" . . . I knew what it was, but how he did it! So there's nothing
> more fun. . . .
>
> I like that *a lot,* when producers take something real common,
> everybody know, and flip it. You know, chop it up, do your own lit-
> tle twist to it. So that's a good thing. (Samson S. 1999)

In Samson S.'s view, it is actually better to recast something well known
than to produce something totally original. Additionally, as with many
of the aesthetic aspects of producing, Samson S. (like most other producers) specifically associates the social value of the practice with "fun"
and "showing off your skills." In a sense, the aesthetic expectations are
akin to the rules of verbal signifyin(g): part of the enjoyment derives
from the challenge of expressing oneself within a variety of self-imposed
constraints.

Flipping a beat, then, isn't about meaning per se; it is about the practitioner's skill in recasting meaning. Much like the appreciation of corny
records I mentioned earlier in this chapter, the value of flipping melodies suggests an underlying aesthetic in which value derives less from
the sampled material or the structure that is imposed on it by the producer than on the process that links the two.

In fact, as Mr. Supreme points out, several producers could conceivably use identical samples and still create very different compositions:
"Everyone has their own signature. I don't care what they do; everyone
has their signature, to the way they put it down. So even if you gave someone the same drums, the same loop, and [said], 'Go put this together,'
they're all gonna be different . . . 'cause they're gonna chop their drums,
right? Everyone's pattern's gonna be different, the way they program 'em
is gonna be different. It's gonna be different" (Mr. Supreme 1998a).

For Specs, the relationship between creativity and the sampled element
goes beyond personal satisfaction and becomes almost spiritual. The producer has a responsibility *to the samples* to organize them creatively.

You're not gonna create something that's totally new on this planet. But at the same time, it's a respect thing. You have to have a little respect for the things that you lift up. Reshape. It's just like clay: you have to be nice to the clay 'cause it's from the earth, which you're from, too. So it's family and you should just treat it with respect, 'cause karmically it's gonna come back up, sooner or later. . . . It's not necessarily trying to prove that you can be original. Because that's pointless, really. Don't make no sense to prove it to anybody. (Specs 1998)

As I mentioned in chapter 5, the primary method by which samples are flipped is known as "chopping." In discussions of its creative value, chopping (the deconstruction and reorganization of samples) is usually counterposed to looping (repeating a sample with little or no alteration). For Vitamin D, the distinction between chopping and looping has significant philosophical implications in terms of ownership and creativity:

I don't wanna take another man's composition . . . 'cause they wrote that with a feeling and a whole spirit behind it. And their intent when they wrote it wasn't for me to sample it, really. So I understand how a guy that's getting sampled out here, he could be brutal about such a thing. 'Cause he didn't write his music for that. So I'm more taking their *texture* and taking what their producer did with them, and taking their *sound*. As opposed to taking their composition. Which, again, it's a thin line between violating and not. (Vitamin D 1998)

For Domino, by contrast, the reasoning is more pragmatic; chopping is a natural outcome of a limited number of old records being sampled to extinction:

I just think that, now, you're getting to the point where . . . you're running out of things to find. And so a lot of the best loops have been used already. I mean, there's some stuff out there, I'm sure. There always will be stuff. But now it's like, in order to stop recycling things, you gotta just take pieces and make 'em into a whole new thing. It's just hard to find records now. So now . . . you just

need to find drum pieces and you can make different styles of
drums, just by like piecing 'em, and making 'em your own thing.
(Domino 1998)

For Mr. Supreme, chopping is a matter of pride and professional standing: "I think producers are different. We listen to records different than
the average person, or even a rapper. We know. And if we know the [origi-
nal] record and he just looped it, we're like, 'Awww, he didn't do nothin',
he just looped that, he's a punk,' you know? But if he took something
and really flipped it? Be like 'Yeah'" (Mr. Supreme 1998). Wordsayer, who
is an MC, sees parallels between producing and rapping in this regard:

> There's just so many different degrees of emceeing. Somebody
> might move you with their delivery, but they're not really sayin'
> nothing. The same thing with producers: somebody might use
> nice sounds, but they didn't really take it any further. That's the
> thing, when I think about producing, that moves me the most is
> when I see that a producer utilized elements of a song and took it
> further. Not just said, "Here's that break," or "Here's that drum
> sound, it's hittin'," and just put it in there, but took that drum sound
> and built upon it, and made something; not necessarily better, but
> took it to another degree. (Wordsayer 1998)

Wordsayer suggests that it is not the quality of the final product that is
most important, but the quality of the manipulation. This is an important point, and one that is reinforced throughout the spectrum of hip-
hop experience. After all, if the quality of the final product were the most
significant aspect, then the best hip-hop song would be one that sampled
another hip-hop song that was highly respected. The fact that producers
reject this practice on both ethical and aesthetic grounds confirms the
significance of process.

While chopping is clearly valued (for both ethical and aesthetic reasons), producers who make a point of chopping records are surprisingly
slow (in most cases) to claim moral or artistic superiority on that basis
alone. Rather, many producers specifically point to chopping's legal and
economic benefits as the major factor in their embrace of it: "I think the
whole chopping phenomenon came about as a direct result of rappers

getting sued, or rappers having to pay way too much, or labels not willing to put out records" (Samson S. 1999). In fact, many producers take offense at the suggestion that looping is not creative:

> I like to loop. Just straight loop stuff . . . I'll chop something up a whole lot and change it around so that you can't hear it. But I'll also just straight loop something. And just use the loop. Especially if it's a loop that's not running through the whole original. And I like that.
>
> But the thing is that we're about to come out with a piece of vinyl on 321 records. And we'll have to clear our samples. So: can't do that. Unless I'm 'a pay somebody or get sued or whatever. But if I could, I would. Not every cut, because it's certain levels of creativity in it. People will think "Oh, that's just a loop—that's not creative." It is, if you . . . it's a couple things. One is if that's not playing through the whole [original] cut. It's what loop you select. But then there's also how you apply it, or use it. Or how the MC uses it. That's part of the art right there. (DJ Kool Akiem 1999)

Phill Stroman also emphatically defends the creativity of looping:

> See, the thing about it is that there's different types of loops. . . . I mean, you can get real creative with just a loop, without even chopping it. You know, it depends on that individual. There's a million ways you can loop something. You can take something and it'll be kinda off-beat and you'll put it to the drums in a certain way that— it's a loop—but it doesn't sound anything like the original record, you know? It's just creativity, how you do it. . . .
>
> You can take something that's like maybe a 5/4 . . . you know, some crazy jazz song. But if you listen to it as it was played, as the original recording, it's like a 5/4 beat. But then you loop that same thing to a 4/4 drum pattern. And it's a loop, but it's playing in a totally different way. It sounds totally different. (Stroman 1999)

Moreover, even producers who do take pride in chopping their samples may still criticize others when they feel that the means have overwhelmed the ends. Jake One, for example, characterizes a fellow producer's approach as "showing off":

He doesn't make music, he makes, like, art for art's sake. He doesn't make music. He seems to be more into, "Well, I chopped it fourteen different times," which I don't care about, personally. That's not me. I care about how it sounds, whether he looped it or not. So there's people like that. There's the segment of the producing population that's like, "Well, I have to chop it fifteen times and throw some reverse angles in there," and that's production to them. . . . But if still sounds weak, then what's the point? If it doesn't really sound good, it doesn't sound good. (Jake One 1998)

Samson S., who values chopping very highly, also does not see it as an end unto itself. If fact, he even goes so far as to defend Sean "Puffy" Combs, the most prominent practitioner of looping:

To be honest with you, man, to me, it's like: what's good is good. . . . I'm not the type of hip-hopper that gets in my little elite shell, and just naturally: "Awww, Puffy," this. Well, that's fine, whatever. Puffy's not necessarily *for* you! He's for the club. When you out kickin' it, you don't wanna hear no damn Company Flow [a self-consciously progressive hip-hop group]! . . . It's different moods.

Like, if you look at my collection, I got all kinds of different hip-hop. I appreciate it all. I can get into the artsy-fartsy shit; I have the little Unkle *Science Fiction* CD. I got Company Flow. I also have Eightball and MJG. And Spice-1. (Samson S. 1999)

Domino agrees:

This may be a little unorthodox of what you might get from most hip-hop producers, but I think that part of being in this industry is knowing and figuring out what has you on top. And finding out what people wanna hear. And that is so hard, in itself. It's easy to say, "Oh, he just took this record, and that's why it happened." But it isn't how it happened, you know what I'm sayin'? So there's a lot that goes along with that, which you gotta respect, in my eyes.

Now, whether or not *I* would do it, is a whole 'nother situation. I feel like I have certain standards of how I do music, and what I wanna do out of music. And I can live with that, and if he can live with *that*, then no one should try to put their own production standards on Puffy. And that's just how I view it. I may not [be] impressed by what he's doing, but I'm not gonna say that he should be doing *anything*. Who am I to say? And who's to say that doin' it the underground way, making something out of scratch, is *the way?* It's just one way, it's one style of doing it. (Domino 1998)

Ultimately, what counts is the level of perceived creativity:

Personally, I like loops. Certain people really have a gift for chopping. You know, like Premier or somebody. But even after a while that starts getting tired, 'cause people start imitating his style and stuff . . . like the same old stuff over and over, you know what I mean? So, I mean, it varies. I think it's all about being creative. And sometimes you can be creative with looping, and sometimes you can be creative with chopping. It all depends on the person doing it. (Stroman 1999)

Taken collectively, the aesthetic aesthetic preferences of sample-based hip-hop define a frame of reference that serves two purposes: it allows the genre to maintain a consistent character despite using samples from a wide variety of sources, and it gives meaning to the choices made by individual producers.

The character of the genre—as represented by looping, the groove-based rhythmic sensibility, repetition and variation, and signifyin(g)— is deeply African American in its conception. It is, in fact, specifically designed to bring diverse musical material into an African American sphere of influence. At the same time, aesthetic reference points provide a framework for interpretation that valorizes record knowledge, processual mastery, compositional creativity, and deejaying skill. The sample-based hip-hop aesthetic is—by its very existence—an exercise of intellectual, social, and artistic power.

chapter 7

The Outer Circle

From Samplers to Ears

Although I have spent the majority of this book discussing the social circle of sample-based hip-hop producers as a discrete community, the people who make beats do not live a cloistered existence. In this chapter I will address the larger social world in which the hip-hop producer operates: that of individuals who, for artistic, social, and economic reasons, facilitate the music's journey from producer to listener. Although their work usually takes place after a recording has been completed, their influence is nevertheless strong: their actions affect an artist's reputation and pocketbook, both of which may be taken into account by producers when they create their next songs.[1]

Most producers work in partnership with one or more MCs (rappers), to whom they submit a number of instrumental beats. The MCs then choose the particular beats which they feel best suit their needs at that time. Once an MC's rhymes have been added, the producer and the MC, along with various record company executives and legal professionals, must decide which of these songs can and should be commercially released. And of all commercially released hip-hop music, only a small number of songs are heard by any given listener; this is largely at the discretion of deejays, whether on the radio or in nightclubs.

Although producers have their own standards for ethical behavior and aesthetic quality, their reputations and potential earnings largely rest in the hands of individuals whose sensibilities lie outside of those standards. As a result, the wishes of individuals outside of the producers' community are also considered when hip-hop music is produced. It is not my intention, however, to suggest that to do so is to compromise one's artistic standards. It would be easy to idealize the process, to speculate about what hip-hop producers *might* produce if not bound by the needs of others. But, as I will show, these apparently "outside" needs are, in fact, fundamental to the nature of hip-hop production. Without them, it would be unlikely to exist at all.

All art, and all evaluative standards for art, exist within a social world, and it is my intention to show how the requirements of that world affect the works produced. In doing so, I draw substantially upon Howard Becker's notion of an "art world" as a community of individuals whose collective activity defines, produces, and appreciates a given art form:

> All artistic work, like all human activity, involves the joint activity of a number, often a large number, of people. Through their cooperation, the art work we eventually see or hear come to be and continues to be. The work always shows signs of that cooperation. The forms of cooperation may be ephemeral, but often become more or less routine, producing patterns of collective activity we can call an art world. The existence of art worlds, as well as the way their existence affects both the production and consumption of art works, suggests a sociological approach to the arts. It is not an approach that produces aesthetic judgements, although that is a task many sociologists of art have set for themselves. It produces, instead, an understanding of the complexity of the cooperative networks through which art happens. (Becker 1982: 1)

In this chapter, I will discuss how a particular group of artworks—hip-hop beats—progress through cooperative networks that allow them to be heard as well as how the values of these networks circle back to influence future beats.

Although there is a growing market for instrumental hip-hop music, the vast majority of commercially released hip-hop songs feature the rhymes of an MC. As a result, producers tend to make beats that they feel will be conducive to rhyming. Any number of factors may come into play in such assessments, from tempo (neither so fast that the MC can't be understood, nor so slow that the song lacks energy) to number of samples (if there are too many different sounds, the MC will be lost in the mix) to the personal preferences of a particular MC with whom the producer is working. Of course, a producer is not required to take such factors into account, but when MCs consistently choose to rhyme over beats with certain characteristics, a producer must learn to provide those characteristics, or become known as someone who doesn't.

Adam Krims (2000) has written extensively about how this interaction may contribute to a broader genre profile, but by making genre his analytical focus he has, to some degree, obscured the actual process by which these decisions are made. This is because in hip-hop, as in other musical forms, the concept of genre is so broad that it is meaningless for most practical purposes. A producer who is not already thoroughly saturated in the aesthetic characteristics of the genre of hip-hop in which he purports to be working stands little chance of meeting the specific needs of any MC. Before they got to the point of having to articulate preferred genre characteristics, most MCs would have long since found a new collaborator.

According to the MC Wordsayer, what an MC needs from a producer can vary considerably, but is often either more abstract or more specific than generic labels can describe:

> You look for something that can support what you've already created, or something where you can say, "OK, this a nice foundation, now I can build on it." And it just depends on how you're feeling, 'cause you might have something already in your mind, where, "I'm just looking for something to put this over," or you might be in a frame of mind where you don't have any preexisting concept, and it's like, "Now, I'm looking for something to build with." (Wordsayer 1998)

In the former case, when the rhyme is already written and the MC is simply looking for a beat that works well under it, the MC's relationship with the producer is primarily that of a critic, choosing the beat that is best for his or her needs. But in the latter case, when the MC is looking for a beat that inspires him or her to write, the interaction is somewhat more complex; in those circumstances, the MC may focus more on the aesthetic factors I discussed in chapter 6.² In fact, aesthetic issues such as rhythmic feel and general "vibe" can become so significant when an MC makes these determinations, that they verge on the spiritual:

> The music within itself contains already the melodies, and [the MC is] just bringing up the particular sounds that are within the beat, whether it be just embellishments or different rhythms or har-monies. And listening to the sound. For me, it's like the music talks, on its own. You hear certain things and they have their own identity within that song. So just finding . . . prominent rhythms and . . . coming up with a counter-rhythm that's in time or in har-mony with your vocal. So using your voice, really, just as another instrument to embellish the track, musically. Not just seeing a beat and just rhyming over it, but sort of feeling [that] each and every beat has a different vibration and feel to it. So just listening to it in that way. (Wordsayer 1998)

MC Kylea supports this analysis, suggesting that the aesthetic "vibe" can affect the process of rhyme composition in specific ways. In the ideal case, music and lyrics will merge into a single organic whole:

Production is about a vibe. . . . I mean, all the way down from the person who's creatin' it, to when you receive it. It's like, "Now this is your child. Raise it. Raise it and just watch it grow." And that's usually what happens with a beat that I receive. I listen to it and it's like, "Oh, yeah." It's weird how it kinda comes to you, 'cause it really does come from beyond.

You sit down and you listen to it, and I write and get to a part, and then, well, I freestyle [improvise] the rest. Because you keep freestylin' to be able to hear what you wanna write. And then when you look back at the whole song, it's like, "Wow, I don't even remem-ber really writing that down, or knowing that the song is gonna be this way." I just heard the music, and the music said, "This is the song." You sit down, and the more you listen to the music, the more you'll be able to write this song. If you don't listen to the music, then you're not gonna write the song. But if you get into that vibe of the music, then you gonna slowly see the song come together. And when you listen to it, it's like, "Wow, that song really makes sense." (Kylea 1998)

For Wordsayer, in fact, openness to this type of creative approach is a major factor in his choice of producers to work with: "The song sort of creates itself. It's not like sitting down and producing with the intent to create so much of a specific sound. But just sitting down and opening yourself up to facilitate whatever particular energy comes through you, creatively. So I feel producers who create in that way" (Wordsayer 1998).

Beyond the general sensibility of the song, MCs may react to different elements within the song. Often, an MC will change the rhythm or tone of their performance to correspond with different samples at various points throughout the song:

> The drum pattern could be one thing, and then there's a bass line that's happening that could just be real funky. And it's like, "Oh man, when I get to this one part—" And then the beat might drop out and the bass line's doin' this. And it's like, "Well I wanna rhyme to the bassline when it does that." And when the beat comes back in, you're just changing your tempo to go back with the beat. You're almost playing, like, see-saw. You're going back and forth and back and forth. And, for myself, doing that, it gets complicated, because you gotta really remember: what are you following, and when are you following it? You know? All the way through the song. I know there's a lot of artists that do that, though. You can listen to their cadence and see that, "Oh, OK, I can hear what they're flowing off of," you know? What part that they're following in the song. (Kylea 1998)

When such thoughts are continually relayed back to the producer, it cannot help but influence their work (assuming that the producer is interested in maintaining a relationship with that MC):

> The producer that you usually work with, you pretty much have a feel for how they create. Not saying that all their beats are the same, but they're gonna give you a beat that, if they know you, and know how you rhyme, and know what you do, they'll know. They'll

make a beat and say, "Here. When I made this beat I was thinking about you." And so then, when you get the beat, it's like "Yeah!" (Kylea 1998)

Wordsayer (whose real name is Jon) agrees: "There's a personal relationship where it's like, they might be producing some music and just through the nature of our relationship, they're able to be like, 'OK, that sounds like Jon,' or 'that feels like Jon,' or 'I can hear Jon on that,' or 'I could see Jon on that.' Then when I get one of their beats, it hits me. I be like, 'I can see myself on that'" (Wordsayer 1998). In a sense, this idea is related to a social convention that was raised in my discussion of digging in the crates: that artists have their own characteristic aesthetics or vibes, and that certain musical materials can be almost predestined for a particular musician. As producer Vitamin D spoke of other producers giving him records that fit his vibe, so he directs his own finished beats to the appropriate MCs.

As a recording-based musical form, there is little room in hip-hop for totally noncommercial music. With the exception of working tapes that are played for other producers or MCs, mix tape exclusives, and so-called "white label" underground releases (which are usually given directly to deejays), almost all hip-hop is commercially released. Once an MC has chosen which songs to rhyme over, therefore, a final decision must be made as to which of those songs to release commercially. This decision is usually made collectively by the producer, the MC, and record executives (in the case of independently released hip-hop, these are often the same individuals). Factors that come into play are the same as for any other form of popular music, such as perceived danceability, ability to fit into preexisting radio formats, and "catchiness," most of which are highly subjective. One somewhat more pragmatic concern that arises at this stage is that of avoiding potential copyright violations, a process generally referred to as "sample clearance."

As I argued in chapter 4, sampling is the foundation of hip-hop music, and producers, left to their own devices, are not particularly interested in justifying its use. When forced by circumstance, however, they are more than willing to articulate a point of view. Sample clearance—the process of obtaining permission from copyright holders for the use of their music—is the primary circumstance that forces them to do so:

It's all about money. I mean, there was times when people didn't try to own this piece of land. You know, try to put some kind of boundary on it. And say, "Well, I own this." The way I look at it, how can you really own a piece of land that's gonna be here after you're gone, and was there before you was there? You can't just come along and say, "This belongs to me, 'cause I wrote this piece of paper." You know what I mean? Anybody could come write a piece of paper, then. What if my paper is bigger than yours?

It's really all about money and how many guns you got to back up the laws you write. It really goes in and shows that all the laws are basically just a sham. . . . I don't have respect for any of the laws. . . .

And that fits in with my sampling law. Once a piece of music is out there, it's in the air. How can you really say you own this vibra- tion that's moving through the air in this configuration? You not around to even see what's happening. How do you own that? I mean, that's like saying you own a certain wavelength of color. . . . It's ridiculous. (DJ Kool Akiem 1999)

Sample clearance raises a difficult methodological issue for the re- searcher: despite many producers' ideological disdain for the sample clear- ance process, one opens oneself to civil liability if one releases music that contains uncleared samples. As a result, many producers are under- standably hesitant to go on record about their practices in this area. Rather than put them in that position, I chose not to even inquire about this issue in interviews. I have, however, spoken off the record with many of my consultants (as well as many others) about sample clearance, and this section tries to reflect the general tenor of the hip-hop perspective, rather than the approach of any individual. In addition, it should go without saying that I am not a lawyer and that anything contained herein should not be taken as legal advice.

In order to clear a sample, the artist (or their agents) must obtain two sets of permissions: publishing rights and master rights (Stim 1999: 66). "Publishing rights" are the ownership of the composition in the abstract, including music and lyrics (Ashburne 1994: 2–3; Stim 1999: 66). These rights are generally split between the composer, lyricist, and publishing company. "Master rights" are the the the ownership of a particular recording of the composition and may be owned by the performer, but are usually owned by the record company (Ashburne 1994: 2). A hip-hop artist may need to clear either or both of these sets of rights in order to release a song.

For instance, a hip-hop song that samples a measure from an original recording, retaining a recognizable melody from that song, would need both permissions. A hip-hop song that uses the melody from an original song but does not sample it (the melody is replayed on a synthesizer, for example) need pay only publishing rights. By the same token, a hip-hop song that uses the lyrics from a copyrighted song would also need to pay publishing rights, unless it could be successfully argued that the lyric was a parody of the original and thus protected under U.S. fair use doctrine as specifically defined by the 7 March 1994 Supreme Court decision in *Luther R. Campbell, aka Luke Skyywalker, et al. v. Acuff-Rose Music, Inc.* (Sanjek 2000b: 1). The decision, as David Sanjek points out, requires that the new work be "transformative" of the old for the purpose of commenting upon it. Works that did not sufficiently change the old version or (presumably) did not sufficiently comment on it would not be protected. What, exactly, constitutes sufficient change or comment is, of course, highly contingent upon cultural norms, and hip-hop producers cannot reasonably be blamed if they suspect that the Supreme Court does not adjudicate from the perspective of hip-hop culture.

The final potential case—a song that samples an original recording, but alters it so that the original composition is unrecognizable—need only pay master rights: the recording is being used, but the composition is not. As Domino says,

> Ultimately, legally, it doesn't matter. You know, there's all this talk about how you gotta use, like, more than three bars—that's all bullshit. On the publishing side, maybe that's true. But on the master side, if you sample *any* piece from a record, no matter what you get . . . Legally, if I took this *khhhhhh* [imitates record static] from this record, they own that master. So anything you sample from their record, no matter what you do with it, legally, they own it. . . . If they find out that that's what it is, then they can pop you, no matter how small a piece you use. (Domino 1998)

The operative phrase here, for many producers, is "if they find out that that's what it is." In practice, such samples are often not cleared at all, on the assumption that the owner of the master rights would not be able to recognize that the song had been sampled in the first place. This is part of the reason why so many producers resent breakbeat compilations; they can alert copyright holders to samples that they may not have been aware of.

Many producers feel that copyright law is more often a matter of money and power than of creativity and artists' rights. Hank Shocklee of the Bomb Squad, for instance, feels that original artists expect an inappropriate share of recording royalties:

> The whole sampling thing has gotten out of proportion anyway because if you use one little lick from somebody, [the sampled artist is] claiming like 50% copyright! I tend to think that the laws should protect the entire composition. I understand that. But when you're starting to protect licks, and [musical] phrases, now you're getting to a [dangerous] point. That's like saying, "Let me copyright the note 'C'" And anytime somebody uses it you're like "Oh! You usin' 'C.' I should get some!" No! Because that might be part of what makes the song, but it's not stealing the entire composition. (Quoted in Chairman Mao 1998:, 113–114)

Once the money and power have been factored out, many producers will argue, the situation becomes much more relative. And when the new artist and the original copyright holder are of equal moral stature, then one's default position should be in favor of increased artistic freedom, rather than monetary rights:

> DJ Kool Akiem: Regardless of what the [original] artist says, to me, once it's recorded, it's out there . . . To me, it's 'hip-hop first,' you know what I'm sayin'? That means, basically, I'm 'a take my side over any musician for any reason. Even the most skilled musician, the one that I praise the most, I'm still sampling.
> Joe: 'Cause hip-hop's more important, you're saying.

DJ Kool Akiem: Right. Not to him; to me. (DJ Kool Akiem
1999)

DJ Kool Akiem is not claiming an absolute moral right to sample. Rather,
he argues, essentially, that old songs are part of the environment ("once
it's recorded, it's out there") and, as such, constitute reasonable material
for artistic manipulation. He is *not* saying that the original musician is
wrong, only that his own position is of equal moral standing. Note that
this approach is quite different from presenting a new model of artistic
ownership: DJ Kool Akiem (along with every other hip-hop artist I have
encountered) still copyrights his own music. This is largely due to the
fact that copyright tends to be viewed by hip-hop producers as a tactic for
dealing with the non-hip-hop world (record companies, lawyers, musicians from other genres). Within the hip-hop producers' community,
such issues are dealt with through the ethical system discussed in chapter 5.

With that in mind, hip-hop artists' approach to copyright tends to be
more reformist than revolutionary, often arguing that the laws simply do
not do what they claim to do: protect the original musician. One version
of this criticism points out that it is the record company (often a trans-
national corporation) that makes the lion's share of the profits from sample clearance:

DJ Kool Akiem: I mean, I understand how it makes sense in a way
to where "Yeah, I sweated and made this, and I deserve to get
paid off it." Yeah, and maybe that's true. But at the same time,
somebody that didn't make [the song] is making a whole lot
more money than you are off it.
Joe: Yeah, you mean from the record company . . .
DJ Kool Akiem: Yeah. Maybe you ain't even makin' none of it and
they makin' all of it, 'cause they bought your rights. (DJ Kool
Akiem 1999)

Another line of reasoning questions the idea of nonmaterial art as a
transferable commodity. If copyright is about protecting the rights of a
creative individual, how then can the moral value of creativity be traded

on the open market? DJ Kool Akiem raises this issue with regard to Michael Jackson, who as of this writing owns the publishing rights to the Beatles catalog: "Why should somebody pay Michael Jackson for sampling the Beatles? How do you *transfer* the ownership of this wave configuration that you only owned because you created it? You can now transfer that to somebody else? It's a lot of ridiculousness" (DJ Kool Akiem 1999).

A more pragmatic objection to the copyright laws is that even when hip-hop artists operate in good faith, they can often be denied clearance out of hand for purely bureaucratic reasons:

> It's too much of a nightmare. People have this mistaken idea that you can go to an artist and say, "Can I use your thing?," and they're like, "Yeah, man. No sweat." But you can't. Even if you're buddies with an artist, and they're like "Sure, man, you can use two bars of this." It's all down to the publishers and the record company, who own the masters. And they couldn't care less who you are. All they know is if you're using something that they own. And sometimes they don't even wanna make a deal. It's, like, not even worth their while to do it; they don't want the paperwork. It's below their radar. Other times, they want a lot [of money], and they want so much it's not worth you paying for it either. It's just a lot of work. It's a lot of administrative clearance work. (The Angel 1998)

If anything, the Angel is understating the difficulties. As Steinski pointed out (conversation with author, New York, 14 March 2003), a substantial number of people, including artists, lawyers, copyright holders, and their various representatives and assistants, must approve any given sample request—and any one of them can veto it by simply ignoring, forgetting, or otherwise failing to respond to it.[3]

One example of this phenomenon that is well known in the hip-hop community is the song "Cabfare" by Souls of Mischief, which samples the theme from the television show *Taxi*. One of the group's producers, Domino, explains what happened:

> Basically, the story behind that was that we tried to put a sample,

and Bob James, who wrote it, didn't want us to use it, basically, because it wasn't how he wanted it to sound. So, initially, that was the reason.

And then Jive [Souls of Mischief's record company at that time] continuously tried to clear it, and, I guess, change his mind. They got him to change his mind, later on. And then, when it looked like it was gonna go through . . . Paramount, the company that owned the TV show, was like, "No." He was the sole writer, but the ownership was jointly, both of them. (Domino 1998)

Nevertheless, sample clearance—in principle—has little effect on how people produce records. Many producers, for example, make beats that they know in advance will be impossible to clear: "I'll make something, and loop a bunch of stuff from one record, and put it on my tape. And shut the sampler off and erase it. . . . I have a song . . . where I looped a four-bar loop, which is something I don't do that often. But I just did it 'cause it sounded cool. . . . I like the beat, I just didn't wanna save it, 'cause it was a four-bar loop" (King Otto 1998). While such songs are not released, they are valued precisely as an indicator that a producer's work is unfettered by legal or monetary restrictions. The fact that producers make music that they know they cannot sell shows their lack of concern for the marketplace. It is for this reason, in fact, that Domino suggests that a strong understanding of the music business could actually cause a producer to second-guess himself:

You do what you do, you know? It's kind of weird because you're able to, on all levels, do things a lot easier when you don't know about the business at all. And then once you find out, then you go, like, "Oh, I can't use this Fantasy record 'cause they want a minimum of five Gs," or whatever. . . . You know what I mean. . . . There's a lot of reasons: James Brown won't let you cuss. Everyone has a different story. (Domino 1998)

As DJ Topspin points out, hip-hop can be heard in several discrete listening environments, each of which has its own flavor: "You know what parameters you are working with. You know this is not gonna fly. Or this will fly only in a certain space. Like a show, or something like that. It's not gonna be bumping in a Jeep that's on the cruise tip. There's a time and place for different types of rhythms, basically" (DJ Topspin 1999). Generally speaking, these environments can be grouped into three categories: nightclubs, personal listening (including home and portable stereo formats) and car stereo systems (radio exists in—and is geared toward —both personal listening and car stereo environments). Because the particular venues have different and sometimes mutually exclusive musical requirements, producers often target their musical output towards one environment, often to the exclusion of the others. As Samson S. notes, "There's different forms of producing, as far as hip-hop. Like, either you wanna do beats for the clubs, to move crowds and make people dance. *Or*, you wanna show off your little skills and shit, you know, show off how you chopped up this sample here, and how you took this and flipped it. I do a little of both" (Samson S. 1999).

Most hip-hop is produced for nightclubs. This state of affairs exists for several reasons, one of which is that the experience of hip-hop music remains closely tied to dancing. As pioneering hip-hop journalist Harry Allen notes, this can have far-reaching implications:

> Harry Allen: Rhythm and danceability. When I first started writing, it was very striking to me that nobody mentioned what it felt like to move to a record. And I tried to address that whenever I could, or at least mention it in an article. And especially with the increased importance of the clubs in terms of records becoming hot. Which is, to me, a really good thing. A really important thing, because live performances, or club-style performances: performances of many people in one place to live music and records . . .
>
> Joe: Do you see, for instance, a bunch of people dancing to a record as a form of performance?
>
> Harry Allen: Oh, absolutely. It's performance for themselves. For each other. And it's a way that people tell each other, "This is an important record." And, as such, these are important ideas. And, by "ideas," I mean [sings the melody from "The 900 Number," by DJ Mark the 45 King]: that's an idea. Or the repre-

> sentation of an idea . . . And, by everybody moving to that, peo-
> ple are saying to each other "We share this." "This is ours."
> And you can have that conversation with your body. (Allen
> 2003)

Hip-hop began as the soundtrack to social dancing and has remained so (George 1998). There are also aesthetic reasons for hip-hop's association with nightclubs: the clubs' elaborate sound systems can provide a more powerful listening experience than virtually any home system.

Finally, there is hip-hop's continued absence from radio playlists, despite its position as one of the best-selling forms of contemporary music, a situation that has multiple causes. First, despite its increasing commercial power, much hip-hop does not conform to FCC regulations regarding profanity and, as a result, cannot be played on the radio. Furthermore, even songs that may be appropriate in terms of language may not be seen as having the broad appeal that advertisers crave. Moreover, even when a song does meet the needs of radio programmers, the increasing consolidation and conservatism of the music industry leaves fewer slots for new music to be played.

Perhaps the most important factor affecting the way hip-hop functions in nightclub settings, as I discussed in chapter 3, is the role of the deejay as aesthetic arbiter. One of the hallmarks of a good deejay is that the audience trusts his or her judgment as far as which hip-hop songs are appropriate to play at any given time. In other words, deejays' understanding of how music serves various social needs is the primary reason that fans pay money to hear them. As Becker has noted, generally,

> A relevant feature of organized art worlds is that, however their po-
> sition is justified, some people are commonly seen by many or most
> interested parties as more entitled to speak on behalf of the art world
> than others; the entitlement stems from their being recognized by
> the other participants in the cooperative activities through which
> that world's works are produced and consumed as the people enti-
> tled to do that. Whether other art world members accept them as
> capable of deciding what art is because they have more experience,
> because they have an innate gift for recognizing art, or simply be-
> cause they are, after all, the people in charge of such things and

therefore ought to know—whatever the reason, what lets them make the distinction and make it stick is that the other participants agree that they should be allowed to do it. (Becker 1982: 151)

The deejays' authority, then, rests on a community's willingness to accept their judgement. If the deejays' judgment begins to falter, the people will turn elsewhere.

The deejays' relationship to individual hip-hop recordings is a hybrid one; in one sense deejays are presenting a program of completed musical works (twelve-inch vinyl singles almost exclusively) to an audience— they are essentially anthologists. But at the same time, deejays are also seen as artists in their own right, creating a collage of hip-hop songs. In this sense, the individual songs function as the raw material for the deejay's art, much like the old records are the raw material for producers. For a song to be heard in the club, then, it must fulfill the needs of both of these roles.[4]

When choosing which records to play, the nightclub deejay must take into account certain factors that may not be at issue in other venues. As DJ B-Mello points out, primary among these is the song's perceived ability to make people dance: "In a club, to move a crowd . . . it's gotta have some kind of bounce to it, you know? I mean, there's a lot of dope records that I like, that I listen to on a Walkman, in the car, but in a club it's just not gonna move anybody, you know? Might be some dope production . . . real eerie or dark—whatever—but it's not gonna do nothin' in the club" (DJ B-Mello 1998). Deejay and label owner Strath Shepard also finds the rhythm to be a significant factor in the equation:

> I just think that there are certain types of beats that work well in a club, and certain types that don't. And I like a lot of both. . . . Really hard kick drums work well in a club. Just because, with the loud system, it's just gonna work well. Like, we were talking about Timbaland yesterday, his kicks are so strong. And they're not the kind of kicks that will hit and your speakers will not be able handle 'em. Any speakers can handle his kick drum . . . but they're just really warm. Those work well, and just like really snappy, bouncy drums. (Shepard 1998)

As both B-Mello and Strath Shepard specifically note, they personally enjoy beats that would not be valuable in a nightclub setting. Again, this supports the idea that the value of a hip-hop composition in one venue does not necessarily carry over to others.

Successful deejays develop a highly sophisticated sense of which records will work and which will not: "I think I could pretty much tell what'll work for what situation. Like when I preview records, I just drop the needle for like a second, and I can usually tell, you know?" (DJ B-Mello 1998). This "drop the needle" process is closely related to the one I described in chapter 5, in which producers preview records for potential samples. Since many producers are also deejays, it is not surprising that such similarities would occur.

The value of a deejay's opinion cannot be overstated. At the time of our interview, Strath Shepard was co-owner of the independent label Conception Records, and he was emphatic on this point: "We place an enormous amount of importance on the deejay. . . . If the deejays are not feeling our record, we will drop the artist" (Shepard 1998). The deejay's concerns— which combine practical and aesthetic factors—are quickly and decisively conveyed to the producers, who, for the most part, respond to them. In addition to such negative practical incentives as being released from one's recording contract for lack of deejay appeal, there are also the converse positive reinforcements, such as increased frequency of play in nightclubs. Furthermore, many producers are themselves also club deejays, so they naturally tend to internalize these factors.

It is difficult to overestimate the seriousness of the deejays' commitment to the dance floor or the lack of sentimentality they show in discarding songs that fail to support that commitment. Prince Paul, for example, will not even play most of *his own* records when he's deejaying, because he feels that they don't work well for dancing:

Deejaying played a big role, because just by hearing certain sounds and hearing how fast something is, or the depth of the kick and the snare, will help you determine kinda what people's reaction's gonna be, especially in a club. And now since I'm deejaying a lot more than I did before, the new record that I'm making . . . is more club-friendly. But I inclined to make it like that because a lot of songs that I would do in the last few years, a lot of them are "listening" records. Like, you listen to them—you can't party to them. I will not play any songs that I made in the last few years at a party, because people will automatically scatter the floor. . . . Conversations will start. Somebody get a drink. Somebody's talking to me, and I'm deejaying! So, with that realization, I'm like "Man, I'd love to play some records that I made at a party, and have people go 'Oooooh.'"[5] (Prince Paul 2002)

Prince Paul's deejaying experience inspired him to make records that would make people dance and gave him a greater sense of the qualities that would accomplish that goal. In addition to general aesthetic principles, which tend to fall in line with those of other listeners, most deejays cite four factors that determine their willingness to play a given song in a nightclub setting: tempo, a song's rhythmic consistency, the ease with which it may be segued into another song, and the relative physical quality of the record itself.

Tempo

While conduciveness to dancing is largely a result of general aesthetic associations and what Charles Keil (1995) has called participatory discrepancies, tempo also plays a major role for hip-hop artists. One reason for this is simply because it can be easily controlled through technology. Most sequencers have the ability to set a tempo precisely, to within at least a tenth of a beat per minute, and many combined sampler-sequencers can alter the tempo of a composition without changing its pitch. As a result, a producer has—for all intents and purposes—total control over the tempo of a song. As Oliver Wang points out, this has led to very specific tempo preferences in a club setting:

Most people will dance fairly easily to anything that's 100 bpms [beats per minute] or higher, but contemporary hip-hop, especially in the last, I'd say, five years or so, has all moved to like 88 bpm as a norm, or maybe the low nineties. And most R&B production is in the low nineties to the high eighties range. It's very groovy, but if you think about it, it's not like up-tempo dance stuff. A lot of peo-

ple who are used to more disco-era speed beats—[which] were like
120, or house beats which crank up to like 130 or so—find it very
hard to dance to something that's at 88 bpm. Because it's so slow.
You can't really get kinetic with it, you just have to groove to it. (Wang
1998)

I have witnessed, on several occasions, club deejays playing songs that
had strong reputations among home listeners but had very slow tempos
(approximately seventy-five to eighty-five beats per minute). In each case,
the dance floor quickly cleared, and I never heard the deejay play that
song again.

Rhythmic Flow

Another important component of danceablity is rhythmic flow. As I discussed in chapter 6, a sense of momentum is key to keeping a crowd
dancing. RZA's habit of not quantizing his beats—which results in a
lack of rhythmic precision—comes up again among deejays in that it
can interfere both with dancing and segues to other songs. By the same
token, however, a good deejay is expected to be able to deal with such
eventualities:

> I don't mind him not doing that specifically. I mean, in a way I do.
> But then at the same time, it's another thing where . . . you have to
> know your songs better. And if you can mix those songs and make
> it sound good, then you're a better DJ. So in a way, I kind of like it.
> And plus, it's just creative, the way he does it. So I don't mind it
> that much. Sometimes it's tough, because if people don't know that
> song, then they'll think *you're* off beat. (Shepard 1998)

Although it may be considered bad form to criticize a producer for
their rhythmic inconsistency, deejays will go out of their way to compliment producers who are more rhythmically reliable. In fact, DJ Mixx
Messiah specifically lauds producer DJ Premier on this point, and (notably) in terms that are more pragmatic that aesthetic; that is, Premier is
a good producer because his rhythms are easier for a deejay to manipulate (a process known as "beat-juggling"):

Mixx Messiah: [DJ Premier's] production was created for beat-
   jugglin'. It's like a beat-juggler's best friend.
Joe: Really? Why is that?
Mixx Messiah: Because of the hard, hard kick drum. And the
   smooth, like, jazzy bass lines. And just the loops. He leave 'em
   wide open, so that you can cut. He leaves just enough space for
   you to cut, bring something in, and bring it back. . . . You can
   tell the deejay influence on his production, because, if you listen to the instrumental, they're just made to cut up. He's like a
   deejay's best friend on production. (DJ Mixx Messiah 1999)

Segue Opportunities

Another important aspect of the deejay's job is to keep a continuous flow
of music going for people to dance to. A deejay's equipment—two turntables and a crossfader—is specifically designed for unbroken segues between records (Allen 1997: 4–9; Brewster and Broughton 2000: 131; Fikentscher 2000: 37–38; George 1998: 5; Hager 1984: 41). In fact, deejays
pride themselves on making their transitions so smoothly that a listener
cannot tell when one record ends and the other begins because they actually overlap for several bars. To accomplish this, the deejay requires
two things (other than skill): records of roughly the same tempo (minor
adjustments can be made by speeding up or slowing down one of the records) and records that have long enough instrumental passages at the
beginnings and ends that the transition can be accomplished before the
vocals begin for the next song.

   Oliver Wang (aka DJ O-Dub) has a deep appreciation for producers
who provide both of these tools: "The producers that we love are the ones
that give us like eight- or sixteen-bar intros and sixteen-bar outros. Like,
Premier is fuckin' great about that. Primo thinks like a deejay in a lot of
ways, because he may not always set you up with a long intro, but you'll
notice on his beats that there'll always be like eight to sixteen bars of
outro beat without anything over it, which is basically the segue opportunity" (Wang 1998). If such an opportunity is not provided, other arrange-
ments must be made:

There are some producers who just launch right into the song, especially ones that have talking in the beginning and then a beat comes in. That totally throws deejays off; it's very difficult to mix like that. Which is a big reason why you need doubles of a twelve-inch, because what you'll end up having to do is you'll basically take the instrumental [version] of one, mix that in, and then once the instrumental is on, then you can go back to the vocal version and find a place where you can cut in the vocals. So it makes it sound a little smoother. (Wang 1998)

In other words, the deejay must buy two copies of the single (which almost always features both instrumental and vocal versions of the song) and then use the instrumental version as a bridge between the previous song and the vocal version that he or she wishes to play.[6]

Although most deejays clearly prefer songs with long introductory and concluding instrumentals, most are hesitant to complain too vigorously if they are not there because a good deejay is expected to be able to respond to such eventualities. In other words, as deejay Karen Dere suggests, too much complaining may call one's own skills into question:

It just depends on how well you listen to your records before you actually play them in a club. I think a lot of people don't spend the time to get to know the song. And I think that's totally vital, because if you don't know exactly what the song sounds like, it could end cold or something like that, and you're screwed. Even Gang Starr did that with "You Know My Steez," and I know there was a lot of silence in a lot of clubs after that, 'cause they [the deejays] didn't know exactly where it ended. (Dere 1998)

Physical Quality of the Record

The relative physical quality of the vinyl record itself may also be a factor in a deejay's willingness to play it in a club:

Strath Shepard: There's also things like just where you get your records pressed up. Because the needles are made so they can go both ways on the record. But there are certain pressing

plants, like the one that comes to mind most is Europadisc,
in New York. Man, they are pressed so crappy. . . . You just
pull the record back, and from then on, that section where you
pulled it back will just be kind of staticy. So that's something.
. . . I'm gonna be reluctant to play [rapper] O.C. in the club because it's like that. And I want to preserve my record, too.
Joe: So how do you know where certain things are pressed?
Strath Shepard: You don't, really. But you just know labels. Like,
for example: Payday, MoWax, everyone at Virgin, basically. They
all press their stuff so bad. You can't scratch with it, because
it'll just ruin the record. You feel like you're burning a hole, like
it's gonna cut through the record. And then there's companies
that, of course, press them really well. Like WEA, all the WEA
stuff is really good. Warner/Elektra/Atlantic, all that is all really
good. Priority is really good. (Shepard 1998)

The significance of this factor to deejays is demonstrated by Shepard's
ability, in response to my question, to specifically characterize different
record labels by the quality of their pressing.

Similarly, DJ B-Mello notes that the amount of material on an album
can also affect the quality of the pressing; he prefers Canadian pressings,
since Canadian record companies, in his experience, are more likely to
press double albums, rather than try to fit a CD-length album on a single
record:

B-Mello: I mean, a lot of the Elektra things, you know, they'd just
press just single albums and it's a terrible pressing. . . . It's
fucked up, really.
Joe: So would . . . that affect whether you'd play the album a lot or
not?
B-Mello: Yeah! Sure! Yeah, if it's just on single vinyl and it's like fifteen tracks or something, you know, it's just not gonna be good.
Even if the vinyl's all right, the pressing's not gonna
be good. You're not gonna be able to play it at a concert or a
club with all the hum in it, you know? So what are you gonna
do with it? That's the good thing about Canada. Epic, Sony . . .

all their little subsidiaries, they press up double vinyl for all
their albums.

Joe: That means they're, like, thicker?

B-Mello: Nah. They spread it out.

Joe: Oh, so the grooves are farther apart.

B-Mello: Yeah, like two pieces of vinyl, or four pieces, rather than
one . . . so that spreads out the grooves, and then it's like havin'
a couple twelve-inches, really. So it's louder.[7] (DJ B-Mello 1998)

Clearly, then, it is to producers' advantage to take these four factors—
tempo, rhythmic flow, segue opportunities, and physical quality of the
record—into account if they want their music to be played in a nightclub
setting. Furthermore, as I mentioned, many producers are themselves
also club deejays, so they have firsthand experience with the way these
factors play out in a live situation:

When I first started making beats or doing production and stuff, I
didn't think of that. It just so happens that, you know, you play
"Me, Myself and I" [one of Prince Paul's early productions for De
La Soul] at a club and people are like "Ohhhh." And I'm like "Wow!
People are dancing to that!"

. . . A lot of things back then are just by accident, by chance, and
still a lot of things are like that today. But you can't help but to
learn stuff. You know, it's like technology and stuff and everything
else. And even though you don't like to apply it all the time, it's just
part of your know-how. So now, if I'm making something like 98
beats per minute, 100 beats per minute—that's dance tempo. OK.
I didn't think of that before. . . . It's fortunate in some ways, but un-
fortunate 'cause it kind of takes the innocence out of production.
(Prince Paul 2002)

Mr. Supreme expresses a similar perspective: "Being a club deejay, it
makes me think about a record, when I'm making a record. Like 'OK,
I should leave the beat ride by itself at the beginning, to make it easy
to mix at a club,' or something like that. So I do think about it. It does
affect it, definitely" (Mr. Supreme 1998a).

In addition to the club environment, there are two other listening environments in which the deejay does not come into play (at least not to the same degree): personal listening and car listening. Each of these environments also has needs and requirements for music. It is worth noting also that although singles are the format of choice for nightclub play, the other two environments tend to favor full-length albums, if only for convenience.

What I would characterize as "personal listening" refers to musical appreciation by an individual or small group in an informal setting; the music is reproduced either on a home stereo or a Walkman. The presumed inferiority of this reproduction technology (relative to the other two settings) is actually liberating to the producer in several specific ways. Free of the need to play to the strengths of a large sound system (particularly the system's bass response), the producer can afford to work throughout the range of audible sound, rather than focusing on chest-thumping bass. Similarly, people do not expect music in this environment to be primarily made for dancing, although that may still be important. This allows producers to work with different tempos and rhythmic structures that might be more difficult to dance to. Finally, a person who is listening to music on headphones is presumed to be more discerning and appreciative of subtlety than a nightclub audience (particularly one that has been drinking alcohol). In many ways the relationship between club listening and personal listening parallels the relationship between the "Top 40" and "album-oriented rock" (AOR) formats of the early 1970s. The AOR listener was presumed to have a deeper connection to the artists, and ideas could be played out over the course of an entire album, rather than in a three-minute single. All of these factors combine to make "personal listening" the environment most conducive to self-consciously artistic hip-hop music.

The significance of elaborately designed car stereo systems to hip-hop production cannot be overstated. The ideal car stereo system has huge subwoofers for increased bass response. The power of the bass to cut through the music and physically affect the listener is celebrated. For this reason, as Mr. Supreme notes, music that is appreciated in a home system may not work at all in this environment:

> It depends, 'cause my favorite producers—like Pete Rock or Large
> Professor—you play their album in a car with a nice system and it

sounds like shit, you know? It's great production, it's a great record, but the recording of it and the quality, it sounds like shit [in a car]. You put, like, a Too $hort record in and it sounds so good.

So it depends on, really, what you're going for, there. . . . But just being sample based . . . with nothing else, usually it can sound like crap . . . in [car stereo] systems. . . . I don't know why. It's just like if you throw an 808 kick under something or a keyboard bass line, it fattens it up tremendously. I don't know why. (Mr. Supreme 1998a)

In light of my comments about home listening, it is significant that Mr. Supreme feels that sample-based hip-hop may be less valuable in a car system than music that makes use of drum machines (such as the Roland TR-808) or synthesizers—especially considering that Mr. Supreme is himself a rather militantly sample-based producer.

DJ Mixx Messiah, who in addition to deejaying also works in music retail, characterizes the car listener as one who is less discerning than the home listener: "I would say people favor more the guys that make the production for the cars. . . . It's almost like their ears are impatient. They want something that's just gonna be the fix for their ears at the time, and then they'll get over it. They don't really look at it from a dissecting point of view" (DJ Mixx Messiah 1999).

Steinski, however, argues that production with the broad appeal necessary to capture the car stereo audience has its own virtues:

Most of the people that I have seen, in terms of independent producers, they can do a lot of great things, but they're not making radio hits. They ain't Timbaland. They're not making the thing that's gonna come boomin' outta the Jeep down the street, necessarily. Or the thing that's gonna show up on Hot 97. Nothing against them.

Nothing against them. But, also, I think there is a great deal to be learned from stuff that shows up on the radio. As awful as Clear Channel is, as awful as the selection process is, as bad as the labels who are buying the time are. All of that aside, you can listen to things and go, "Damn, that's a hot record. And that beat is great. And that rap is terrific." And here it is, it's connecting with a *zillion* people. . . . That's hip-hop too, I got no problem with that. (Stein 2002)

From the MC's need for a "rhymable" beat to the deejay's need for a well-pressed record, there are a variety of concerns that affect the passage of music from producer to fan. Rather than presenting these concerns as peripheral to an idealized musical form, I suggest that these specific social forces are as integral to the music as abstract aesthetics or general political issues. They give the music its shape and quality and are not generally seen as undue constraints by producers. In fact, they are integral to the process of hip-hop production; the music of hip-hop producers cannot be understood outside of this larger social environment.

Conclusions

Hip-hop producers make no apologies for sampling. In fact, as I have tried to demonstrate, they consistently show great pride and commitment to their approach in myriad ways. This, I argue, is primarily due to the complementary influences of social and aesthetic forces in the community of sample-based hip-hop producers. As the community preserves the aesthetic, so the aesthetic preserves the community.

At the most basic level, I hope that this study has shown one way in which ethnography may be valuable for the study of popular culture. No matter how significant the pressures applied by base and superstructure, nationalism, capitalism, and ethnicity, it is still individual human beings (and their friends) who must navigate this course, and it is therefore individuals who usually have the most incisive stories to tell. It is the strategies they use to assimilate the larger concerns into their lives—concerns of politics, class, culture, gender, and morality—that provide the most nuanced pictures of how and why music works. In this book, I have presented a variety of strategies that hip-hop producers use to hold together both their community and their aesthetic.

The power of history is invoked in hip-hop music through producers' commitment to an aesthetic that was originally developed by deejays using turntables. This dedication operates across a spectrum of specific concerns that ranges from the highly abstract to the thoroughly practical. On the abstract end of the scale, the use of a cyclic structure to isolate and reinterpret the most satisfying moments of popular songs is one of the foundations of hip-hop music. Part of the reason for its significance is its reinscription of hip-hop history in any given moment through the self-consciously "traditional" use of deejaying methodology. On the more pragmatic end, the immediate social value of the music is also beholden to the role of the deejay: the music must be responsive to the needs of the listeners, dancers, and head-nodders. It has to rock the crowd.

The very use of sampling in the first place is a strategy for preserving the artistic integrity of this approach. Many producers believe that if music uses live instruments, it has lost its connection to deejaying and therefore its essence as hip-hop. As with many such conventions, the social commitment that this belief necessitates is a major part of its appeal, easily separating the insider from the outsider. For hip-hop producers, purism is its own reward.

In the material realm, the purist's dues are paid through the act of digging in the crates. The elaborate networks, attitudes, and strategies that hip-hop record collectors have created reinforce the ties that bind the social to the material to the aesthetic. Digging demonstrates an abstract commitment to the hip-hop tradition while it provides raw material for artistic expression. At the same time, digging provides a broad-based musical education that helps contextualize hip-hop within larger traditions. Moreover, digging is a social activity that producers can use as a venue for discussion of a variety of issues concerning larger sampling practices—particularly ethics and aesthetics. This social opportunity also provides a counterbalance to the sometimes-isolating practice of making beats by oneself in a home studio.

The creation of a system of producers' ethics to guide the hip-hop composer's actions is another strategy that illuminates the connection between the social and artistic realms. The rules represent a community exerting moral pressure to preserve a valued aesthetic. But at the same time, the continued relevance of music that follows these rules shows that the aesthetic also exerts a reciprocal moral pressure to preserve the community. The specific rules (one must sample from vinyl records, one cannot sample from compilations or other hip-hop records, and so on) create parameters within which creativity may be assessed.

And the creativity that is being assessed—and preserved—is not some random collection of gestures and sounds. It is an aesthetic that conflates deejaying and verbal signifying into a complex musical form. By turning samples of single notes and linear musical phrases into cycles and using virtually all material in an ambiguous or double-voiced way, hip-hop can simultaneously "Africanize" material from any source and hide its African sensibility. At the same time, producers must be cognizant of the very real economic and social forces that come from outside their small community. The balance must be maintained.

Ultimately, sample-based hip-hop preserves both its community and itself through the Zen-like paradox it embodies: the assimilation of radical new material is the core practice around which a deeply conservative tradition has been built. To rest on one's laurels—to be traditional in a superficial way—is to violate the tradition; to be a purist is to preserve the value of the new, the unexpected, and the bizarre. The aesthetic, social, cultural, and political power that such an outlook offers cannot be overestimated, as hip-hop's rapid conquest of the planet clearly shows. The world embraces hip-hop because hip-hop—through the logic of its production—increasingly becomes the world.

Epilogue—20 September 2002

Tomorrow morning I will spell-check this book, print it out, and send the manuscript off to Wesleyan University Press. But tonight I am attending a celebration of the twentieth anniversary of the groundbreaking feature film *Wild Style,* which was filmed primarily in the South Bronx and featured many of hip-hop's earliest practitioners as themselves. The main attraction tonight is to be a showing of a 35-mm print of the film in the Lower East Side amphitheater where the last quarter of the movie takes place. Before the film begins, however, many old school innovators take the stage to warm up the crowd, and almost all note with pride the diversity of the audience.

Prince Whipper Whip of the Fantastic 5, caught up in the moment, begins to list the many neighborhoods, ethnicities, nationalities, cultures, and subcultures that have come together to celebrate hip-hop history: "We're representing Harlem! We're representing the South Bronx! We're representing Puerto Rico! We're representing b-boys and b-girls! We're representing Japan!" He concludes with an exuberant declaration: "We . . . represent . . . *everything!*"

And, indeed, we do.

New Afterword

Looking Back at *Making Beats*

Though I didn't know it at the time, *Making Beats: The Art of Sample-Based Hip-Hop* was written at the end of an era.[1] Even as I completed my research, hip-hop music was being reshaped by the same profound technological and cultural changes that were transforming the rest of America at the turn of the millennium. As a result, the period covered in the book has subsequently come to be viewed as a distinctive and significant stage in the history of hip-hop sampling, the last moment when hip-hop production was still the province of a small, insular community whose traditions were unknown to most outsiders. Ten years later, although the philosophies and practices I discussed in *Making Beats* no longer form the central axis of a cohesive subculture, they still stand as important stylistic and symbolic resources for individual hip-hop producers. In fact, within hip-hop, the producers' subculture of the nineties may actually be more widely appreciated in retrospect than it was in its own time. Moreover, as hip-hop itself has become more central to popular music in general, the underlying principles of sample-based production have made their influence felt far beyond the genre in which they first developed. The relatively obscure approach to musicianship that I described in the book ultimately gave rise to a diverse array of musical styles around the globe. As I predicted in the epilogue, hip-hop did indeed become the world.

As hip-hop has become more accepted, its mythologies have been integrated into the larger canon of pop music culture. But in order to fit this new frame, hip-hop's rough edges have often been sanded down, its contradictions resolved, and its sensibilities reinterpreted from a more mainstream point of view. The emergence of the sample-based hip-hop aesthetic has come to seem as if it were natural and obvious, almost inevitable. It was none of these things, and we forget this at our own peril. Because there was a reason hip-hop was weird and creative, and that reason still lingers in its heart, though it may be increasingly difficult to see.

*   *   *

I have three goals for this new afterword. First, I want to discuss some of the specific changes that have come about in hip-hop production over the decade since *Making Beats* was originally published, and explore the implications of those changes. Second, with the benefit of ten years of hindsight, I want to reevaluate some of the choices I made as to how to actually present the material, in order to provide some perspective on the way I—and others—have framed major issues in hip-hop scholarship. Third, I want to explore the specific value of ethnography to the larger field of hip-hop studies, and share some thoughts on what it may have to offer to future scholars.

Changes

Over the last ten years, hip-hop production has evolved in many ways, most of which are related to larger changes in the relationship between culture and technology in contemporary society. The three most significant developments in sample-based hip-hop have been a shift from hardware- to software-based production methods, increased access to sample sources, and the growing public availability of information about the process of hip-hop production itself.

The shift from hardware to software is not unique to hip-hop (or even to music). We now take it for granted that our smartphones will contain a variety of technologies—such as calculators, cameras, and music players—that until recently would only have existed in the form of separate physical machines. Similarly, the widespread availability of sampling software for personal computers and other digital devices has changed the practice of hip-hop production on technical, aesthetic, and social levels. When a quick search of Apple's "App Store" yields hundreds of free programs that promise to instantly turn any iPad into a fully functional drum machine, it is easy to forget that a sampler was once an obscure, hard-to-find, hard-to-use, and extremely expensive piece of studio equipment. In the original text, I noted that the Akai MPC 2000, the state-of-the-art sampler at that time, had a manufacturer's suggested retail price of $1,649 (Schloss 2004: 30). Akai now offers the downloadable "iMPC" app for the iPad—essentially a digital simulacrum of an MPC sampler—for $6.99.

In retrospect, samplers' rarity and high price may actually have been among their most socially significant qualities. In the eighties and nineties, samplers were costly, highly technical pieces of studio equipment that were not marketed to the general public. Even if you knew what a sampler was and could afford the investment, you still might not know where to actually buy one. Now, sampling software can easily be found with a simple Google search, and even professional-level platforms can be purchased for only a few hundred dollars. In addition to affordability, such software offers increased options for processing and organizing samples, including the ability to work with sounds visually (on a computer screen) rather than auditorily.

At the same time, producers have not rejected hardware samplers altogether. It is common for serious producers to use a kind of hybrid studio arrangement, often consisting of a vintage hardware sampler connected to a modern computer. Notably, these samplers can be as much as twenty years or more out of date (many use floppy discs for data storage, for example), and thus require elaborate technological workarounds in order to communicate effectively with modern software systems. The fact that producers would bother with such a cumbersome arrangement in order to preserve their ability to work with outdated hardware suggests that, while the newer technology has clearly been embraced, the older machines still have something distinctive to offer modern hip-hop producers.

Archaic hardware samplers are valued for several reasons. At the most basic level, simply having the sampler as a physical object is an indicator of authenticity and tradition. In addition, many producers consider their kinetic interactions with the sampler to be an essential part of their creative process. They also often cite the hardware's so-called workflow—the way that its physical layout and procedural organization facilitate the natural development of a producer's ideas—as something that cannot be replicated with software. Moreover, the circuitry and programming of different models of samplers are believed to impart special characteristics to the music (perhaps the best known of these characteristics is the legendary "MPC swing," a rhythmic idiosyncrasy first noted in the Akai MPC 60 sampler, circa 1988). This, in turn, bleeds into a kind of romantic nostalgia for vintage samplers in general—even including their "retro" appearance—that is reminiscent of the symbolic value associated with vintage guitars by rock musicians. Like guitar players, many hip-hop producers have an almost spiritual connection not only to certain models of sampler but also to the individual samplers themselves.

Electronics manufacturers have responded to this trend by developing products that are intended to reproduce this experience via an integrated system that combines software for a PC or Mac with a hardware controller designed to look and feel like a stand-alone sampler. The best known of these products as of this writing is the Native Instruments "Maschine," released in 2009. Akai responded in 2012 with the similar MPC Renaissance, which had the added benefit of being able to leverage Akai's preexisting reputation in the hip-hop production world. Since many of the old-fashioned samplers that these products are intended to imitate were actually designed by Akai in the first place, the company made the most of this advantage, branding its version with the respected "MPC" name and providing a hardware controller whose look and feel were almost indistinguishable from one of the older MPC samplers. In fact, the simulation was so accurate that it was actually criticized in some quarters as being misleading. Virtually all of the reviews I found made a point of noting that, unlike previous models in the MPC line (and contrary to its appearance), the MPC Renaissance could not be used as a freestanding sampler without being attached to a computer. As if to emphasize the idiosyncratic value of old samplers even further, both the Maschine and the Renaissance feature a "Vintage Mode," which allows them to emulate the distinctive characteristics of classic samplers, including the Emu SP 1200 (c. 1987) and the Akai MPC 60 (c. 1988), among others.

When I did the original research for the book, most of the producers I spoke with were adamant about the idea that original—preferably rare—vinyl records were the only legitimate source for sampling. This was true for several reasons: First, most of the music that people wanted to sample was only available on vinyl. Second, the practice of locating rare vinyl to sample was seen as an important part of the hip-hop production process in itself. "Digging in the crates"[2] for used records was not only a practical necessity but also an educational opportunity, a rite of passage and a form of socialization. And since most producers were also deejays, the records could do double duty as sampling material and material for deejay sets, thus increasing the aesthetic cross-pollination between those two pursuits. All of these conditions have changed substantially in the intervening years.

First of all, the range of what is considered appropriate to sample has broadened notably, and much of the material sampled today was never available on vinyl to begin with, if only because the original music was released in the compact disc era. Faced with the prospect of declaring a growing body of music permanently off-limits, hip-hop producers opted to change the rules. Secondly, even when one searches for vinyl— which many still do—the wide availability of information about records on the Internet has altered the digging experience considerably. On a practical level, this has changed record shopping in much the same way as it has changed all shopping. It has made it easier for buyers and sellers to connect with each other, and thus diminished the relative benefits of searching for things in the physical world. If you are looking for something rare, you are simply more likely to find it on the Internet than in any given physical location. It has also changed the experience on a more indirect level, by allowing sellers greater access to pricing information. Before the rise of the Internet, there was a general sense that the monetary value of a record was linked to its cultural value, and that this cultural value was defined by a more-or-less universally recognized set of standards. This worked to the advantage of hip-hop producers, since they were operating according to a totally different set of cultural expectations. The most valuable records to hip-hop producers were often considered worthless by mainstream listeners and critics, and were priced accordingly. Any hip-hop producer who was willing to put effort into record shopping could thus expect to regularly find astounding bargains. In the modern era, record sellers need only Google the name of a record to see what it is currently selling for. They do not need to know why.

These factors, combined with the rise of downloadable digital files, have also served to diminish the overall symbolic capital associated with developing an extensive record collection. In the nineties, virtually the only way one could have a song available to sample was to physically own the record, and the only way to own the record was to have done the work to find it. Every sample used in a hip-hop song was thus implicitly a demonstration of the producer's connoisseurship and effort. Tools that undercut this principle—such as compilations—were largely rejected on that basis. In fact, as I discussed in the book, producers developed an entire system of ethics to maintain a level playing field in that regard. Now, by contrast, most songs are easily available online in digital form, and even if one wants to find the original vinyl record, that can also usually be accomplished online with a small amount of research.

Theoretically, the community could have maintained its ethical system in spite of these developments, but for the most part it did not. I'm not sure there is any single explanation for this change, but my sense is that the opportunity costs of maintaining the system became too great. As the Internet offered increasingly simple methods for acquiring rare music—often for free—producers began to see it as foolish to deny themselves such easy access to music they loved just for the sake of maintaining a philosophical principle. This was especially true for a younger generation of producers who had been raised in the Internet era, and had already come to rely on those tools before they became producers in the first place. It is one thing to expect someone to maintain their devotion to an existing vinyl record collection; it is another to expect them to throw away music they already have, simply because it is not on vinyl. While it's true that many producers do still hold themselves to the old rules, such a position is now seen more as an individual choice than a collective principle.

Finally, the connection between deejaying and hip-hop production is no longer as intimate as it once was. At the time of my research, virtually all hip-hop producers had started out as deejays, and most considered sample-based production to be a natural evolution of that process. Now, as a result of the technological changes I just discussed, it is much easier to move directly into hip-hop production without being a deejay first.[3] At the same time, deejaying itself has changed. The vast majority of professional deejays now use digital sound files rather than vinyl records as source material, which has also served to divorce the experience of hip-hop music making from that of collecting records.[4]

In the original book, I noted that record shopping, as an activity, also had many social and cultural functions, including reinforcing producers' commitment to the idea of hip-hop tradition itself, "paying dues" in order to be taken seriously by other members of the community, musical education, and just as a way of socializing with other producers. All these things still apply, but they are now optional, simply because one no longer needs to be a member of the "hip-hop producers community" to be a hip-hop producer. Activities that reinforce the idea of community are therefore less essential to the process of hip-hop production.

It may be hard to imagine now, but at the time I wrote the original book, virtually all significant hip-hop producers knew each other personally. Though it is true that some people have worked to maintain that sense of community in the years since, it is no longer necessary to participate in it to be a hip-hop producer. Information about the history and technique of hip-hop production that was once only transmitted personally from teacher to student is now easily available in many forms on the Internet. And since there is no longer a common lineage, there is no longer a common body of knowledge that is inculcated in beginning hip-hop producers. The relative benefits or liabilities associated with this social, intellectual, and conceptual fragmentation are difficult to judge objectively. The simple fact is that many people who did not previously have access to knowledge about sampling now do. While to some that may represent the breakdown of a beloved artistic community, to others it represents increased openness and diversity.[5]

Choices

Of all the decisions I made when compiling the book, the one that seems to have been the most surprising to readers was that I devoted very little space to the legal issues associated with sampling. There were three major reasons for this. The first was simply that I felt the topic had already received an outsized amount of attention relative to its significance to producers at that time. The second was that, precisely because the legal questions were so central to most other discussions of sampling at that time, I felt that if I were to make them a centerpiece of my own discussion, their very presence would naturally tend to distort the subjects I was trying to address by implicitly framing them according to the terms set by those other conversations. And the third was that it was essentially impossible to research the issue ethnographically without putting my consultants at legal risk. I still think I made the right choice, but I also understand why readers may have wished for more explicit discussion of the subject. Luckily, Kembrew McLeod and Peter DiCola's *Creative License* (2011) has subsequently done a wonderful job of covering the relevant arguments for those who are interested, so I would direct readers to that work as a companion to the current one.

My reticence on the subject doesn't mean I actually disagreed with the arguments that others were making, however, and it was certainly never my intention to minimize the many significant legal issues associated with sampling. Over the last decade, as hip-hop-influenced music has become more central to popular music overall, it has become increasingly apparent that current laws regarding sampling are wildly out of step with reality. My feeling is that the problem is basically an ideological one. Although our society's concept of intellectual property is clearly the result of cultural, economic, and social forces that are specific to this particular historical moment, we are expected to treat it as if it were a timeless and unchanging reality. But the truth is that "intellectual property" is only a metaphor; samples are simply not the same as physical property. There are some ways in which the two categories are similar, and some ways in which they are not. But the complexities and contradictions of that analogy must be addressed before any reasonable discussion of sampling law can even be attempted. Unfortunately, this rarely happens. More commonly, America's current definition of intellectual property is simply accepted as a given before the discussion even begins. But to accept that definition is to place the forces that produced it outside the scope of the argument, and thus tacitly reinforce their legitimacy. In its own approach to sampling, hip-hop has refused to do that, and it is no accident. Hip-hop is an art that questions its own frame. And those questions, though often subtle, can be extremely powerful.

In retrospect, this concept—the way social critiques may be embedded in the musical processes themselves—was actually one of the main themes of *Making Beats*. Seen in that light, my decision to focus on the aesthetic and ethical questions that hip-hop producers were debating at that time had a very clear political intention. It was part of a larger reflex-ivist attempt on my part to allow my ethnographic experience to frame my inquiries, as a way of challenging my own assumptions about what is—or should be—interesting to scholars about hip-hop. I will discuss this as a more general proposition shortly, but I think it had specific im-plications with regard to the way I treated issues of gender and race.

Since hip-hop scholarship in general has tended to see hip-hop through the lens of mass media and popular culture, it is not surprising that its gender scholarship would tend to reflect this orientation, often centering on analyses of media imagery. This has left a space for the study of gender in other hip-hop contexts, especially those in which gen-der roles are negotiated in face-to-face social interactions. Ethnography in particular provides an opportunity to reflect upon these negotiations, because it foregrounds the way gender is lived as much as the way gen-der is conceptualized, so the relationship between the two is immedi-ately apparent.[6] Though I did not emphasize it in the original text, I have always considered this tension to be an important aspect of the processes I was describing.[7] I was especially interested in how the role of the producer might reflect a much more complex understanding of mas-culinity than hip-hop is generally given credit for. The qualities that make for a good hip-hop producer may be quite different from the quali-ties that make a good rapper, yet both are still considered to be quintes-sentially masculine roles. Of course that has its own implications, but I believe the fact that hip-hop has made space for both—and the way it has done so—is not insignificant.

Similarly, my approach to race was an attempt to turn the lens back on the scholarly discourse itself, to push myself to consider the racial politics of *the way we talk about racial politics* in hip-hop. After all, one of the primary goals of hip-hop's pioneers was to liberate themselves from the ideological frames imposed upon them by mainstream culture, and this very much includes the frames imposed upon them by the institu-tional culture of academia. To be more specific, the notion that hip-hop should be interpreted primarily in terms of its racial politics *is itself polit-ical*, and not always in a way that is beneficial to hip-hop or to the com-munities that produce it. I did my best to maintain an awareness of that fact throughout the book, and let it inform my decisions as appropriate. Perhaps the most fundamental way that this influenced my analysis was that I took the basic legitimacy of hip-hop culture as a given, rather than preemptively trying to prove it to those who might disagree. In other words, my intent in focusing on the details of the hip-hop producers' culture was not so much to overturn specific stereotypes of hip-hop or the communities from which it emerged as it was to broaden the discourse in such a way that the *idea* of stereotyping wouldn't make sense in the first place. So, for example, the goal of writing in a detailed way about the complex ethical discourses that producers maintained around sampling was not to win a debate about whether or not hip-hop was made by amoral musical thieves. It was to show that the debate itself was ridiculous and irrelevant.

Ethnography

This book was one of the first ethnographic studies of hip-hop culture. Ten years later, although studies that utilize participant observation still constitute a minority of hip-hop scholarship overall, they represent an increasingly significant voice within hip-hop studies.[8] In fact, there is now a substantial enough body of ethnographic hip-hop scholarship that it can actually be subdivided into three general categories.[9]

The first category consists of relatively traditional ethnographies that draw on the theories and research methods of anthropology and qualitative sociology. The communities that these works portray are usually associated with a specific geographical location (often outside the United States) and also tend to be defined by specific cultural commonalities other than hip-hop itself (often ethnicity). On a practical level, the researchers are usually working within a well-defined physical field site in which a series of larger cultural intersections are taking place. These intersections are then understood and negotiated by community members through hip-hop culture. Some prominent examples of this approach include Ian Condry's *Hip-Hop Japan* (2006), Ali Colleen Neff's *Let the World Listen Right* (2009), Anthony Kwame Harrison's *Hip-Hop Underground* (2009), Marcyliena Morgan's *The Real Hiphop* (2009), Nitasha Sharma's *Hip-Hop Desis* (2010), and Sujatha Fernandes's *Close to the Edge* (2011).[10]

The second category of ethnographic hip-hop studies—which includes my own work—blends the social science methodologies of the previous group with analyses drawn from the humanities, generally from fields associated with the particular expressive form they are studying (e.g., musicology, ethnomusicology, art history, dance history, literature).[11] These works often combine a deep interest in the aesthetics and techniques articulated by the artists themselves with a desire to locate the artists' choices within a broader social, cultural, economic, or historical context. The subject of these studies is usually a specific practice within hip-hop, such as deejaying or dance. Though these works do not necessarily present a traditional anthropological field site per se, practitioners of particular art forms often do organize themselves into what Bennett and Peterson (2004) have characterized as "translocal" communities based on their common interests. Although such communities tend to be less geographically specific than those of the first category, that very fact makes them particularly useful for studying the idea of community itself from a poststructuralist perspective. Aside from this book and my second book, *Foundation: B-Boys, B-Girls and Hip-Hop Culture in New York* (2009), well-known works in this category include Craig Castleman's *Getting Up* (1982), Ivor L. Miller's *Aerosol Kingdom* (2002), Felicia Miyakawa's *Five Percenter Rap* (2005), Kyra Gaunt's *The Games Black Girls Play* (2006), Gregory Snyder's *Graffiti Lives* (2009), and Mark Katz's *Groove Music* (2012).

The final category includes studies of hip-hop's influence on education and social development, usually from a sociological or educational studies perspective. This research, quite naturally, tends to be of a more practical or prescriptive bent, and tends to engage less frequently with the kinds of anthropological questions raised by the first two categories. For me, these works are useful precisely because they are so practical and detail-oriented. Prominent examples of this type of study include Greg Dimitriadis's *Performing Identity/Performing Culture* (2001), H. Samy Alim's *Roc the Mic Right* (2006), Marc Lamont Hill's *Beats, Rhymes, and Classroom Life* (2009), Michael Jeffries's *Thug Life* (2011), Emery Petchauer's *Hip-Hop Culture in College Students' Lives* (2012), Andreana Clay's *The Hip-Hop Generation Fights Back* (2012), and Bettina Love's *Hip Hop's Li'l Sistas Speak* (2012).

What all of these studies hold in common is that the researchers must develop and articulate a personal relationship to the communities they study as an integral part of the work itself. This offers many advantages for the study of hip-hop culture, but I would like to take a moment here to highlight three specific areas where I think the benefits are particularly noteworthy.

The first is that, by being in the community, ethnographic researchers have access to the community's internal discourses, and particularly to its internal scholarship. Generally speaking, this scholarship consists primarily of a combination of memoir and historical research that is produced by hip-hop practitioners seeking to deepen their understanding of their own art. Much of it is unpublished, self-published, or published by very small independent presses, and is informally publicized and distributed within the community or on the Internet. Books that fall into this category include Amir Said's *The Beat Tips Manual* (2002), Mabusha "Push" Cooper's *Push Hip Hop History, Volume 1: The Brooklyn Scene* (2003), Martha Cooper's *Hip-Hop Files* (2004), Adisa Banjoko's *Lyrical Swords*, volumes I and II (2004 and 2009, respectively), Julius Cavero's *The Nasty Terrible T-KID 170* (2005), Vincent Fedorchak's *FUZZ ONE: A Bronx Childhood* (2005), Johan Kugelberg and Joe Conzo's *Born in the Bronx* (2007), Ivan Sanchez and Luis Cedeno's *It's Just Begun* (2009), Alien Ness's *Art of Battle* (2009) (for which I wrote the introduction), Luis De Jesus's *The Kings of Dance: The History of Bronx Rock* (2013), and Christian P. Acker's *Flip the Script* (2013). Other works of independent scholarship include a virtually infinite number of short documentaries available on YouTube and many websites devoted to specific aspects of hip-hop history and practice. Finally, there is a substantial oral tradition within hip-hop, particularly with regard to history and aesthetics. This scholarship is increasingly found in the form of "panels"—usually roundtables featuring historically significant figures—that are organized as part of b-boy battles, graffiti exhibitions, and other nonacademic hip-hop events. And of course some of this information is embodied in the art itself. To be sure, this research often has a different agenda from that of academic scholarship, and certainly operates according to different standards (which, in some ways, are actually more stringent), but it remains a valuable source of insight for those who engage with it. More importantly, the very act of engaging with this scholarly discourse can itself be part of the ethnographic experience. Understanding the parameters and goals of these discussions is an important way to gain insight into the individual and collective agendas at work in the community.

A related benefit of ethnography is that it is particularly well suited to studying the way hip-hop functions as a cultural tradition. A common thread throughout all my work has been the idea that hip-hop is "traditional" in two different senses. It represents the reintegration of deep cultural practices drawn from throughout the African Diaspora, and it has also developed its own internal sense of tradition over the four decades of its existence. Though both of these ideas are accepted in principle by most hip-hop researchers, they are rarely studied in detail. As a result, conclusions that are drawn in these areas are often unnecessarily speculative.[12] But both can be more effectively studied via ethnography. This is mainly because the traditional aspects of hip-hop tend to be expressed in the context of mentor relationships centered on specific practices, so the information is more available to people who participate in those practices. If one is studying hip-hop primarily through the interpretation of music videos or recordings, by contrast, the traditional aspects—even of those endeavors—may simply be rendered invisible. This also has larger theoretical implications, in that any theoretical material we develop will naturally reflect our level of consciousness about these concerns. If we do not engage these questions, then we will not develop bodies of theory to address them.

A third notable advantage of an ethnographic approach is that the author's relationships with individuals in the community constitute the actual mechanism of research, so the social, political, and cultural tenor of those relationships is made apparent in the research, and thus available for criticism. This provides opportunities for self-reflection that are largely absent in other forms of hip-hop scholarship.[13] To take one example from my own experience: In researching hip-hop dance for my second book, I was surprised to hear many early b-boys make reference to the Hollywood musical *West Side Story*. But why was I surprised? *West Side Story* was one of the only films of its era to make any attempt at all to sympathetically reflect the experience of young Puerto Rican gang members in New York. If I had assumed that such a film would not have been of interest to hip-hop pioneers (many of whom were themselves young Puerto Rican gang members interested in music or dance), that assumption says more about me than it does about them. More to the point, I was not even aware that I was making an assumption in the first place until I had these conversations. When our experiences contradict our expectations, it provides a valuable opportunity to interrogate our own biases. But that can only happen if you actually have experiences. If we are going to ascribe significance to other people's lives, we should at least be interpreting their actual lives, not imagined lives built from our own preconceptions. Considering that hip-hop was specifically created to give a voice to the voiceless, it is particularly problematic for hip-hop scholarship to brush aside the complexity and contradictions of these individual perspectives in our rush to make grand statements.

It is also important to remember that our assumptions aren't random; in fact, they are often part of the precise culture that hip-hop was designed to critique. As such, they are shaped by a wide variety of ideologies about art, culture, race, class, gender, sexuality, economics, and many other factors. Attempting to disentangle ourselves from such biases is part of all hip-hop scholarship of course, but it is especially central to ethnographic research, since the researcher's identity—and thus his or her personal relationship to such ideologies—is so central to the process itself.

One of the stranger aspects of writing a book that challenges the conventional wisdom of your field—as I believe *Making Beats* did—is that if your perspective eventually becomes accepted, its very success tends to obscure the contribution that it made. The last ten years have seen an explosion of ethnographic research in popular music, and the idea that one should need to explain the idea of living in the same social world as one's consultants, as I did, now seems almost quaint. In fact, much of the methodological discussion in the original book is devoted to explaining ideas that in retrospect seem like they should not require explanation: Poverty cannot be directly transformed into art without creativity on someone's part. All members of a culture do not necessarily share the same goals and agendas. A good way to find out what someone is thinking is to ask them what they are thinking. All of these were arguments that I made in the original book, and all of them now seem so obvious as to be absurd. But at the time, these basic ethnographic ideas really did need to be expressed, which I think is a good indication of how marginal ethnographic approaches were to hip-hop studies in those days. Conversely, the fact that these ideas now seem self-evident indicates that that is no longer the case. We have clearly moved into a new era of hip-hop scholarship.

Journalistic histories like Jeff Chang's *Can't Stop Won't Stop* and Dan Charnas's *The Big Payback* have established the general historical facts of hip-hop as both a cultural practice and a form of popular music. Academic works, including those I mentioned earlier and many others, have sketched out the general theoretical questions that define the field. Research is increasingly being done by scholars who have a preexisting personal commitment to hip-hop culture. Our task now is to build on this foundation, through a careful combination of research and self-critique. Our politics needs to become more subtle, more nuanced, and more intersectional. Our methodologies and theoretical orientations need to become more diverse. We need more studies of counternarratives *within* hip-hop.

In our understandable quest for credible sources, we have sometimes created a kind of king-of-the-hill situation where only the most "authentic" voices are to be trusted, without looking at how our concept of authenticity was constructed in the first place. There are virtually unlimited perspectives that one could take on even a single event in hip-hop history, and that needs to be encouraged, not thrown aside in a quest to establish a standard story. As I suggested before, we need *more* contradictions and rough edges, not fewer. We need more studies of hip-hop in specific times, in specific places, in specific communities, from specific points of view. We need more studies of specific aspects of hip-hop; not just the elements, but also the way those elements are practiced in different social and cultural environments. We need more discussion of the way artistic choices are being made in different contexts—especially musical choices—and what's at stake when those choices are made. In an ever-increasing range of settings, it is important to talk about what hip-hop *is* before we talk about what hip-hop *means*. When we focus on such things—the particulars of hip-hop culture and the aesthetic principles they reflect—we may seem to be neglecting the bigger social or economic picture. But it is those very details that can help us to see the bigger picture in a new way. In fact, that's why they are there.

For me, one of the clearest examples of this occurred when I invited Alien Ness (president of the Mighty Zulu Kings, the b-boy division of the Universal Zulu Nation) to speak to one of my classes. A student asked him if he could describe the hip-hop aesthetic in one word. "I can do it in *no* words," he replied, and proceeded to silently jump up and wave his arms in imitation of a person desperately hoping to be acknowledged, a person using every tool at his disposal to avoid being forgotten and abandoned. That was a very real danger in the South Bronx in the seventies, and for many people around the world it still is.

That's why hip-hop was weird and creative: because it was made by people whose lives depended on being noticed. Hip-hop's idiosyncrasies were designed to represent the spirit and intelligence and individuality of its many creators, in a world that would have preferred to ignore them. So when we focus on the seemingly minor artistic and practical choices that go into hip-hop production—or any other aspect of the culture—we are not minimizing hip-hop's social or political significance. We are celebrating its humanity. And that may be the most liberating position that a scholar could take.

> Joseph Schloss
> Brooklyn, NY
> January 12, 2014

Notes

1. I would like to thank the following people for their insights and feedback on the issues I discuss here: Alien Ness, Shaheen Ariefdien, Laylah Amatullah Barrayn, Regina Bradley, Jalylah Burrell, Raquel Cepeda, Jeff Chang, Michael Dorfman, Kyra Gaunt, Carolina Gonzales, Karl Haas, Anthony Kwame Harrison, Tim Hughes, David J. Leonard, Arthur Lewin, Adam Mansbach, Moe Mitchell, Mark Anthony Neal, Ali Colleen Neff, Dan Tres Omi, MiRi Park, Emery Petchauer, Guthrie Ramsey, Peaches Rodriguez, Gabriel Solis, Trac 2, Cristina Veran, and Oliver Wang.

2. Over the last ten years, the phrase "digging in the crates" has become so overused that I now virtually cringe every time I see it in this text. At the time, however, the phrase was really only known among insiders to the hip-hop production community. In fact, I would argue that the phrase's journey to becoming a cliché is itself evidence of hip-hop's ever-widening cultural influence.

3. While many of the people I interviewed no longer make beats professionally, many of them still make all or part of their living as deejays. Mr. Supreme—now using the name Supreme LaRock—in particular remains a sought-after international deejay. And virtually all of them still keep up on

the latest technology and continue to produce music as a hobby. In terms of production specifically, by far the biggest subsequent success story among the individuals interviewed for this book has been Jake One. When I interviewed him for *Making Beats*, he was a young producer who by his own admission "thought about this stuff way too much," as evidenced by my extensive quoting of him in the book. But over the last decade, he has become one of the most well-respected producers in hip-hop, having released four full-length solo or collaborative albums, numerous mix tapes, and hundreds of songs for a diverse list of clients including 50 Cent, Rick Ross, Brother Ali, and Snoop Dogg. In 2013, he was nominated for two Grammy Awards, one for Record of the Year for his production work on the album *Some Nights* by Fun., and the other for Best Rap Album, for his work on Rick Ross's album *God Forgives, I Don't*.

4. Many deejays split the difference by creating these sound files through the digitization of vinyl records that they own. See Katz 2012 (pp. 220–226) for an excellent discussion of the influence of digital media on hip-hop deejaying.

5. One of the great ironies of this new openness is that the intellectual and material tools of hip-hop production are actually far more accessible to working-class urban youth *now* than they were when the music was viewed as an exclusively inner-city pursuit. This can—and should—complicate our increasingly standardized narratives of what it means to be an insider or outsider to hip-hop. Thanks to Emery Petchauer for his insights on this point (p.c. 7/21/13).

6. It can also be useful in addressing the meta-issue of how these questions are framed discursively. For example, we often begin our inquiries by designating the areas of hip-hop associated with men as being the most significant, and then asking why women aren't better represented in those roles. Roles that are more frequently associated with women, such as publicists, personal managers, and magazine editors, often go unexamined, in spite of the fact that without them the entire hip-hop industry would have ground to a halt long ago.

7. Kyra Gaunt's *The Games Black Girls Play* (2006) provides a wonderful template for what this type of scholarship has to offer. Much of my own approach to these issues was profoundly shaped by conversations I had with her over the course of writing the book.

8. Forman and Neal's *That's the Joint!* (Routledge, 2012) is the preeminent anthology of hip-hop scholarship and is an excellent representation of the

current shape of the field. By my admittedly subjective criteria (which exclude interview-based journalism but include ethnographic works by self-trained researchers), eight of the forty-four readings (18 percent) are works of ethnography. That percentage is consistent with my own sense of the role that ethnography plays in contemporary hip-hop studies.

9. These categories remain surprisingly consistent regardless of whether one attempts to group studies by disciplinary/theoretical orientation or subject area. I think this is simply because people tend to choose methodologies that are appropriate to what they want to study (or vice versa).

10. These lists are intended to give a general sense of the range of works in the field. They are in no way meant to be comprehensive.

11. Of course the modern theoretical orientations of many of these fields often bridge this gap within themselves.

12. Just to take one example: based on observable similarities between the two practices, scholars sometimes hypothesize that b-boying (widely, though wrongly, known as "breakdancing") might be derived from Brazilian capoeira. Most b-boys and b-girls, however, reject this claim on the strength of a relatively straightforward argument: no hip-hop dancers from that era recall being influenced by capoeira. Moreover, Jelon Vieira, the first person known to have taught capoeira in New York City, didn't arrive there until 1975, by which point b-boying had already existed for several years. Therefore, unless scholars can document a previously unknown line of transmission from a specific capoeira practitioner to a specific b-boy or b-girl that challenges this timetable, the default assumption must be that there was not a direct influence. It is significant that the b-boys' analysis is defined in terms that are far more precise—and thus more researchable—than that of the academics. This is largely because it is designed to serve a different goal: the b-boys are primarily interested in giving credit where credit is due, while the scholars are more interested in broader cultural continuities. For more discussion of the implications of this distinction, see Schloss 2009 (pp. 125–54).

13. On a more basic level, it can also go a long way toward ensuring a work's accuracy. My relationships in the hip-hop community allowed me to share this book with people who were in a position to critique it before it was published, including—but not limited to—the people whom I had interviewed. In fact, I actually offered my consultants the opportunity to directly respond within the text to anything they disagreed with. As it turned out, this never became necessary, since I always either took their criticism to heart,

and corrected what I had written, or integrated the disagreement itself back into my larger argument. Regardless, the result of this approach was that, to the best of my knowledge, the book contains only one significant factual error: I failed to give the proper credit to "Breakbeat Lou" Flores for his role in compiling the Ultimate Breaks and Beats record series with Lenny Roberts. My apologies to him for the oversight.

Sources Cited

Acker, Christian P. 2013. *Flip the Script*. Gingko Press in association with Upper Playground.

Alien Ness. 2009. *The Art of Battle*. New York: Self-published.

Alim, H. Samy. 2006. *Roc the Mic Right*. New York: Routledge.

Banjoko, Adisa. 2004. *Lyrical Swords, Vol. I*. YinSumi Press.

———. 2009. *Lyrical Swords, Vol. II*. YinSumi Press.

Bennett, Andy, and Richard A. Peterson, eds. 2004. *Music Scenes*. Nashville: Vanderbilt University Press.

Castleman, Craig. 1982. *Getting Up: Subway Graffiti in New York*. Cambridge, Mass.: MIT Press.

Cavero, Julius. 2009. *The Nasty Terrible T-KID 170*. New York: From Here to Fame.

Clay, Andreana. 2012. *The Hip-Hop Generation Fights Back*. New York: New York University Press.

Condry, Ian. 2006. *Hip-Hop Japan*. Durham, N.C.: Duke University Press.

Cooper, Mabusha "Push." 2003. *Push Hip Hop History, Volume 1: The Brooklyn Scene*. 1st Books Library.

Cooper, Martha. 2004. *Hip-Hop Files*. Cologne, Germany: From Here to Fame.

De Jesus, Luis. 2013. *The Kings of Dance: The History of Bronx Rock*. Wake Up Write Publishing Company.

Dimitriadis, Greg. 2001. *Performing Identity/Performing Culture*. New York: Peter Lang Publishing.

Fedorchak, Vincent. 2005. *FUZZ ONE: A Bronx Childhood*. New York: Testify Books.

Fernandes, Sujatha. 2011. *Close to the Edge*. New York: Verso.

Forman, Murray, and Mark Anthony Neal. 2012. *That's the Joint!* 2nd ed. New York: Routledge. 2012.

Gaunt, Kyra. 2009. *The Games Black Girls Play*. New York: New York University Press.

Harrison, Anthony Kwame. 2009. *Hip-Hop Underground*. Philadelphia: Temple University Press.

Hill, Marc Lamont. 2009. *Beats, Rhymes, and Classroom Life*. New York: Teachers College Press.

Jeffries, Michael. 2011. *Thug Life*. Chicago: University of Chicago Press.

Katz, Mark. 2012. *Groove Music*. New York: Oxford University Press.

Kugelberg, Johan, and Joe Conzo. 2007. *Born in the Bronx*. New York: Rizzoli International Publications, Inc.

Love, Bettina. 2012. *Hip Hop's Li'l Sistas Speak*. New York: Peter Lang Publishing.

McLeod, Kembrew, and Peter DiCola. 2011. *Creative License*. Durham, N.C.: Duke University Press.

Miller, Ivor L. 2002. *Aerosol Kingdom*. Jackson, MS: University Press of Mississippi.

Miyakawa, Felicia. 2005. *Five Percenter Rap*. Bloomington: Indiana University Press.

Morgan, Marcyliena. 2009. *The Real Hiphop*. Durham, N.C.: Duke University Press.

Neff, Ali Colleen. 2009. *Let the World Listen Right*. Jackson: University Press of Mississippi. 2009.

Petchauer, Emery. 2012. *Hip-Hop Culture in College Students' Lives*. New York: Routledge.

Said, Amir. 2002. *The Beat Tips Manual*. Superchamp Books.

Sanchez, Ivan, and Luis Cedeno. 2009. *It's Just Begun*. New York: Miss Rosen Editions.

Schloss, Joseph. 2004. *Making Beats: The Art of Sample-Based Hip-Hop*. Middletown, CT: Wesleyan University Press.

———. 2009. *Foundation: B-Boys, B-Girls and Hip-Hop Culture in New York*. New York: Oxford University Press.

Sharma, Nitasha. 2010. *Hip-Hop Desis*. Durham, N.C.: Duke University Press.

Snyder, Gregory. 2009. *Graffiti Lives*. New York: New York University Press.

Endnotes

Chapter 1: Introduction

1. As a result, while there are still many deejays who do not produce, virtually all producers deejay.

2. The extent to which this process has influenced this work is easy to overlook but was brought home to me by the following recent experience: A friend of mine introduced me to the legendary producer Steinski in a club in New York. It seemed like a very local and unremarkable phenomenon until I mentally traced the chain of social interactions that had led me to that moment. The friend who introduced us was Jeff Chang, aka DJ Zen (who lives in the San Franciso Bay Area), whom I had met through Lizz Mendez-Berry (who lives in New York), whom I had met through Oliver Wang, aka DJ O-Dub (who also lives in the Bay Area), whom I had met through S. K. Honda (who lives in New York), who was one of the editors in the mid-nineties of Seattle's *Flavor* magazine, which I had begun to write for after meeting Strath Shepard, another editor and cofounder of Seattle-based Conception Records, at a Seattle book signing for Chicago-based author William "Upski" Wimsatt's book, *Bomb the Suburbs*.

3. The relationship between genre and production technique in hip-hop has often been overlooked. Mainstream journalists, for example, spent several years in the early 1990s trying to define "gangsta rap" by its lyrical content, inevitably settling on a definition that was either too narrow (music that contains references to specific gang activities or sets) or too broad (music that contains violent lyrics of any kind). For its listeners, however, "gangsta rap" —to the extent that it existed at all—was defined by the relationship between the lyrics and two other characteristics: its heavy reliance on synthesizers and the vocal delivery, or "flow," of its MCs. See Krims 2000 for an excellent analysis of how these factors define genre in hip-hop.

4. In addition, there continue to emerge sample-based genres—such as drum and bass—that are not considered hip-hop, either by their own practitioners or by those who consider themselves to be bearers of a hip-hop aesthetic. These genres will not be addressed here.

5. While the relevance of such definitional issues to the specific act of performing fieldwork in one's native environment has been apparent since at least the early 1970s, a cohesive body of literature has not developed (or, at least, I have not been able to find it). This is largely due to the simultaneously specific and abstract nature of the issues that arise. While there have been several notable anthologies concerning the nature of fieldwork itself that have touched on such questions (Okely and Callaway 1992, Fowler and Hardesty 1994, Barz and Cooley 1997), most of the work that has been done can be found in the introductions to a wildly diverse group of doctoral dissertations. As a result, those who wish to address these issues have little easily available material to draw on aside from their own intuition and practical experience. Fortunately, both of these sources have much to offer the researcher who wishes to use them.

6. By my observation, a slight majority of my consultants are African American. The rest are white, Latino, and Asian.

7. Many of the most prominent innovators of contemporary experimental deejaying (or "turntablism") are Filipino American. GrandWizzard Theodore, who is African American, is credited with the invention of "scratching," or creating percussive sounds with records.

8. In fact, in some—though not most—cases, producers actually articulated their educational lineage to me. More commonly, it was older producers who cited the younger producers whom they had taught.

9. Although three of my consultants did make brief pejorative references to "suburban kids," which I took to be a euphemism for "white kids."

10. Upon reading this section, Kyra Gaunt rather astutely asked me if all of my consultants who used African American English were in fact African American (Gaunt, conversation with author, 20 August 2002). They were not. Clearly this is a phenomenon that is far too complex to address here, but which—I believe—is intimately related to the influence of hip-hop culture on American culture generally. At the very least, it supports the idea that hip-hop producers, regardless of race, are committed (in some deep way) to an African American cultural outlook.

11. Though both deal with the relationship of European American writers to African American culture, their analyses are, in many regards, more broadly applicable.

12. As Serlin is focusing on explicitly educational television, he does not emphasize *Fat Albert and the Cosby Kids,* but this was certainly an influence

as well. The animated show, which debuted in the early 1970s, featured musical numbers influenced by Sly Stone and Funkadelic at the end of each episode, which were designed to emphasize the lessons that had been learned from that week's adventure. The show's motto, which often comes to mind when I'm feeling idealistic about hip-hop, was delivered by Bill Cosby in proto-rap style over a break in the opening theme: "It's Bill Cosby comin' at ya with music and fun / and if you're not careful, you may learn something before it's done / So let's get ready, OK? / Hey, Hey, Hey!"

13. In 1956, Bill Buchanan and Dickie Goodman released "The Flying Saucer," a novelty record that consisted of a "reporter" asking questions that were answered with snippets from popular songs of the day. It was a hit, and it was soon followed by two similarly named sequels. Goodman continued to create such records until his death in the 1980s and is listed in the Guinness Book of World Records as the most successful novelty artist of all time (www.dickiegoodman.com, cited 24 August 2002).

14. Gaunt's more recent work is more explicitly ethnomusicological, but it does not directly address hip-hop sampling.

15. And to that end, it is worth noting that instrumental hip-hop (i.e., music without rapping) is so widespread that it virtually constitutes a genre unto itself. By contrast, I have *never* heard an album that consisted of rapping without music.

16. This formulation also requires that all who are creative are ethical, which may seem odd at first. But the reason for this is that the ethics are required for admission to the community in which creativity is judged. Unethical people may be creative, but they are not creative *as sample-based hip-hop producers.*

17. Because I am interested in hip-hop production, this model represents a perspective that is intentionally "producer-centric." Others in the hip-hop community would be unlikely to put producers at the center of their philosophical worlds.

18. The first is "What's the difference between rap and hip-hop?"

Chapter 2: History

1. The SP-12 and its more expensive sister, the SP-1200, were the samplers of choice for such hip-hop innovators as Marley Marl, Public Enemy, and Ced G of the Ultramagnetic MCs.

2. It is also worth noting that the predominance of generational conflict,

class determinism, and cultural determinism as explanations for hip-hop's development are not always misunderstandings on the part of scholars; in many cases, hip-hop participants actively promote these myths about themselves.

3. The term "stabs," usually expressed as "guitar stabs" or "horn stabs," is an evocative one. It suggests quick, knifelike, intense sounds that puncture the surface texture of the music before quickly receding.

4. Although finding rare records is highly valued, it is significant that one of the highest compliments a producer can give to another is to credit him with the discovery of a break that no one else had noticed in a *common* record.

5. Of course, shortly after I wrote this, Missy Elliott used this break on her single "Work It" (2002). The manner in which it is deployed (a few bars at the end of the song), however, suggests that it is being used as a tribute to the early days of hip-hop.

6. "Synthetic Substitution," by Melvin Bliss, a song that was officially released only as the b-side of a rare 45 rpm single in 1973 (Mason 2002: 48), but which appears on *Ultimate Breaks and Beats, Volume 5*, which was released in 1986. Although I have not been able to independently verify this, several people have told me that there are a number of hip-hop songs from the late eighties whose samples can all be traced to a single volume of the *Ultimate Breaks and Beats* series. This adds another level of mediation to the interpretive process. Even someone who recognized the original songs from which the samples were taken still might not be aware of the relationship that they shared with each other by appearing on the same underground compilation.

7. As I discuss later in this chapter, these techniques can, in theory, be reproduced by deejays through the use of multitrack recording and overdubbing. But aside from being incredibly arduous, such techniques are so far removed from live deejaying practices that it probably would not have even occurred to anyone to attempt them before digital sampling arose.

8. I would compare this to the bond that exists between aficionados of lesser-known but highly respected jazz musicians, such as Eric Dolphy.

9. This is to some degree circular in that it assumes that producers should want to do this in the first place.

10. In my experience, this term is always used generically in a manner analogous to the way jazz musicians refer to "the woodshed," a practice space defined by its function. There is never a specific "lab"; the term refers to any space in which studio work is undertaken.

II. It's also worth noting that although he is best known as a producer, he still calls himself "DJ" Kool Akiem. This is true for many producers (e.g., DJ Quik, DJ Premier). In fact, DJ Premier is probably the single most-respected producer in hip-hop, but he's not called "Producer Premier." More to the point, the phrase "Producer Premier" sounds strange to the hip-hop trained ear. Which is another way of sayng that the community has internalized the identification of deejaying with production.

12. Back to backs are two copies of the same record used so that the break in question can be played on one record while the other is being pulled back.

13. This is my own perception and was not stated to me in this way by any of my consultants.

14. It is for this reason, as I noted earlier, that I have chosen to follow the practice of virtually all male hip-hop producers and use the masculine pronoun when referring to producers generically.

Chapter 3: Live Instrumentation versus Hip-Hop Purism

I. I use the neologism "live instrumentation" in accordance with hip-hop usage: acoustic, electric, or electronic instruments that do not use previously recorded sound, which is to say, virtually everything but turntables and samplers. It is interesting to note that while many in the hip-hop community would argue that both turntables and samplers are in fact musical instruments, they implicitly make a distinction by not including them when they refer to "live instruments." In fact, some producers have told me that they do not even consider keyboards to be a "live instrument"; this is apparently due to the fact that they are more often used by producers to trigger samples than to play extended figures.

2. It might seem contradictory that I would devote an entire chapter to sampling ethics and then claim that hip-hop producers do not believe that "there are certain uses of sampling which are undeniably unethical." I would argue, however, that the ethics to which hip-hop producers subscribe are not about sampling *itself* being right or wrong, but about particular musical material being used in an appropriate or creative manner.

3. For the listeners' part, not only are most unaware of the specific sources of hip-hop's samples (in my experience), at any given moment they are not even particularly cognizant that the sounds they are hearing are samples in the first place.

4. Interestingly, even producers who take pride in altering the sound of their samples still place enormous value on the original sound of the albums

they use. I have, for example, personally seen Showbiz and DJ Premier—two of the most respected exponents of sample manipulation—spend almost two hours digging through records in a ninety-five-degree, cockroach-infested basement. This suggests a profound commitment to the ideas of sampling and finding the "right sound" that goes far beyond its practical value. I would also associate this phenomenon with the historical value of deejaying that I described in chapter 2.

5. Note that both Kylea and Strath conflate the role of the producer with that of the deejay. See chapter 2 for a general discussion of the historical significance of this move.

Chapter 4: Materials and Inspiration

1. Incidentally, I have heard more than one hip-hop producer describe himself as a "record nerd."

2. One well-known example of this phenomenon is a version of the Mickey Mouse Club theme from the 1970s, which begins with a particularly hard-edged drum break.

3. Such tapes are not unheard of; Kon and Amir and Phill Stroman each have a long-running series of similar tapes.

Chapter 5: Sampling Ethics

1. A fourth possibility, that a usage is a tribute or homage to an earlier hip-hop song, does not apply here; the "No biting" rule only applies to songs that are released at roughly the same time. Tributes must be created several years later to be acceptable.

2. Flipping is also valued for its own sake, aesthetically, as opposed to as an indicator of an ethical orientation. This aspect will be addressed in chapter 6. This is a somewhat arbitrary distinction that I'm making for the sake of clarity and does not necessarily reflect the views of the producers.

3. Note the telling phrase "that I have on vinyl, that I found." This suggests that, even if he were to sample from CDs, he would only sample material that he had also found on vinyl, thus fulfilling the ethical obligation to search out one's records.

4. Producers are proud of the combination of listening skills and background knowledge necessary to perform such tasks. Beni B (in the conversation to which I refer in the section of this chapter regarding compilations) berated a producer for sampling a song from a compilation rather than from

the original release. He could tell, he explained, because he owned both the original and the compilation and could hear the difference: The compilation version was slightly distorted.

5. In fact, they make the same exception: the bass drum sound of the TR-808 drum machine. This is apparently based on a distinction between sampling the sound of a musician playing an instrument and sampling the sound of a machine. Human performances are all different, so a producer must invest effort to find the proper performance to sample; if another producer then samples *that*, then the first producer's effort has been exploited. Drum machine sounds, by contrast, are all the same, so sampling one from a record is essentially the same as using the actual machine—no one is being exploited. See Theberge (1997: 196–198) and Rose (1994: 75–67) for extensive discussions of the TR-808.

6. This is a song in which Ice Cube rhymed over the instrumentals of various other songs that were popular at that time. The title locates it as self-referential parody—the song is about stealing beats.

7. Wang conflates the role of the deejay with that of the producer. This is common practice in the hip-hop world, and is dealt with in chapter 2.

Chapter 6: Elements of Style

1. The significance that hip-hop producers place upon this cyclic sensibility is demonstrated by the fact that even when looping is *not* the technique of choice, the formal structure is designed specifically to create the impression that it is. In fact, without knowing the original song, it is often impossible to tell whether a sample has been extensively manipulated by the producer or simply looped. Moreover, even when live instruments are used in hip-hop, the musicians meticulously adhere to a loop-based aesthetic.

2. It's interesting to note that in Mr. Supreme's conception, the drums are on top of the other instruments, precisely the opposite of the conventional Western view. This initially seemed to be a clue to the compositional outlook of sample-based hip-hop producers, but when I asked other producers about how they would visually represent a hip-hop beat, no consistent view on this issue emerged. Also note that in this case Mr. Supreme is using the term "beat" to refer only to the drum samples in an instrumental hip-hop composition. The semantic slippage between uses of this term to mean anything from a set of drum samples to an entire composition demonstrates the significance of percussion and rhythm to the compositional process.

3. "Live" in this context means "rhythmically exciting," not "played on live instruments." See Kyra Gaunt (1995: 118) for extensive discussion of this term's use in hip-hop.

4. The overemphasis of this factor can be seen in the vastly disproportionate amount of scholarly literature on sampling that has focused on samples of speech (which account for a relatively small number of the total samples used in hip-hop music, but which are conducive to literary interpretation) as opposed to samples of music (which make up the vast majority of samples, but which tend to resist such interpretations; see Potter 1995: 42–45; Rose 1994: 165–166; Theberge 1997: 205).

5. Producers do use records based on what they represent to other producers, but this is largely based on symbolic associations with the record itself, rather than the music.

6. This change is due to a variety of factors, including changing tastes and the expense of sampling from multiple copyrighted sources.

7. When I presented this comparison to Negus I, who is a graphic artist as well as a sample-based producer, he responded that Romare Bearden was his biggest influence as an artist.

8. The normativity of this element is attested to by MC Lauren Hill's comparison on the 1996 Fugees song "How Many Mics", "Me without a mic is like a beat without a snare"—that is, it never happens.

9. It is significant, however, that RZA's work is rarely played by nightclub deejays; it is not generally seen as conducive to dancing. His primary is audience is the home listener (I discuss these distinctions in chapter 7).

10. The Roy Ayers Music Project. As the group's name suggests, this was a side project of the jazz and funk vibraphonist Roy Ayers.

11. In hip-hop, this technique is often termed a "subliminal dis." The extreme subtlety of such insults not only allows some comments to pass unnoticed, but also torments the victim by leading them to become hypersensitive to other potential insults, a process that often leads them to find criticisms where none were actually intended.

Chapter 7: The Outer Circle

1. And it is a song-by-song process; hip-hop is a musical form that is based on the singles format.

2. The producers' ethics, discussed in chapter 5, are distinctly secondary to this process and only come into play when an MC doesn't want to be associ-

ated with an egregious ethical violation. And the violation must be egregious; most MCs (in my experience) have only a glancing familiarity with producers' ethics.

3. An experience I had while attempting to research this issue may help to illustrate the extent of these obstacles: I telephoned the New York offices of a well-known rock group, identified myself as the author of a book about sampling, and asked how one might obtain permission to sample the group's songs. I was told that the artists in question did not own the publishing rights to songs they had written in the early years of their career, nor did they own the master rights to many of their other recordings, most of which were owned by the record company they were signed to at the time the recordings were made. In short, the rights to each of their songs are jointly controlled by a variety of individuals and corporations located in several different countries. In order to streamline the process, all of the group's sample clearance requests are fielded by a single company—based in Amsterdam—which directs the requests to the appropriate parties. It is then up to each copyright holder to approve the use of the sample (and, again, *all* of them must approve it for the usage to be legal). After telling me this, the individual with whom I was speaking asked not to be identified in my book on the grounds that (for reasons that were not entirely clear to me) those who worked in the offices were not supposed to be providing this information to the public! One need only imagine trying to obtain similar information for the hundreds of samples that a producer wanted to use—and then actually going through the clearance process for each one—to appreciate the difficulties involved in releasing a sample-based recording. There are sample clearance firms that producers can hire to do the work for them, but that merely changes the burden from time to money. For most producers who are not signed to a major label, either is prohibitive.

4. See Fikentscher 2000 and Brewster and Broughton 2000 for insightful discussion of these issues in non-hip-hop contexts.

5. Several weeks after conducting this interview, I attended a party at which Prince Paul was deejaying with DJ Premier, who is also noted for making "listening" records. Both played sets of notably crowd-pleasing dance music, featuring classic hip-hop hits and mainstream R&B artists including Michael Jackson, Prince, and the Commodores.

6. Strath Shepard suspects that, in certain cases, this may actually be a conscious strategy on the part of producers to force the deejay to purchase

twice as many records: "In some ways, I think, maybe people at times do that on purpose. . . . I think, like, 'Yeah, I'm gonna buy two copies of that record.' And if it wasn't like that, I wouldn't necessarily buy two copies, unless there was something I wanted to cut up on it. So . . . I'll spend more money on it" (Shepard 1998).

7. It is interesting that B-Mello (at the begininning of this excerpt from the conversation) cites Elektra as a particularly poor label in this regard, yet Strath Shepard singles them out as exemplary.

Bibliography

Aaron, Charles. 1989. Gettin' paid: Is sampling higher education or grand theft audio? *Village Voice Rock & Roll Quarterly* (fall): 22–26.

Abrahams, Roger. 1964. *Deep Down in the Jungle: Negro Narrative Folklore From the Streets of Philadelphia*. Hatboro, Penn.: Folklore Associates.

———. 1970. *Positively Black*. Englewood Cliffs, N.J.: Prentice-Hall.

Abrahams, Roger, ed. 1969. *Jump-Rope Rhymes: A Dictionary*. New York: Pantheon Books.

Adorno, Theodor W. 1990. On popular music. 1941. Reprinted in *On The Record*, edited by Simon Frith and Andrew Goodman. New York: Pantheon Books.

Allen, Ernest, Jr. 1996. Making the strong survive: The contours and contradictions of message rap. In *Droppin' Science: Critical Essays on Rap Music and Hip-Hop Culture*, edited by William Eric Perkins. Philadelphia: Temple University Press.

Allen, Harry. 1988. Invisible band. *Village Voice Electromag* (October): 10–11.

Allen, Joe. 1997. *"He's the DJ, I'm the Turntablist": The Progressive Art of Hip Hop DJs*. Muncie, Ind.: Mississinewa Press.

Anderson, Benedict. 1983. *Imagined Communities*. New York: Verso.

Appadurai, Arjun. 1990. Disjuncture and difference in the global cultural economy. In *Gobal Culture*, edited by Mike Featherstone. London: Sage Publications.

Arom, Simha. 1985. *African Polyphony and Polyrhythm*. Translated by Martin Thom, Barbara Tuckett, and Raymond Boyd. New York: Cambridge University Press.

Ashburne, Michael. 1994. *Sampling in the Record Industry*. Oakland, Calif.: Law Offices of Michael Ashburne.

Attali, Jacques. 1996. *Noise: The Political Economy of Music*. Translated by Brian Massumi. Minneapolis: University of Minnesota Press. Originally published under the title *Bruits: Essai sur l'économie politique de la musique* (Presses Universitaires de France, 1977).

Austin, Joe. 1998. Knowing their place: Local knowledge, social prestige, and the writing formation in New York City. In *Generations of Youth*, edited by Joe Austin and Michael Nevin Willard. New York: New York University Press.

Awadu, Keidi Obi. 1997. *Rap, Hip-Hop, and the New World Order*. Long Beach, Calif.: Conscious Rasta Press.

Barz, Gregory F., and Timothy J. Cooley, eds. 1997. *Shadows in the Field*. New York: Oxford University Press.

Beadle, Jeremy J. 1993. *Will Pop Eat Itself?* Boston: Faber & Faber.

Becker, Howard. 1982. *Art Worlds*. Berkeley: University of California Press.

———. 1997. The culture of a deviant group: The "jazz" musician. In *The Subcultures Reader*, edited by Ken Gelder and Sarah Thornton. New York: Routledge.

———. 1998. *Tricks of the Trade*. Chicago: University of Chicago Press.

Berger, Harris M. 1999. *Metal, Rock, and Jazz*. Hanover, N.H.: Wesleyan University Press.

Boyarin, Daniel. 1997. *Unheroic Conduct: The Rise of Heterosexuality and the Invention of the Jewish Man*. Berkeley: University of California Press.

Brewster, Bill, and Frank Broughton. 2000. *Last Night a DJ Saved My Life: The History of the Disc Jockey*. New York: Grove Press.

Burnett, Robert. 1990. *Concentration and Diversity in the International Phonogram Industry*. Gothenburg, Sweden: Gothenburg Studies in Journalism and Mass Communication.

Buskin, Richard. 1999. *Inside Tracks*. New York: Avon Books.

Castleman, Craig. 1982. *Getting Up: Subway Graffiti in New York*. Cambridge, Mass.: MIT Press.

Chairman Mao. 1997. The legacy of Marley Marl. *Ego Trip* 3, no. 3: 88–89.

———. 1998. Behind the boards with the Bomb Squad. *Ego Trip* 4, no. 1: 112–115.

Chernoff, John Miller. 1979. *African Rhythm and African Sensibility*. Chicago: University of Chicago Press.

Clifford, James. 1992. Traveling cultures. In *Cultural Studies*, edited by Lawrence Grossberg, Cary Nelson, and Paula A. Treichler. New York: Routledge.

Considine, J. D. 1995. Larcenous art? 1990. Reprinted in *Rap on Rap*, edited by Adam Sexton. New York: Dell Publishing.

Costello, Mark, and David Foster Wallace. 1990. *Signifying Rappers*. Boston: Ecco Press.

Crowley, Daniel J., ed. 1977. *African Folklore in the New World*. Austin: University of Texas Press.

Dance, Daryl Cumber. 1978. *Shuckin' and Jivin': Folklore from Contemporary Black Americans*. Bloomington: Indiana University Press.

Decker, Jeffrey Louis. 1994. The state of rap: Time and place in hip hop nationalism. In *Microphone Fiends*. New York: Routledge.

Del Barco, Mandalit. 1996. Rap's Latin Sabor. In *Droppin' Science: Critical Essays on Rap Music and Hip-Hop Culture,* edited by William Eric Perkins. Philadelphia: Temple University Press.

DuBois, W. E. B. 1965. The souls of black folk. 1903. Reprinted in *Three Negro Classics*. New York: Avon Books.

Dudley, Shannon. 1996. Judging 'by the beat': Calypso versus soca. *Ethnomusicology* 40, no. 2: 269–298.

Dyson, Michael Eric. 1994. *Between God and Gangsta Rap*. New York: Oxford University Press.

Ellingson, Ter. 2001. *The Myth of the Noble Savage*. Berkeley: University of California Press.

Epstein, Dena J. 1977. *Sinful Tunes and Spirituals*. Chicago: University of Illinois Press.

Eshun, Kodwo. 1999. *More Brilliant Than the Sun: Adventures in Sonic Fiction*. London: Quartet Books.

Fabian, Johannes. 1983. *Time and the Other: How Anthropology Makes Its Object*. New York: Columbia University Press.

Fernando, S. H., Jr. 1994. *The New Beats*. New York: Anchor Books.

Fikentscher, Kai. 2000. *"You better work!": Underground Dance Music in New York City*. Hanover, N.H.: Wesleyan University Press.

Finnegan, Ruth. 1970. *Oral Literature in Africa*. New York: Oxford University Press.

Flores, Juan. 1996. Puerto rocks: New York Ricans stake their claim. In *Droppin' Science: Critical Essays on Rap Music and Hip-Hop Culture,* edited by William Eric Perkins. Philadelphia: Temple University Press.

Forman, Murray. 2002a. *The 'Hood Comes First: Race, Space, and Place in Rap and Hip-Hop*. Hanover, N.H.: Wesleyan University Press.

———. 2002b. Unpublished manuscript.

Fowler, Don D., and Donald L. Hardesty. 1994. *Others Knowing Others*. Washington, D.C.: Smithsonian Institution Press.

Gates, Henry Louis, Jr. 1988. *The Signifying Monkey: A Theory of Afro-American Literary Criticism*. New York: Oxford University Press.

Gaunt, Kyra D. 1995. The veneration of James Brown and George Clinton in hip-hop music: Is it live! Or is it re-memory? In *Popular Music: Style and*

Identity. Montreal, Quebec: Centre for Research on Canadian Cultural Industries and Institutions.

———. 1997. The games black girls play: Music, body, and "soul." Ph.D. diss., University of Michigan.

Gilroy, Paul. 1991. Sounds authentic: Black music, ethnicity, and the challenge of a *changing* same. *Black Music Research Journal* 11, no. 2: 111–136.

———. 1992. *Black Atlantic: Modernity and Double Consciousness*. New York: Oxford University Press.

Gladstone, Eric. 1995. Top 10 tips for searching out 7" singles. *Grand Royal* 2: 32.

George, Nelson. 1998. *Hip-Hop America*. New York: Viking Press.

Goodwin, Andrew. 1990. Sample and hold: Pop music and the digital age of reproduction. In *On the Record*. New York: Pantheon Books.

Guerasseva, Stacy. 1999. Things come together. *XXL* (April): 88–99.

Gupta, Akhil, and James Ferguson, eds. 1997. *Anthropological Locations*. Berkeley: University of California Press.

Hager, Steven. 1984. *Hip-Hop*. New York: St. Martin's Press.

Harlambos, Michael. 1974. *Right On: From Blues to Soul in Black America*. London: Edison Press.

Harrison, Faye V., ed. 1991. *Decolonizing Anthropology*. Washington, D.C.: Association of Black Anthropologists/American Anthropological Association.

Herman, Andrew, John Sloop, and Thomas Swiss. 1998. Mapping the beat: Spaces of noise and places of music. In *Mapping the Beat,* edited by Thomas Smith, John Sloop, and Andrew Herman. Malden, Mass.: Blackwell Publishers.

Heron, Gil-Scott. 1990. *So Far, So Good*. Chicago, Ill.: Third World Press.

Herskovits, Melville. 1990. *The Myth of the Negro Past*. 1941. Reprint, Boston: Beacon Press.

Horwitz, Devin. 1999. The original beat box. *URB* 68: 150.

Jameson, Frederic. 1991. *Postmodernism, or The Cultural Logic of Late Capitalism*. Durham, N.C.: Duke University Press.

Jones, Del. 1990. *Culture Bandits*. Volume 1. Philadelpia, Penn.: Hikeka Press.

Keil, Charles. 1991. *Urban Blues*. 1961. Reprint, Chicago: University of Chicago Press.

———. 1995. The theory of participatory discrepancies: A progress report. *Ethnomusicology* 39, no. 1:1–20.

Keil, Charles, and Steven Feld. 1994. *Music Grooves*. Chicago: University of Chicago Press.

Kelley, Robin D. G. 1996. Kickin' reality, kickin' ballistics: Gangsta rap and postindustrial Los Angeles. In *Droppin' Science: Critical Essays on Rap Music and Hip-Hop Culture*, edited by William Eric Perkins. Philadelphia: Temple University Press.

————. 1997. *Yo' Mama's Disfunktional!* Boston: Beacon Press.

Keyes, Cheryl. 1996. At the crossroads: Rap music and its African nexus. *Ethnomusicology* 40, no. 2: 223–248.

KPW Festschrift Committee. 1977. *Essays for a Humanist: An Offering to Klaus Wachsmann.* New York: Townhouse Press.

Krims, Adam. 2000. *Rap Music and the Poetics of Identity.* New York: Cambridge University Press.

Leland, John, and Steve Stein. 1987. What it is. *Village Voice* 33, no. 3: 24–30.

Levine, Lawrence W. 1977. *Black Culture and Black Consciousness.* New York: Oxford University Press.

Lipsitz, George. 1994. *Dangerous Crossroads.* New York: Verso.

Marcus, George E., and Michael M. J. Fischer, eds. 1986. *Anthropology as Cultural Critique.* Chicago: University of Chicago Press.

Mason, Andrew. 2002. Building blocks. *Wax Poetics* 1, no. 1 (winter): 44–51.

Melberg, Jerald L., and Milton J. Bloch, eds. 1980. *Romare Bearden: 1970–1980.* Charlotte, N.C.: Mint Museum.

Merriam, Alan. 1982. *African Music in Perspective.* New York: Garland Publishing.

Mitchell-Kernan, Claudia. 1999. Signifying, Loud-Talking, and Marking. 1972. Reprinted in *Signifyin(g), Sanctifyin', and Slam Dunking,* edited by Gena Dagel Caponi. Amherst: University of Massachussets Press.

Monson, Ingrid. 1996. *Saying Something: Jazz Improvisation and Interaction.* Chicago: University of Chicago Press.

Musician's Friend Catalogue. 2002. Summer.

Nelson, Havelock, and Michael Gonzales. 1991. *Bring the Noise.* New York: Harmony Books.

Norfleet, Dawn. 1997. "Hip-hop culture" in New York City: The role of verbal musical performance in defining a community. Ph.D. diss., Columbia University.

Okediji, Moyo. 1992. *Principles of "Traditional" African Culture.* Ibidan, Nigeria: Bard Books.

Okely, Judith, and Helen Callaway. 1992. *Anthropology and Autobiography.* New York: Routledge.

Oliver, Paul. 1970. *Savannah Syncopators: African Retentions in the Blues*. London: November Books.

Oppenheimer, Larry. 1986. The E-mu SP-12. *Electronic Musician* (July): 84–90.

Pareles, Jon. 1995. Rap moves to television's beat. In *Rap on Rap*, edited by Adam Sexton. New York: Dell Publishing.

Passaro, Joanne. 1997. "You can't take the subway to the field!": "Village" epistemologies in the global village. In *Anthropological Locations*, edited by Akhil Gupta and James Ferguson. Berkeley: University of California Press.

P. Brothers. 2002. Heavy Bronx Experience: Jazzy Jay. *Big Daddy* 11: 8–14.

Perkins, William Eric. 1996. *Droppin' Science: Critical Essays on Rap Music and Hip Hop Culture*. Philadelphia: Temple University Press.

Porcello, Thomas. 1991. The ethics of digital audio-sampling: Engineers' discourse. *Popular Music* 10, no. 1: 69–84.

Potter, Russell A. 1995. *Spectacular Vernaculars*. New York: State University of New York Press.

———.1998. Not the same: Race, repetition, and difference in hip-hop and dance music. In *Mapping the Beat*, edited by Thomas Swiss, John Sloop, and Andrew Herman. Malden, Mass.: Blackwell Publishers.

Pressing, Jeff. 1992. *Synthesizer Performance and Real-Time Techniques*. Madison, Wis.: A-R Editions.

Progler, J. A. 1995. Searching for swing: Participatory discrepancies in the jazz rhythm section. *Ethnomusicology* 39, no. 1: 21–54.

Rogin, Michael. 1996. *Blackface, White Noise*. Berkeley: University of California Press.

Rose, Tricia. 1994. *Black Noise*. Hanover, N.H.: Weslyan University Press.

Said, Edward. 1978. *Orientalism*. New York: Vintage Books.

Sanjek, David. 2000a. Mourning becomes electronic: Memory and digital culture. Unpublished manuscript.

———. 2000b. Ridiculing the "white bread" original. Unpublished manuscript.

Scherman, Tony. 2001. Strike the band: Pop music without musicians. *New York Times*. 11 February, national edition: 1, 32.

Schrader, Barry. 1982. *Introduction to Electro-Acoustic Music*. Englewood Cliffs, N.J.: Prentice-Hall.

Serlin, David. 1998. From *Sesame Street* to *Schoolhouse Rock:* Urban pedagogy and soul iconography in the 1970s. In *Soul*, edited by Monique Guillory and Richard C. Green. New York: New York University Press.

Sexton, Adam. 1995. *Rap on Rap.* New York: Del Publishing.

Shomari, Hashim. 1995. *From the Underground: Hip Hop Culture as an Agent of Social Change.* Fanwood, N.J.: X-Factor Publications.

Slobin, Mark. 1992. Micromusics of the West: A comparative approach. *Ethnomusicology* 36, no. 1: 1–87.

Smitherman, Geneva. 1997. *Talkin and Testifyin: The Language of Black America.* Detroit: Wayne State University Press.

Snead, James A. 1984. Repetition as a figure of black culture. In *Black Literature and Literary Theory,* edited by Henry Louis Gates Jr. New York: Methuen.

Sour, Eddie. 1999. People under the stairs. *URB* 64: 76.

Spencer, Jon Michael, ed. 1991. *The Emergency of Black and the Emergence of Rap.* Special issue of *Black Sacred Music: A Journal of Theomusicology* 5, no. 1.

Stim, Rich. 1999. Safe sampling: How to secure the permissions you need. *Keyboard* (April): 66–68.

Stolzoff, Norman C. 2000. *Wake the Town and Tell The People: Dancehall Culture in Jamaica.* Durham, N.C.: Duke University Press.

Straw, Will. 1997. Sizing up record collections: Gender and connoisseurship in rock music culture. In *Sexing the Groove,* edited by Sheila Whitley. New York: Routledge.

Tate, Greg. 1992. *Flyboy in the Buttermilk.* New York: Simon & Schuster.

Theberge, Paul. 1997. *Any Sound You Can Imagine: Making Music/Consuming Technology.* Hanover, N.H.: Weslyan University Press.

Thompson, Robert Farris. 1996. Hip-Hop 101. In *Droppin' Science: Critical Essays on Rap Music and Hip Hop Culture,* edited by William Eric Perkins. Philadelphia: Temple University Press.

Toop, David. 1991. *Rap Attack 2.* 1984. New York: Serpent's Tail.

Toure. 1998. Wyclef. *Rolling Stone* 798: 38.

Tully, Tim. 1986. Choosing the right sampler. *Electronic Musician* (December): 27–34.

Turner, Ike. 2000. Gettin' Dusty. *Elemental* 2, no. 12: 64.

Van Deburg, William L. 1992 *New Day in Babylon.* Chicago: University of Chicago Press.

Walser, Robert. 1995. Rhythm, rhyme, and rhetoric in the music of Public Enemy. *Ethnomusicology* 39, no. 2: 193–218.

Washington, Booker T. 1965. Up from slavery. 1901. Reprinted in *Three Negro Classics.* New York: Avon Books.

Wheeler, Elizabeth A. 1991. "Most of my heroes don't appear on no stamps": The dialogics of rap music. *Black Music Research Journal* 11, no. 2: 193–215.

White, Miles. 1996. *The World the Music Made: Hip-Hop and Its Milieu.* Master's thesis, University of Washington.

Wilson, Olly. 1992. The heterogeneous sound ideal in African-American music. In *New Perspectives in Music,* edited by Josephine Wright. [No city], Mich.: Harmonie Park Press.

Wimsatt, William Upski. 1994. *Bomb the Suburbs.* Chicago: Subway and Elevated Press.

Interviews by Author

Allen, Harry. 2003. Telephone interview by author. Tape recording.
10 January.

The Angel. 1998. Telephone interview by author. Tape recording. 9 October.

Beni B. 2002. Telephone interview by author. Tape recording. 25 February.

Dere, Karen. 1998. Interview by author. Tape recording. Seattle, Wash.,
31 August.

DJ B-Mello. 1998. Interview by author. Tape recording. Seattle, Wash.,
20 August.

DJ Kool Akiem. 1999. Telephone interview by author. Tape recording.
4 March.

DJ Topspin. 1999. Interview by author. Tape recording. Seattle, Wash.,
17 January.

Domino. 1998. Telephone interview by author. Tape recording. 5 November.

Jake One. 1998. Interview by author. Tape recording. Seattle, Wash., 14 July.

King Otto. 1998. Interview by author. Tape recording. Seattle, Wash.,
4 October.

Kylea. 1998. Interview by author. Tape recording. Seattle, Wash., 21 September.

DJ Mixx Messiah. 1999. Telephone interview by author. Tape recording.
19 January.

Mr. Supreme. 1998a. Interview by author. Tape recording. Seattle, Wash.,
16 July.

———. 1998b. Interview by author. Tape recording. Seattle, Wash., 10 August.

Negus I. 1998. Interview by author. Tape recording. Seattle, Wash.,
8 September.

Prince Paul. 2002. Interview by author. Tape recording. New York, N.Y., 8
June.

Samson S. 1999. Interview by author. Tape recording. Seattle, Wash.,
5 January.

Specs. 1998. Interview by author. Tape recording. Seattle, Wash., 24 August.

Stein, Steve [Steinski]. 2002. Interview by author. Tape recording. New York,
N.Y. 7 August.

Shepard, Strath. 1998. Interview by author. Tape recording. Seattle, Wash.,
    15 July.

Stroman, Phill. 1999. Telephone interview by author. 2 September.

Vitamin D. 1998. Interview by author. Tape recording. Seattle, Wash.,
    13 August.

Wang, Oliver. 1998. Interview by author. Tape recording. Oakland, Calif., 28
    August.

Wordsayer. 1998. Interview by author. Tape recording. Seattle, Wash.,
    27 September.

Clockwise from top left:
Domino and Karen Dere. Photo by Viviane Oh
Wordsayer and Kylea with son Upendo. Photo by author
Specs. Photo by Brian Whalen for LOOK records
DJ Kool Akiem with turntable, vinyl records and Akai MPC2000 sampler.
    Photo by Akiem Allah Elisra

Clockwise from top left:
Steve Stein a/k/a Steinski. Photo by Doug Di Franco
Oliver Wang. Photo by Jessica Miller
Mr. Supreme. Photo by Carlos Imani
King Otto. Photo by Joe Courtemanche

Discography

Beach Boys. 1966. *Pet Sounds*. Capitol Records DT-2458.

Beatles. 1967. *Sgt. Pepper's Lonely Hearts Club Band*. Parlophone 46442.

Brown, James. 1987. Funky drummer. *In the Jungle Groove*. Polydor Records 829 624.

Conmen. 1998. *Smooth Criminals on Beatbreaks, Vol. I* [No label, no number]

Elliot, Missy. 2002. Work it. *Under Construction*. Elektra 62813.

Fugees. 1996. How many mics. *The Score*. Ruffhouse/Columbia CK67147.

Gang Starr. 1998. Moment of Truth. Noo Tribe Records 45585.

Handsome Boy Modeling School. 1999. Holy calamity (Bear witness II). *So . . . How's Your Girl?* Tommy Boy Records TBCD 1258.

James, Bob. Take me to the Mardi Gras. *Two*. CTI Records CTI 6057.

Keys, Alicia. Girlfriend. *Songs in A-Minor*. J Records 80813-20002.

Jeru tha Damaja. 1995. Ya playin' yaself. Payday/FFRR 697-124-119.

Junior M.A.F.I.A. 1995. Player's anthem. *Conspiracy*. Atlantic 92614.

Old Dirty Bastard. 1995. Brooklyn zoo. Elektra PRCD 91082.

RAMP [Roy Ayers Music Project]. 1977. Daylight. *Come into My Knowledge*. ABC Records, BT6208.

Rock, Pete, and C. L. Smooth. 1992. They Reminisce Over You (T.R.O.Y.). *Mecca and the Soul Brother*. Elektra 7559-60948.

Run-DMC. 1986. Peter Piper. *Raising Hell*. Profile/Arista Records 16408.

Tribe Called Quest. 1990. *People's Instinctive Travels and the Paths of Rhythm*. RCA/BMG 1331.

Yesterday's New Quintet. Daylight. *Angles without Edges*. Stones Throw Records STH2042.

Index

African American English, 11–12, 220n10
Akai MPC 2000, 30
Allen, Harry, 25–26, 131–32, 135, 151, 181–82
ambiguity, 159–168
Angel, The, 58–59, 73–74, 111–12, 179
authenticity, 10, 63–65

Bambaataa, Afrika, 32
Bearden, Romare 152–53, 226n7
beat digging. *See* crate digging
Beatles, 41, 49
Beatminerz. *See* Mr. Walt
Beni B, 94, 96, 122, 224n4
biting, 105–9, 224n1
Bomb Squad, 39–40, 177
"Bonita Applebaum" (song by A Tribe Called Quest), 159
breakbeat (break), 31–33, 36–39, 50, 85, 98–99, 112, 136–39
Brown, James, 180. *See also* "Funky Drummer"
Buchanan and Goodman, 19–20, 221n13

"Cabfare" (song by Souls of Mischief), 179–80
car stereo, 191–93
Ced G, 40
chopping, 98, 106, 150–51, 165–68
class determinism, 27–30
compilations (breakbeat records), 120–30

"corny" records 147–50
crates, 81–82
crate digging, 79–100
    as abstract commitment to hip-hop tradition, 92–93
    educational benefits of, 95–96
    as "paying dues," 93–94
    recent changes in, 98–100
    as socialization, 97–98
    techniques, 82–91
CTI (Creed Taylor International), 84, 94
cultural determinism, 27
cutting, 118

dance, 143–44, 181
"Daylight" (song by RAMP), 158–59
deejaying, 2, 20, 52–57, 75, 92–93, 110, 117, 124, 182–91, 223n11, 224n5, 225n7, 227n5
De La Soul. *See* Prince Paul
Dere, Karen, 60, 69, 80, 88, 119, 145, 188
digging in the crates. *See* crate digging
DJ B-Mello, 183, 184, 189–90, 228n7
DJ Jazzy Jay, 37, 157
DJ Kool Akiem (DJ Kool Akiem Allah Elisra), 29, 50, 51, 52, 53, 54, 97, 103, 104, 106, 111, 114, 116, 118, 120, 123, 130–31, 137, 152, 157, 166, 175, 177–78, 179, 223n11
DJ Mixx Messiah, 53, 56, 57, 86, 88, 93–94, 187, 192
DJ O-Dub. *See* Oliver Wang

MUSIC/CULTURE

A series from Wesleyan University Press

Edited by Deborah Wong, Sherrie Tucker, and Jeremy Wallach
Originating editors: George Lipsitz, Susan McClary, and Robert Walser

A Thousand Honey Creeks Later:
My Life in Music from Basie to
Motown—and Beyond
by Preston Love

Music and Technoculture
edited by René T.A. Lysloff and Leslie
C. Gay, Jr.

Songs, Dreamings, and Ghosts:
The Wangga of North Australia
by Allan Marett

Phat Beats, Dope Rhymes:
Hip Hop Down Under Comin' Upper
by Ian Maxwell

Some Liked It Hot:
Jazz Women in Film and Television,
1928–1959
by Kristin A. McGee

Carriacou String Band Serenade:
Performing Identity in the Eastern
Caribbean
by Rebecca S. Miller

Global Noise:
Rap and Hip-Hop outside the USA
edited by Tony Mitchell

Popular Music in Theory:
An Introduction
by Keith Negus

Upside Your Head!
Rhythm and Blues on Central Avenue
by Johnny Otis

Coming to You Wherever You Are:
MuchMusic, MTV, and Youth Identities
by Kip Pegley

Musicking Bodies:
Gesture and Voice in Hindustani Music
by Matthew Rahaim

Singing Archaeology:
Philip Glass's Akhnaten
by John Richardson

Black Noise:
Rap Music and Black Culture in
Contemporary America
by Tricia Rose

The Book of Music and Nature:
An Anthology of Sounds, Words,
Thoughts
edited by David Rothenberg and
Marta Ulvaeus

Angora Matta:
Fatal Acts of North-South Translation
by Marta Elena Savigliano

Making Beats:
The Art of Sample-Based Hip-Hop
by Joseph G. Schloss

Dissonant Identities:
The Rock 'n' Roll Scene in Austin, Texas
by Barry Shank

Among the Jasmine Trees:
Music and Modernity in Contemporary
Syria
by Jonathan Holt Shannon

Between Nostalgia and Apocalypse:
Popular Music and the Staging of Brazil
by Daniel B. Sharp

Banda:
Mexican Musical Life across Borders
by Helena Simonett

About the Authors

Joseph G. Schloss is an adjunct associate professor of Black and Latino studies and sociology at City University of New York. He is also author of *Foundation: B-Boys, B-Girls and Hip-Hop Culture in New York*. His writing has appeared in *URB*, *Vibe*, *Seattle Weekly*, *The Flavor*, and the anthologies *Classic Material* and *Total Chaos*.

Jeff Chang is the executive director of the Institute for Diversity in the Arts + Committee on Black Performing Arts at Stanford University. He is the author of *Can't Stop Won't Stop*, winner of the American Book Award and the Asian American Literary Award.